W9-CCO-454

THE NIGHT OF THE GUN

OF THE GUN

DAVID CARR

A REPORTER INVESTIGATES THE DARKEST STORY OF HIS LIFE. HIS OWN.

SIMON & SCHUSTER   New York   London   Toronto   Sydney

SIMON & SCHUSTER
1230 Avenue of the Americas
New York, NY 10020

Copyright © 2008 by David Carr

All rights reserved, including the right to reproduce this book or
portions thereof in any form whatsoever. For information, address
Simon & Schuster Subsidiary Rights Department,
1230 Avenue of the Americas, New York, NY 10020.

First Simon & Schuster hardcover edition September 2008

SIMON & SCHUSTER and colophon are registered trademarks of Simon & Schuster, Inc.

For information about special discounts for bulk purchases,
please contact Simon & Schuster Special Sales at
1-800-456-6798 or business@simonandschuster.com.

Designed by Jaime Putorti

Manufactured in the United States of America

10   9   8   7   6   5   4   3   2   1

Library of Congress Cataloging-in-Publication Data
Carr, David.
 The night of the gun : a reporter investigates the darkest story of his life, his own / David
Carr.
     p. cm.
1. Carr, David. 2. Drug addicts—United States—Biography. 3. Cocaine abuse—United
States—Case studies. 4. Journalists—New York (State)—New York—Biography. I. Title.
 HV5805.C356A3 2008
 616.860092—dc22
 [B]   2008012178

ISBN-13: 978-1-4165-4152-3
ISBN-10:   1-4165-4152-7

To the magic fairies
Jill, Meagan, Erin, and Madeline

AUTHOR'S NOTE

The following book is based on sixty interviews conducted over three years, most of which were recorded on video and/or audio and then transcribed by a third party. The events represented are primarily the product of mutual recollection and discussion. Hundreds of medical files, legal documents, journals, and published reports were used as source material in reconstructing personal history. Every effort was made to corroborate memory with fact and in significant instances where that was not possible, it is noted in the text. (Go to nightofthegun.com for more information concerning methodology.) All of which is not to say that every word of this book is true—all human stories are subject to errors of omission, fact, or interpretation regardless of intent—only that it is as true as I could make it.

It is quite a common thing to be thus annoyed with the ringing in our ears, or rather in our memories, of the burden of some ordinary song, or some unimpressive snatches from an opera. Nor will we be the less tormented if the song in itself be good, or the opera air meritorious. In this manner, at last, I would perpetually catch myself pondering upon my security, and repeating, in a low undertone, the phrase, "I am safe."

One day, whilst sauntering along the streets, I arrested myself in the act of murmuring, half aloud, these customary syllables. In a fit of petulance, I remodeled them thus:

"I am safe—I am safe—yes—if I be not fool enough to make open confession!"

—EDGAR ALLAN POE, "THE IMP OF THE PERVERSE"

PART ONE

1

GUN PLAY

Sure as a gun.

—*DON QUIXOTE*

The voice came from a long distance off, like a far-flung radio signal, all crackle and mystery with just an occasional word coming through. And then it was as if a hill had been crested and the signal locked. The voice was suddenly clear.

"You can get up from this chair, go to treatment, and keep your job. There's a bed waiting for you. Just go," said the editor, a friendly guy, sitting behind the desk. "Or you can refuse and be fired." Friendly but firm.

The static returned, but now he had my attention. I knew about treatment—I had mumbled the slogans, eaten the Jell-O, and worn the paper slippers, twice. I was at the end of my monthlong probation at a business magazine in Minneapolis; it had begun with grave promises to reform, to show up at work like a normal person, and I had almost made it. But the day before, March 17, 1987, was Saint Patrick's Day. Obeisance was required for my shanty Irish heritage. I twisted off the middle of the workday to celebrate my genetic loading with green beer and Jameson Irish whiskey. And cocaine. Lots and lots of coke. There was a van, friends from the office, and a call to some pals, including Tom, a comedian I knew. We decided to attend a small but brave Saint

Patrick's Day parade in Hopkins, Minnesota, the suburban town where I grew up.

My mother made the parade happen through sheer force of will. She blew a whistle, and people came. There were no floats, just a bunch of drunk Irish-for-a-days and their kids, yelling and waving banners to unsuspecting locals who set up folding chairs as if there were going to be a real parade. After we walked down Main Street accompanied only by those sad little metal noisemakers, we all filed into the Knights of Columbus hall. The adults did standup drinking while the kids assembled for some entertainment. I told my mom that Tom the comedian had some good material for the kids. He immediately began spraying purple jokes in all directions and was wrestled off the stage by a few nearby adults. I remember telling my mom we were sorry as we left, but I don't remember precisely what happened after that.

I know we did lots of "more." That's what we called coke. We called it more because it was the operative metaphor for the drug. Even if it was the first call of the night, we would say, "You got any more?" because there would always be more—more need, more coke, more calls.

After the Knights of Columbus debacle—it was rendered as a triumph after we got in the van—we went downtown to McCready's, an Irish bar in name only that was kind of a clubhouse for our crowd. We had some more, along with shots of Irish whiskey. We kept calling it "just a wee taste" in honor of the occasion. The shot glasses piled up between trips to the back room for line after line of coke, and at closing time we moved to a house party. Then the dreaded walk home accompanied by the chirping of birds.

That's how it always went, wheeling through bars, selling, cadging, or giving away coke, drinking like a sailor and swearing like a pirate. And then somehow slinking into work as a reporter. Maybe it took a line or two off the bottom of the desk drawer to achieve battle readiness in the morning, but hey, I was there, wasn't I?

On the day I got fired—it would be some time before I worked again—I was on the last vapors of a young career that demonstrated real aptitude. Even as I was getting busy with the coke at night, I was happy to hold the cops and government officials to account in my day job. Getting loaded, acting the fool, seemed like a part of the job description, at least the way I did it. Editors dealt with my idiosyncrasies—covering the city council in a bowling shirt and red visor sunglasses—because I was well sourced in what was essentially a small town and wrote a great deal of copy. I saw my bifurcated existence as the best of both worlds, no worries. But now that mad run seemed to be over. I sat with my hands on the arms of the chair that suddenly seemed wired with very strong current.

There was no time to panic, but the panic came anyway. *Holy shit. They are on to me.*

The editor prodded me gently for an answer. Treatment or professional unallotment? For an addict the choice between sanity and chaos is sometimes a riddle, but my mind was suddenly epically clear.

"I'm not done yet."

Things moved quickly after that. After a stop at my desk, I went down the elevator and out into a brutally clear morning. Magically, my friend Paul was walking down the street in front of my office building, looking ravaged in a leather coat and sunglasses. He hadn't even beaten the birds home. I told him I had just been fired, which was clinically true but not the whole story. A folk singer of significant talent and many virulent songs about the wages of working for The Man, Paul understood immediately. He had some pills of iffy provenance—neither he nor I knew much about pills—maybe they were muscle relaxers. I ate them.

Freshly, emphatically fired, I was suffused with a rush of sudden liberation. A celebration was in order. I called Donald, my trusty wingman. A pal from college, he was tall, dark, and compliant, a boon companion once he got a couple of pops in him. We had first met at a crappy state college in Wisconsin, where we tucked dozens of capers under our belts. We had been washed down a mountain in the Smokies inside a tent, created a campfire out of four stacked picnic tables at Wolf River, and casually taken out picket fences and toppled mailboxes during road trips all over Wisconsin. Our shared taste for skipping classes in lieu of hikes, Frisbee, and dropping acid during college had been replaced by new frolics once we both moved on to Minneapolis.

We worked restaurant jobs, pouring and downing liquor, spending the ready cash as fast as it came in. "Make some calls!" became the warm-up line for many a night of grand foolishness. We shared friends, money, and, once, a woman named Signe, a worldly cocktail waitress who found herself wanly amused by the two guys tripping on acid one night at closing time at a bar called Moby Dick's. "Let me know when you boys are finished," she said in a bored voice as Donald and I grinned madly at each other from either end of her. We didn't care. He was a painter and photographer when he wasn't getting shit faced. And at a certain point, I became a journalist when I wasn't ingesting all the substances I could get my hands on. We were a fine pair. Now that I had been fired for cause, there was no doubt that Donald would know what to say.

"Fuck 'em," he said when he met me at McCready's to toast my first day between opportunities. The pills had made me a little hinky, but I shook it off with a snort of coke. Nicely prepped, we went to the Cabooze, a Minneapolis blues bar. Details are unclear, but there was some sort of beef inside, and we were asked to leave. Donald complained on the way out that I was always getting us 86'd, and my response included throwing him across the expansive hood of his battered '75 LTD. Seeing the trend, he drove away, leaving me standing with thirty-four cents in my pocket. That detail I remember.

I was pissed: Not about losing my job—they'd be sorry. Not about getting 86'd—that was routine. But my best friend had abandoned me. I was livid, and somebody was going to get it. I walked the few miles back to McCready's to refuel and called Donald at home.

"I'm coming over." Hearing the quiet menace in my voice, he advised me against it; that he had a gun.

"Oh really? Now I'm coming over for sure."

He and his sister Ann Marie had a nice rental on Nicollet Avenue in a rugged neighborhood on the south side of Minneapolis, not far from where I lived. I don't remember how I got there, but I stormed up to the front door—a thick one of wood and glass—and after no one answered, I tried kicking my way in. My right knee started to give way before my sneaker did any damage. Ann Marie, finally giving in to the commotion, came to the door and asked me what I was going to do if I came in.

"I just want to talk to him."

Donald came to the door and, true to his word, had a handgun at his side. With genuine regret on his face, he said he was going to call the cops. I had been in that house dozens of times and knew the phone was in his bedroom. I limped around the corner and put my fist through the window, grabbed the phone, and held it aloft in my bloody arm. "All right, call 'em, motherfucker! Call 'em! Call the goddamn cops!" I felt like Jack Fucking Nicholson. Momentarily impressed, Donald recovered long enough to grab the phone out of my bloody hand and do just that.

When we met again through the glass of the front door, he still had the gun, but his voice was now friendly. "You should leave. They're coming right now." I looked down Nicollet toward Lake Street and saw a fast-moving squad car with the cherries lit, no siren.

I wasn't limping anymore. I had eight blocks to go to my apartment, full tilt all the way. Off the steps, 'round the house, and into the alleys. Several squads were crisscrossing. *What the hell did Donald tell them?* I thought as I sprinted. I dove behind a Dumpster to avoid one squad coming around the corner, opening up a flap of jeans and skin on my other knee. I had to hit the bushes and be very still as the cops strafed the area with their searchlights, but I made it, scurrying up the back steps to my apartment in a fourplex on Garfield Avenue. I was bleeding, covered in sweat, and suddenly very hungry. I decided to heat up some leftover ribs, turned the oven on high, and left the door of it open so I could smell the ribs when they heated up. And then I passed out on my couch.

Every hangover begins with an inventory. The next morning mine began with my mouth. I had been baking all night, and it was as dry as a two-year-old chicken bone. My head was a small prison, all yelps of pain and alarm, each movement seeming to shift bits of broken glass in my skull. My right arm came into view for inspection, caked in blood, and then I saw it had a few actual pieces of glass still embedded in it. So much for metaphor. My legs both hurt, but in remarkably different ways.

Three quadrants in significant disrepair—that must have been some night, I thought absently. Then I remembered I had jumped my best friend outside a bar. And now that I thought about it, that was before I tried to kick down his door and broke a window in his house. And then I recalled, just for a second, the look of horror and fear on his sister's face, a woman I adored. In fact, I had been such a jerk that my best friend had to point a gun at me to make me go away. Then I remembered I'd lost my job.

It was a daylight waterfall of regret known to all addicts. It can't get worse, but it does. When the bottom arrives, the cold fact of it all, it is always a surprise. Over fifteen years, I had made a seemingly organic journey from pothead to party boy, from knockaround guy to friendless thug. At thirty-one, I was washed out of my profession, morally and physically corrupt, but I still had almost a year left in the Life. I wasn't done yet.

In the pantheon of "worst days of my life," getting fired was right up there, but I don't remember precisely how bad it was. You would think that I would recall getting canned with a great deal of acuity. But it was twenty years ago.

Even if I had amazing recall, and I don't, recollection is often just self-fashioning. Some of it is reflexive, designed to bury truths that cannot be swallowed, but other "memories" are just redemption myths writ small. Personal narrative is not simply opening up a vein and letting the blood flow toward anyone willing to stare. The historical self is created to keep dissonance at bay and render the subject palatable in the present.

But my past does not connect to my present. There was That Guy, a dynamo of hilarity and then misery, and then there is This Guy, the one with a family, a house, and a good job as a reporter and columnist for *The New York Times*. Connecting the two will take a lot more than typing. The first-date version of my story would suggest that I took a short detour into narcotics, went through an aberrant period of buying, selling, snorting, smoking, and finally shooting cocaine, and once I knocked that off, well, all was well.

The meme of abasement followed by salvation is a durable device in literature, but does it abide the complexity of how things really happened? Everyone is told just as much as he needs to know, including the self. In *Notes from Underground*, Fyodor Dostoevsky explains that recollection—memory, even—is fungible, and often leaves out unspeakable truths, saying, "Man is bound to lie about himself."

I am not an enthusiastic or adept liar. Even so, can I tell you a true story about the worst day of my life? No. To begin with, it was far from the worst day of my life. And those who were there swear it did not happen the way I recall, on that day and on many others. And if I can't tell a true story about one of the worst days of my life, what about the rest of those days, that life, this story?

Nearly twenty years later, in the summer of 2006, I sat in a two-room shack in Newport, a town outside of the Twin Cities, near the stock-yards where Donald now lived and worked at a tree farm. He was still handsome, still a boon companion. We hadn't seen each other in years, but what knit us together—an abiding bond hatched in reckless glory—was in the room with us.

I told him the story about the Night of the Gun. He listened care-fully and patiently, taking an occasional swig out of a whiskey bottle and laughing at the funny parts. He said it was all true, except the part about the gun. "I never owned a gun," he said. "I think *you* might have had it."

This is a story about who had the gun.

2

POSSESSION

Who by now could know where was what? Liars controlled the locks.

—NORMAN MAILER, *THE ARMIES OF THE NIGHT*

I am not a gun guy. That is bedrock. And that includes buying one, carrying one, and, most especially, pointing one. I've been on the wrong end a few times, squirming and asking people to calm the fuck down. But walking over to my best friend's house with a gun jammed in my pants? No chance. That did not fit my story, the one about the white boy who took a self-guided tour of some of life's less savory hobbies before becoming an upright citizen. Being the guy who waved a gun around made me a crook, or worse, a full-on nut ball.

Still, there it was: "I think *you* might have had it."

We were not having an argument, we were trying to remember. I had gone to his house with a video camera and a tape recorder in pursuit of the past. By now the statutes were up, no charges in abeyance, no friendship at stake.

Donald is not prone to lies. He has his faults: He has wasted a gorgeous mug and his abundant talent on whiskey and worse, but he is a stand-up guy, and I have seen him bullshit only when the law is involved. Still, I know what I know—Descartes called it "the holy music of the self"—and I believe that I was not a person who owned or used a gun. The Night of the Gun had stuck in my head because it suggested that I was such a menace that my best friend not only had to call the cops on me but wave a piece in my face.

I didn't hold it against him—Donald was far from violent, and maybe I had it coming. I doubt that he would have shot me no matter what I did. But now that memory lay between us. Sort of like that gun.

Memories are like that. They live between synapses and between the people who hold them. Memories, even epic ones, are perishable from their very formation even in people who don't soak their brains in mood-altering chemicals. There is only so much space on any one person's hard drive, and old memories are prone to replacement by newer ones. There's even a formula for the phenomena:

$$R = e^{-\frac{t}{s}}$$

In the Ebbinghaus curve, or forgetting curve, R stands for memory retention, s is the relative strength of memory, and t is time. The power of a memory can be built through repetition, but it is the memory we are recalling when we speak, not the event. And stories are annealed in the telling, edited by turns each time they are recalled until they become little more than chimeras. People remember what they can live with more often than how they lived. I loathe guns and, with some exceptions, the people who carry them, so therefore I was not a person who held a gun. Perhaps in the course of transforming from That Guy to This Guy, there is a shedding of old selves that requires a kind of self-induced Alzheimer's.

In this instance, the truth didn't seem knowable. At best, there was a note on a long-lost precinct nightly sheet about some lunatic at Thirty-first and Nicollet. In the matter of the gun, Donald and I are both unreliable witnesses, given the passage of years and our chemical résumés. But Ann Marie was there. I called her in the midst of my attempt to report something in dispute. She said that she remembers me showing up in a state of complete agitation, but nothing about a gun. Then again, she said, "I didn't exactly stick around." Perhaps her brother or I had the decency not to wave one around in her presence. The change in custody of the weapon made no sense. It's true that I was fully involved in the drug lifestyle at the time, buying and selling coke, but weapons were not part of my corner of that scene.

Bat-shit crazy or not, the weight of a large-caliber handgun in your hand is not something you're likely to forget. I've held a few as a cop reporter, and I was always stunned by how dense and formidable a gun felt. As I thought about it, I realized I would have had to walk over to his house with one jammed in my pants. I'm not obsessed with my own privates, but I'm not one to point a pistol at them, either.

Donald was the first person I went to see when I decided to put my own memories up against those of others. By turns, it became a kind of journalistic ghost dancing, trying to conjure spirits past, including mine. Donald was my first stop because he was and is incredibly dear to me. And if I were being honest, I thought that addiction, which had come close to killing me, would take him out, and I would miss my shot. He was plenty lucid and hilarious while we talked, but the bottle was winning over the longer haul, exacerbated by a methadone habit that served as a rubber band, always pulling him back to that same terrible place. (Sometimes addiction seems more like possession, a death grip from Satan that requires supernatural intervention. Absolution from end-stage chemical obsession tends to force otherwise faithless men to their knees.)

Other mysteries would pile up as I made my way, but the Night of the Gun stuck with me. Maybe Donald didn't know what he was talking about. Perhaps his memory was even more compromised than my own. Those were very busy days—I was on the run a lot—but I remember some of it with a great deal of acuity.

In that same year, near the end of 1987, I got in a fight with my girlfriend. The last time we had fought, I ended up going to jail because I assaulted her, so this time I was smart enough to call my friend Chris to pick me up. Chris was one of the saner people I knew, and I used to call him whenever I got in a jam. That night, I called him for a ride, threw my stuff in some garbage bags, and fled out the back of my apartment. It's the kind of thing you see on *Cops*—I was even shirtless, to add to the verisimilitude. Chris was and is a kind man, and he never seemed to run out of patience with me. As I panted in the cab of that truck, he told me everything would be OK even though we both knew better.

In the summer of 2007, a year after I talked with Donald about the gun, I went to New Orleans to see Chris. He is now a professor of creative writing at Loyola University and the godfather to one of my children. Sitting in his backyard, we caught up on family stuff, and then I asked him about that night.

"I remember showing up," he said. "I had this GMC pickup truck. You put the garbage bags in the back, and that was it."

Then he said something else: "I went back into your place once you'd taken off. You sent me back to get a gun that you'd left there . . ."

Oops.

"You were worried about the cops going through the place, and so you'd asked me to go back and get some things that you had stashed. You had, I think, a .38 special," he said evenly. "I don't know where you got it. It was toward the very end, and you were starting to act real . . ."

He didn't finish the sentence, but he didn't have to.

"Yeah, you did have one—for I don't know how long," he said. "Somewhere in the closet, up above the shelf or something. And up above the refrigerator you had some drug paraphernalia or something, and you wanted me to just go there and clear out anything that would be incriminating."

Given that Chris was able to describe where the gun was stashed in the closet of my apartment near Donald's house, it probably happened the way Donald remembers it. It started to ring some distant, alarming bell. Oh yeah, my gun. Maybe so.

But if I was wrong about the gun, what else was I wrong about?

3

WHO YOU GONNA BELIEVE, ME OR YOUR LYING EYES?

The moral question of whether you are lying or not is not settled by establishing the truth or falsity of what you say. In order to settle this question, we must know whether you intend your statement to mislead.

—SISSELA BOK, *MORAL CHOICES IN PUBLIC AND PRIVATE LIFE*

On the face of it, I am no more qualified to take my own historical inventory than the addict with the fetid dreads who spare-changes people on the subway while singing "Stand by Me." Ask him how he ended up sweating people for quarters with off-key singing, and he may have an answer, but it won't be the whole story. He doesn't know it and probably couldn't bear it if he did.

To be an addict is to be something of a cognitive acrobat. You spread versions of yourself around, giving each person the truth he or she needs—you need, actually—to keep them at one remove. How, then, to reassemble that montage of deceit into a truthful past?

Addiction, which Oliver Sacks defines as "a form of self-induced catatonia, a repetitive action bordering on hysteria," is a little preoccupying. And if the apparatus is impaired, what of the will to be truthful? Let's stipulate that I do not have a good memory, having recklessly sautéed my brain in fistfuls of pharmaceutical spices. I generally test well for intelligence, but if you caught me after a punishing night-and-day run back then with a simple "What happened to you?" I was usually stumped.

I learned early on as that it was probably OK to lie to my parents, but once I had skipped out into the world, not so much. It is dumb to lie to cops, a lesson that was tattooed into me at a tender age. Later on, when a cop asked me a direct question about something that would implicate me, I would always say the same thing: "I can't help you with that, officer."

Even so, give or take a died-in-the-diagnosis sociopath, there may be no more unreliable narrator than an addict. Recovered or not, you are in the hands of someone who used his mouth and his words to constantly create one more opportunity to get high. But my version of events is worth knowing, if for no other reason than I was there.

———

HERE IS WHAT I DESERVED: Hepatitis C, federal prison time, HIV, a cold park bench, an early, addled death.

HERE IS WHAT I GOT: A nice house, a good job, three lovely children.

HERE IS WHAT I REMEMBER ABOUT HOW THAT GUY BECAME THIS GUY: Not much. Junkies don't generally put stuff in boxes, they wear the boxes on their heads, so that everything around them—the sky, the future, the house down the street—is lost to them.

To the extent that I remember, this is what I know: I was born a middle kid in a family of seven into a John Cheever novel set on the border of Hopkins and Minnetonka on the western edge of Minneapolis. It was a suburban idyll where any mayhem was hidden in the rear rooms of large split-level homes. I sought trouble even though I had to walk a long way to find it. My home was a good one, my parents were wonderful, no one slipped me a Mickey, and if they did, I would have grabbed it with both hands and asked for more. I drank and drugged for the same reason that a four-year-old spins around past the point of dizziness: I liked feeling different. Three of my siblings have the allergy to alcohol. My dad is in recovery, and while my mother may not have been an alcoholic, she knew her way around a party. That girl could go.

Let's skip high school. I mostly did, smoking doobies like they were Pall Malls every single day of those four years. I went to an all-boys school I loathed and hid behind red eyes and long hair that hung in my face. The day after I finished high school, my friend Greg and I hitch-hiked to the yippie camp-in at Spokane, Washington, near the site of the 1974 World's Fair. I became a hippie at precisely the instant that it had lost cultural salience. The camp-in was pathetic—Nixon was on the way out, the draft and the war were over, it was mostly just loadies trading food stamps for pot and eating the gruel that the Krishnas were handing out with beatific smiles. I ended up hopping a bus of the so-called Rainbow Tribe, and on the ensuing ride, they gifted me with peyote, a profound sense of life's psychedelic possibilities, and a tenacious case of crabs.

I came back and was working in a jelly bean factory, Powell's Candy, where we wore helmets, beard guards, and earmuffs while we cranked out trays of rolled sugar. My foreman called me Curlicue because of my long ringlets and rarely spoke to me without using his index finger on my sternum as a punctuation device. I worked in a hydraulic tube assembly plant where my boss was a dwarf named George who took Dolly Parton's breasts as his central religious icons. Here and there I dug ditches, worked at a golf course, and washed dishes.

Obviously on a roll, I decided that the time was not right for college, but my father thought otherwise. He drove me to a branch of the University of Wisconsin at River Falls, a small farming town near the Minnesota border. He dropped me off in the middle of campus with my beanbag chair and chest of bongs and gave me a check for $20. It bounced.

My crowning achievement came early: As a brand-new freshman, I won the beer-chugging contest, drinking five twelve-ounce beers in under twenty seconds. My new pals clapped me on the back as I vomited minutes later. I stayed for two years and moved in with a lovely girl, Lizbeth, whom I soon wore out. I ended up working at a local nursing home, where I found myself the lone male on night shifts full of townie girls. It was a good life until one night when I was doing laundry at one of their trailers and the ex-husband came by drunk as a goat and pointed a gun at me. I left town soon afterward. (Never, ever get mixed up with townies.)

After some months of traveling in the West, I came back to Minneapolis and enrolled at the University of Minnesota, a massive campus in the middle of the city. I worked nights in a restaurant called the Little Prince—one of two straight guys on a very large gay and female staff, so, again, I was blessed with friendly odds—and during the day, I hung out in parking garages at school with pals, mostly lesbians and pot smokers. Throughout college I had many friends, very little money, and what Pavlov called "the blind force of the subcortex." Ring the getting-high bell, and I was right there.

I subsisted on Pop-Tarts and Mountain Dew, along with less nutritious substances: LSD, peyote, pot, mushrooms, mescaline, amphetamines, quaaludes, valium, opium, hash, liquor of all kinds, and—this is embarrassing—morning glory seeds. (Rumored to have psychedelic properties, they didn't work.) Total garbage head.

———

On my twenty-first birthday, I went out with Kim, who worked at the Little Prince and would become my wife. I also did coke for the first time. The relationship with the coke was far more enduring and would define the next decade.

A dealer who dropped his money on Dom Pérignon at the restaurant palmed me a Balkan Sobranie cigarette tin when he found out it was my birthday. He told me to open it in the bathroom. I saw the powder and knew what to do.

It was a Helen Keller hand-under-the-water moment. Lordy, I can finally see! Cold fusion, right here in the bathroom stall; it was the greatest thing ever. My endorphins leaped at this new opportunity, hugging it and feeling all its splendid corners. *My, that's better.* You can laugh all you want, but Proust had a similar epiphany eating a madeleine: " . . . a shudder ran through me, and I stopped, intent upon the extraordinary thing that had happened to me. An exquisite pleasure invaded my senses, something isolated, detached, with no suggestion of its origin."

Every addict is formed in the crucible of the memory of that first hit. Even as the available endorphins attenuate, the memory is *right there.* The chase is on, sometimes for hours, sometimes for days—in my case, for years on end. I could get high just having coke in my pocket, knowing that I had a little edge that few others had. I had spent my life terrified that I would miss out on something, and now I didn't have to. If I had delved deeper, I might have also noticed that coke accessed something in me that was unruly and ungovernable, but there would be time for that later.

In school and out—I attended classes when I could while working at the Little Prince—I told people I was a journalist, with only that uttered noun as evidence. Then I caught a real actual story for the *Twin Cities Reader*, a local alternative weekly, and the fever to go with it. I developed an intense interest in the craft immediately.

But working on stories and the attention that came with them was never enough. Tucked in safe suburban redoubts, kids who had it soft like me manufactured peril. When there is no edge, we make our own, reaching for something that would approximate the cliché of being fully alive because we could die at any minute. That search for sensation leads to the self divorcing from the body, à la Descartes, and a life of faux peril. Everything that brought me joy involved risk. *Yes, let's do mescaline, and, sure, let's wander out onto that trestle bridge hundreds of feet over the St. Croix River. I'm pretty sure we'll hear a train if it comes, right?* My friends would do LSD and stare at the marvel of their own hands. I'd drop acid and organize a road trip.

Early in 1986 I tried this newfangled thing called freebasing and, later, crack cocaine. Another eureka moment—*This is, like, the best. Only better, faster.* The smoke became a pharmacological rocket in about four and a half seconds. I quickly became an autodidact, learning to make crack, dropping some coke and baking soda into a spoon over the stove, and, voilà, we were rocking.

During the day, I was doing stories for the *Twin Cities Reader.* I took the recalcitrance and slipperiness of public officials personally—my moral dungeon at the time is freighted with irony in retrospect—and aligned myself with sources who I thought were doing the people's work.

Crime stories riveted me from the beginning—it is often a short walk from cops to robbers. But when I got in a jam of my own, I never worked any connections within the department, I just tried to lay low and duck any uniforms I knew while wheeling through booking. Some of the wiseguy stuff I picked up at night helped me in my day job, but I prospered mostly in spite of my addiction.

In the fall of 1983, I did a story about a food bank that was mismanaging funds and its mission, and, later that year, a story about a neighborhood's effort to shut down a huge food line for the homeless. In 1984 there was a piece about a massive federal civil trial that suggested the makers of the Dalkon Shield had knowingly distributed a product its own research had shown was dangerous. That year I covered politics extensively, including local favorite Walter Mondale's campaign for president. I also exposed a prolific con man who had charmed his way through others' millions.

My worlds began to collide a bit in 1985 and 1986 when I did very detailed reporting at a large detox center—I would later be back as a customer—and, along with another reporter, came up with a lavish and loving portrait of Block E, a downtown square block of urban pathology and lore. I did investigations of the supercomputer firm Control Data Corporation's extensive role in supplying infrastructure for the government of South Africa and broke news about the rise of big-city street gangs in what had been a fairly quiet Midwestern burg.

There were signs early on that the center would not hold. During this time, I was working on a running story about a tough cop who ran the decoy unit of the Minneapolis police. A suspect had been shot accidentally while being taken into custody, and another reporter and I investigated and found out that the cop who ran the unit had entered, but not completed, chemical dependency treatment. State laws required that he give up his gun for a period, and when I called he was civil and serious. But a few days later, my phone rang and he said—I am recalling this decades later—"You know, I've been asking around and your life is not without blemish. You better watch your step." For weeks afterward, I would drive somewhere and see the van that the decoy unit used in my rearview. It both scared me and cramped my style. I eventually had a very uncomfortable conversation with the police chief complaining that some of his officers were following me around. He made them stop.

But for much of the 1980s, I was about my business, all of it, simultaneously. In my little provincial world of Minneapolis, I felt like a king. I had a job, coke, and lots of friends. On my thirtieth birthday, September 8, 1986, a friend gave me some mushrooms and took me into the back room of McCready's for a quick snort. The door opened, revealing a band, streamers, and more than a hundred people—rockers, comedians, drug dealers, lawyers, journalists, and wiseguys—all wearing T-shirts that said, "I Am a Close Personal Friend of David Carr."

You don't say.

In this time, many of my friends went to prison, but I was more of a misdemeanant, spending hours—and every once in a while, days—in various county jails. When things got way out of round, my family—usually my dad—would swoop in and intervene. After long, tortured family discussions about all the promise I was frittering away and all the misery I was spreading around, I would go to treatment (four times in all) and promise to mend my ways. But treatment or not, I continued to live by Emerson's credo: moderation in all things, especially moderation.

But as time wore on, I combined a life of early promise as a writer with dark nights full of half-baked gangsters and full-blown addiction. I became a steady dealer for the creative community in Minneapolis, selling coke to musicians, comedians, and club kids. I moved grams, eight balls, ounces, quarter pounds—no one trusted me with a kilo for more than a few minutes.

I did not date women, I took hostages. I married Kim for all the wrong reasons and pillaged our bank account with an ATM card. (I half-believed at the time that ATMs were invented by a drug cartel to keep the hard cash flowing at night.) There were nights when I would come in and go to bed like a normal person next to her, and once she fell asleep, I would slip out of bed and go between the houses across the street to a woman I knew. Once Kim and I divorced, I fell into a relationship with a woman named Doolie and slowly drove her insane. She was gorgeous, witty as hell, and drew stares in the bar, which led to many ensuing beefs. My duplicity around women was towering and chronic. I conned and manipulated myself into their beds and then treated them as human jewelry, something to be worn for effect. It certainly did not have much to do with how I looked. Far from clinically handsome, I have a face that looks like it could have been carved out of mashed potatoes, and my idea of exercise was running the length of my body.

One night in 1986, I was at a party for Phil, a long-time coke connection who was going away to federal prison. I met Anna, who had better coke than Phil and soon developed a fondness for me. We were an appalling mix, metastasized by her unlimited supply of coke. I taught Anna how to smoke it. Later, in 1987, she came home one day with a needle in her pocket, and I joined in the fun. I lost my job, she lost her business.

It would have ended there, but on April 15, 1988, Anna had twin girls. My daughters. Our remaining friends had begged us, quite reasonably, to abort them. We were smoking crack the day Anna's water broke, and they were born two and a half months premature, fewer than three pounds each. Friends began to boycott our house because it had become such a grim, near-scientific tableau of addiction's progression.

Eventually we both went to treatment, and our kids went into foster care. I sobered up, Anna didn't, and I got the twins, Erin and Meagan. I then lived most of the last two decades at the end of a firehouse of those promises that recovery delivers, with luck, industry, and fate guiding me to a life beyond all expectation.

———

But was it really all thus? Shakespeare describes memory as the warder of the brain, but it is also its courtesan. We all remember the parts of the past that allow us to meet the future. The prototypes of the lie—white, grievous, practical—make themselves known when memory is called to answer. Memory usually answers back with bullshit. Everyone likes a good story, especially the one who is telling it, and the historical facts are generally sullied in the process. All men mean well, and clearly most people who set out to tell the truth do not lie on purpose. How is it, then, that every warm bar stool contains a hero, a star of his own epic, who is the sum of his amazing stories?

Most of my stories are not nice ones, their heroic aspects dimmed by the fact that the hand which struck me was my own. Truly ennobling personal narratives describe a person overcoming the bad hand that fate has dealt him, not someone like me, who takes good cards and sets them on fire. I can easily admit that I did bad things for no good reason but stop at copping to being overtly evil. I was a screwup who took aim on himself and may have created collateral damage along the way. What I found twenty years later was darker, more meretricious, but in the memory, those stories tended to be bathed in pathos, coating the pieces of the past in rich goo that make them go down smooth. Even absent the urge to tart up the past, there are practical impediments to communicating the baseline reality of addiction, because when every day is built around obtaining and consuming a substance, those days run together and fail to gain traction in the memory.

There is also an almost irresistible consistency bias. Memory is an expression of hindsight as much as recollection, so my rear view must incorporate the fact that I was eventually redeemed from a life of drugs, alcohol, and mania. In this construct, the moments when I stumbled across a life-changing epiphany are vividly preserved, while the more corrosive aspects are lost to a kind of self-preserving amnesia. To be fully cognizant of the wreckage of one's past can be paralyzing, so we, or at least I, minimize as we go. Nowhere is that imperative more manifest than in memoir. Popular literature requires framing a sympathetic character, someone we can root for or who is, as they say on the studio lot, relatable.

If I said I was a fat thug who beat up women and sold bad coke, would you like my story? What if instead I wrote I was a recovered addict who obtained custody of my twin girls, got us off welfare, and raised them by myself, even though I had a little touch of cancer? Now we're talking. Both are equally true, but as a member of a self-interpreting species, one that fights to keep disharmony at a remove, I'm inclined to mention my tenderhearted attentions to my children as a single parent before I get around to the fact that I hit their mother when we were together.

So what if I had the gun? A drunken rampage after getting fired has its charms, but waving a gun in the face of a best friend? That behavior creates a large rift in the bigger narrative of me as a knucklehead who was pulled along by a ring in my nose into matters that were beyond my ken. If the gun story is as Donald and Chris remember it, it would put me on the far end of the continuum from victim to perpetrator.

We tell ourselves that we lie to protect others, but the self usually comes out looking damn good in the process. "Stories are for books," Phil, my dealer once upon a time, said to me. I was plaintively explaining how despite my best intentions, things had gone wrong, people had disappeared, and I did not have his money. He put me into collections, sending his boys over to talk to me. Stories are for books.

And so they are. Even if you are a civilian who leaves a few gulps in the bottom of the second glass of wine, you know them by heart. The arc of the addict has become as warm and familiar as a Hallmark movie: the textured childhood, the abasement, the epiphany, the relapse, the ultimate surrender. Dead addicts don't leave behind an uplifting tract, so the narratives are generally told by people who can go on *Oprah* and stand like a barker in front of their abasement.

In the convention of the recovery narrative, readers will want to scan past the tick-tock, looking for the yucky part so that they can feel better about themselves. (Here's a taste: When I got to detox for what I thought was the last time, they took one look at my arms and brought me a tub filled with lukewarm water and Dreft detergent to soak my scabrous, pus-filled track marks. Even the wet-brain drunks wouldn't come near me. See how that works?)

I read some of the classics of the genre, debunked and not. After reading four pages of continuous ten-year-old dialogue magically re-called by someone who was in the throes of alcohol withdrawal at the time, I wondered how he did it. No I didn't. I knew he made it up. It was easy and defendable, really, sublimating and eliding the past in ser-vice of a larger Emotional Truth. Truth is singular and lies are plural, but history—the facts of what happened—is both immutable and mostly unknowable. Can I somehow remember enough to type my way to an unvarnished recitation of what happened to me? No chance.

As I sit today, I am a genuine, often pleasant person. I am able to imitate a human being for long spurts of time, do solid work for a rep-utable organization, and have, over the breadth of time, proven to be an attentive father and husband. So how to reconcile my past with my current circumstance? Drugs, it seems to me, do not conjure demons, they access them. Was I faking it then, or am I faking it now? Which, you might ask, of my two selves did I make up?

But there is a way, not to Truth, but fewer lies. When I set out to write a memoir, I decided to fact-check my life using the prosaic tools of journalism. For the past thirty years, give or take time served as a drunk and a lunatic, I have used those tools with alacrity. I decided to go back and ask the people who were there: the dealers I worked for, the friends I had, the women I dated, the bosses I screwed over. There would be police reports, mug shots from my short career as a crook, and some medical records from my serial treatments.

Left to their own devices, addicts—or people who are attempting to impersonate them for reasons I have never fully understood—end up in the business of wish fulfillment, becoming a composite of their own making to feed specific public appetites. I have always thought that reporting, while onerous, was easier than making it up: There are many great reporters and very few truly remarkable novelists. As a writer, I prefer to get bossed around by my notebook and the facts contained therein. They may not lead to a perfect, seamless arc, but they yield a story that coheres in another way, because it is mostly true. As many of the cold facts as I can uncover and lean on, woven with the networked memories of the people I interviewed, will produce enough seeming fantasy and unreality as it is. But to report out a story I was this close to I would need reinforcements.

In the spring of 2006, I went to Best Buy outside Minneapolis. I told the kid who was helping me that I wanted a set of gadgets that would help me document every inch of a book I was reporting. This time, I thought, I want to remember everything, or at least put it somewhere it can be found. He sold me a video camera, a digital tape recorder, and an external drive to capture all of it. The devices would do what I could not, which is remember everything, code it into ones and zeroes and serve as digital witnesses.

For two years on and off, I would call a long-lost person, set up a time, and then come in with a bunch of questions, the video camera and a voice recorder. I would engage in small talk and then point to some huge scab from the past. "Do you mind tearing that off?" It was a profoundly embarrassing exercise, but it brought with it no small number of epiphanies. I was wrong about a lot of things. In the novelized version of my life, I was basically a good guy who took a couple of wrong turns and ended up in the ditch. In the reported version, I was a person who saw the sign that said dangerous curves ahead and floored it, heedlessly mowing down all sorts of people at every turn.

Some people I interviewed wanted me to say I was sorry—I am and I did. Some people wanted me to say that I remembered—I did and I did not. And some people wanted me to say it was all a mistake—it was and it was not. It felt less like journalism than archaeology, a job that required shovels and axes, hacking my way into dark, little-used passages and feeling my way around, finding other pieces that did not fit, and figuring out that I was working off the wrong map to begin with. It would prove to be an enlightening and sickening enterprise, a new frontier in the annals of self-involvement. I would show up at the doorsteps of people I had not seen in two decades and ask them to explain myself to me.

This is what they told me.

4

TIME'S WINGED FEET

Because I once worked in nursing homes and spent a lot of time with people on the way out, I learned early on that the passage of time does not accumulate, that it does not transform into something corporeal that you can rest on and be comforted by. We are prisoners of the moment—"bugs trapped in amber," as Vonnegut wrote—some looking forward, others looking back.

I took care of a guy named Seth in a River Falls nursing home where I worked during college in the midseventies. Time's winged feet had had their way with him, and he was a tiny, curled-up ball of a man. A human C. But despite his circumstance, he was consistently cheerful, not one to go on about his needs or discomforts. One night I was feeding him lime green Jell-O that had been cut up days before and had developed a rubbery exterior. He began choking on one of the cubes, and by his color, it was clear that his windpipe was completely obstructed. I ran to the door of the room, yelled for the duty nurse—it was an understaffed place— and no one responded. I tore back to the bed, came up behind Seth, and put my arms around his midsection, giving it the quick thrust of the so-called Heimlich maneuver. The pellet of Jell-O shot six feet and bounced off his old black-and-white TV. I asked him if he was all right.

"Yeah, I'm fine," he said, in a nasal Norwegian accent. And then he added, almost as if it were beside the point, "I think you broke my ribs, though."

And so I had. He was still grateful, because he knew he would have been a goner otherwise, and I was proud that I had osmotically absorbed enough medical training as an orderly to be of service to another human being. I worked nights, and Seth was not much of a sleeper, so I would find myself in his room, chatting and rowing back through the years with him. As a young man, I had an affinity for old people, demonstrating an interest in the ancient that I never displayed toward my contemporaries.

The details of Seth's history—the journey from Norway with his parents as a young man, a hard life of farming, the girl he met and married at church, the cows that they milked, her death that left him alone for the last twenty years of his life—were stories I was happy to listen to. He had led a good life; no big splashes for the highlight reel other than farming accidents and the occasional battle with the pig farmer next door, but still, not a bad run.

At the end of one of these nights, his milky eyes looked into mine, and he pointed at me, as if in a Dickens novel, and said, more by way of observation than complaint: "It goes so fast; so, so fast. Never forget that it goes by very fast. One minute you're sitting there, just like you, a young man, big and strong, and the next, you are lying here like me, all dried up and almost done. I have memories, but my life is mostly gone."

Driving home from work that night in a '65 Mustang with rotted-out fenders, careening up Happy Valley Road, where I rented a farmhouse with my girlfriend Lizbeth, I can remember thinking about what he had said. *It goes so fast.* Even then I was terrified of missing anything. I wondered whether my own personal velocity, the mad to-ing and fro-ing of my everyday life, was a fearful response to the thought that life would get away from me.

Somewhere in there, maybe as a sophomore in college, something changed inside me. Bumping along, hanging out with my adopted tribe, smoking pot, and taking classes was not going to get it. I began to think of possibilities, of growing up, of having jobs that didn't involve name tags and bosses whose tiny lives found meaning only in ordering me around. I wanted to be something besides a pothead who played a remarkably inept harmonica. I decided to leave River Falls.

On my way out of town in 1976, I stopped to see Professor Robert in his office. His fingers and beard were tattooed with nicotine. His eyes peered into me with a kindness, but they unnerved me. He tapped out a Pall Mall for me and indicated matches next to an ashtray that looked like a Paul Manship sculpture, almost heroic in its texture and abundance. I was leaving, not so much for greener pastures but someplace where you could smell them with a little less acuity.

After slinking around the small Wisconsin campus for the first few quarters, I had enrolled in Robert's literature class. People, including the stoner in the corner of the room with the beaded roach clip attached to greasy jeans, sat up when he spoke. Professor Robert died in 1996, twenty years after we talked, so this may have been gussied up a bit by the passage of time, but not intentionally. When I stopped to see him before I left, he tilted me toward my future by having the decency to tell me the truth about the heedlessness of my current state.

"The last time I saw you, you were riding around in a convertible late at night on the sidewalks in the middle of campus, waving madly like you were in a parade. It was, um, impressive," he said in his mid-Atlantic lilt. Again with the kind eyes, which I avoided. "You're a smart boy, David. Very bright, actually, but you don't *know* anything. You haven't *read* anything."

That wasn't precisely true. After a nun in fourth grade told me no, my parents would not be in heaven when I got there, I laid awake long into the night for about a year, chewing through all of the Hardy Boys, Nancy Drews, and Black Stallions my parents' basement could hold. They filled my head with words and stories, and I have been spitting them back ever since. But sitting there with Professor Robert, I had no concept of writers, let alone of being one myself. Professor Robert reached into a drawer and handed me a list of sixty contemporary American authors. This, he said, is just a tiny slice of literature, but read this, and at least you will know *something*.

Over the next few years, I read the books on the list. Faulkner, Mailer, Brautigan, Vonnegut, Wolfe, Hemingway. I read them in a hammock with headphones on and Led Zeppelin cranking. I read them on break from smashing up patios with a 100-pound jackhammer. I read them when everyone else went to sleep. It wasn't that I wanted to be a writer. I just didn't want to be stupid.

The journalism part, well, that was just something I told people. An art and English teacher at my high school had sent me to a journalism day at River Falls, and I noticed that people's estimation of me seemed to rise when I mentioned that major. A few years after Woodward and Bernstein had done a number on a sitting president—saved the goddamn republic by typing, fer Chrissakes—reporting was still viewed as something to be admired.

Not that I did any. My only real experience was my tenure as editor of my eighth-grade paper. Handing off the baton at the end of the year,

I was typically modest—"We are proud of our achievement and would like to see it go on"—but after that I never actually wrote anything other than reports for class. I did short internships required by school at weekly papers—"Local students took a bite out of the Big Apple last week"—but I avoided the school newspapers and the nerdy can-do people who worked there. Too square. Too uptight. Too intimidating. But I was looking for something like they had.

"You were full of enthusiasm and joy of life," Lizbeth told me on a visit to New York in 2007. "We were sophomores and juniors in college. I think you had as many hopes and dreams as anybody else. That's how I remember it. We were all together and moving along. I was more surprised that you ended up tipping off the deep end than that you ended up being successful."

I traveled a lot after River Falls, all domestic, but saw people and things that had nothing to do with my little world of suburban Minneapolis. I sensed all kinds of possibilities, but not my place in them. I spent a lot of nights alone on the road, traveling in the West, checking out star-filled skies and making plans that contained no real plans.

5

MUSKIE TALE

... Gifted with such wondrous power and velocity in swimming
as to defy all present pursuit from man; this leviathan seems the
banished and unconquerable Cain of his race ...

—HERMAN MELVILLE, *MOBY-DICK*

When you go to those meetings, the ones with the shitty coffee that are knee-deep in aphorisms that keep millions alive, including me, they never talk about the fun part. Bad form, not done, not in keeping with the spirit of the occasion. But when chemicals and karma combusted into bliss, it was mad, mad fun. If not for those moments, why would people spend the rest of their lives chasing that feeling? Rats—humans too—continue to push on the bar in the cage of our existence looking for a reward past the point of reason because, every once in a while, something unthinkably delicious comes down the tube.

For the record, I had fun, some of it with David B. He is a friend, a professional colleague, and the guy who sat over my shoulder when I wrote my first story. David taught me a lot, including that *a lot* was two words, not one. He is one of the many people in my life who hung a right or a left long before I went down a road that ended with a bridge out and twisted human wreckage. Happily situated with a family and a freelance career, he agreed to meet with me, and we found ourselves ruminating not on the wages of sin but its splendors. It was a fun hour.

"There was one epic experience where we were up, I think, at your place or your parents' place, some place up north," he said, remembering an old fishing camp my family had bought, but I actually think it was my friend Joel's cabin. Both locales were the scene of multiple capers, and, like a lot of them, this one involved watercraft, LSD, fireworks, and long peals of laughter. He was out on the water with Brownie, a dear friend of ours who was almost always game for organized foolishness.

"All of us were around on the Fourth of July weekend," David said, probably recalling a night in 1983 or '84. "Brownie and I, we were all on the same green blotter. It had been done a lot around town, so we all knew it was good. And Brownie and I took a canoe out into the middle of the lake to get a look at the fireworks that were going on over the tree line all around us. And we were having a great old time being just high in the right way on acid, just the colors and all of that. Super sensory perception.

"And all of a sudden, *Boom!* Turns out you and Donald, maybe Eddie, all you guys are on the dock shooting big fucking bottle rockets at us," he said. "So here we are, we're blissing out, and the fucking criminals on the dock are trying to hit us with fireworks." I told him we were trying to make it better.

"And you did. It was meaningful, and it definitely added. So I turned to Brownie while we're out on the canoe—we're on acid, so once we get over the shock, we're kind of digging it—and I say, 'You know what, they're higher than we are. Something is going to happen.' And sure enough, we look over and the dock is on fire. One of the rockets had gotten into your fireworks stash, and they were all going up. And you guys were just screaming and running in all directions.

"Pretty much all of my near-death experiences have come with you," he said. "I don't know how close we ever were. I remember skittering over some back roads and into the drainage ditches in Wisconsin with you driving, not knowing how we were going to fucking live. I can still remember that vividly."

Another time David and I were in Mankato covering Minnesota

Vikings training camp, and we got pulled over one night when David was driving. They gave him the once-over, and he got back in the car. "We're driving away, and I'm sure my heart's beating a hundred miles an hour. And you say something along the lines of, 'Yeah, I'm really glad you passed that test, because there's a big spoonful of cocaine right under the front seat.'"

In those days, there was always one more edge to run the fingers along, no matter how dumb or ill considered. David, who had and has more common sense than many of us back in those days, said he tried smoking crack back then because he wanted to inhabit my skin for a night.

"People might not believe me, but part of the reason that I wanted to do it, aside from just innate curiosity, was that I wanted to see what was going on with you, because you were at a whole different level. I don't know how to describe it. There were always complications, and it was complicated, right? Being with you is complicated. A lot of fun, but a lot of logistics. Some emotional ups and downs, some legal complications. But there was just a whole level of foregoneness, of hollow-eyed looking around, absorption, self-absorption. It was just different. It was clearly beyond the power of any of us to do anything about it."

So in addition to teaching David to just keep typing until a lead came to him, I showed him how to smoke crack. "I'd done cocaine plenty by that point, but this was like—this was surprisingly smooth and powerful and nice," he said. "The second time I did it was where I kind of learned the difference between the addictive gene and the non-addictive gene."

Smart boy. He never smoked coke again.

David was incredibly supportive when I sobered up. There came a time after that when the editorship of the *Twin Cities Reader*, which we'd both worked for, came open. David campaigned openly and loudly for the job. He often talked to me about what he might do with the paper. I stayed in the cut, quietly sending the publisher a note saying that if I got the job, I would change most of the people there. I got the job.

"I kind of laid out my hopes and dreams and plans, and you nodded and gave me some feedback and whatever, and the truth is that you were getting ready to bust a move," he said, not huffy, just matter-of-fact. "And what I thought was, well Jesus, if you're even thinking about doing it at that point, a friend says, 'Hey, shut the fuck up, I'm going for the same job.' And you didn't do that. And later on when I got up the nerve to confront you—you who was the alpha male in my life—the answer I got back was I should have known better. It was my fault."

I didn't tell David because I did not want to put the people who had doubts about me—they were legion, and their skepticism was well founded—on notice that I was gunning for the job.

Of course, it would be easy to say that David's memory is now being bent in service of the present, but when I asked my wife, Jill, about his version of events, she said, "You should have told him."

In the early eighties, I threw a boys' weekend. The party invite had a picture of a muskie—a large, predatory freshwater fish—and Senator Ed Muskie. The copy read, "Your chances of seeing either muskie on this weekend are about equal."

Muskie fishing is an apt metaphor for the lot of the common man. You could make as many as twelve thousand casts on average before you caught one. If Sisyphus were still around, he'd be a muskie man. In Hayward, Wisconsin, it was not uncommon for people to get lawn chairs and binoculars when someone got a big one on, because it could take hours. Epic Saturday fishing show shit. Muskies were blurry fast, ferocious fighters, and overfished to the point of rarity, but they loved to eat: I saw an item in the Hayward paper about a forty-nine-inch muskie that was caught, and when they opened him up, there was a twenty-nine-inch fish inside him. And he was still eating, still going for the bait. That's a fish.

Jim, a pal at the time who signed up for the ride, was a gifted and funny writer, but he did not strike me as a guy born to wrangle bait, live or otherwise. Still, before we went, he insisted, "I'm going to catch

36

one of those damn things." For a while, I patiently explained that the trip was not actually about catching a muskie—"It's a metaphor, numbnuts"—but he still kept talking smack.

We had a little problem with pacing on Friday night. There were psychedelics and coke, and we all got drunk as goats. We went to a stripper bar near the cabins, the kind of joint where they handed out miners' helmets for those who wanted to sit close and shine a light on the talent. Two of the dancers came back to the cabin, but it was social, not business. Once they had their clothes on, the boys were curiously bashful and polite. I can remember shaking hands with one of the dancers at the end of the evening, saying it was a pleasure to make her acquaintance. It was three-thirty in the morning. We tumbled into five ramshackle cabins for a few hours of sleep.

There were over a dozen of us, and at seven o'clock—it was a freezing fall day, raining intermittently, and *hungover* is not an expansive enough term to cover the collective gestalt—we traveled to Lac Courte Oreilles, a chain of interconnected lakes, to meet our lone guide. A former fighter pilot, he took one look at us and asked who was in charge. I wobbled to the front.

"Only three of you in my boat at once," he said quietly. "Anybody pukes in my boat, they are out."

There was a fair amount of puking once we all got underway in a number of boats. Some of the people had never laid hands on an outboard and scattered into a vast horizon of bays, floating islands, and mysterious lakes. I never got in the guide's boat, and it fell to me to round up the truly lost boys at the end of the day. I finally found the last boat—"Thank God you're here, we're down to our last two beers"—and we caravanned to shore. There stood Jim, next to the guide. Next to the muskie they were weighing. I came up for a look. It was a keeper, but looked grim. Something about the eyes. I asked the guide about the fight to land this whopper, and he focused on the sunset while he told me that it "just sort of came straight in."

"I got one! Told you I was going to get one! And I did," Jim interrupted, doing a happy dance.

That night, we went to the Ojibwa Club, a grand Wisconsin supper club, and all ordered Fred Flintstone–sized rib eyes that overwhelmed the plates and dripped grease onto the oilcloth. Much tribute was paid to me at the head of the table, the mighty one, the one who had organized the splendid hunt.

A few weeks later, Donald and I were out at the bar, and I was boring someone for the hundredth time about the amazing muskie posse I had organized. I saw Donald giggling out of the corner of my eye. I've known him for a long time and sweated him until he finally told me that Jim had brought along a dead muskie that he had somehow acquired. Everyone on the trip knew except me. The righteous punking I took taught me that even those things that I thought I knew, that I had seen with my very own eyes, were subject to revision.

In 2007 Jim was in New York City because he had been nominated for a National Magazine Award, and we sat down in Bryant Park to walk back the cat on the Muskie Tale. Jim has an amazing memory and the storyteller's voice to make it all sound real.

I remembered one of the strippers as genial and cute, especially given the rustic backwater she was working in. Jim remembered a few other things.

"There was one that was skinny, no cosmetic enhancement," he said. "But her tits looked like she could have fed Romulus and Remus, the ones that were nourished by that wolf. She had a very smiling, kind-looking face.

"There was this big, fat, drooling guy who was giving her money, and he was sitting near the catwalk. At one point, he reached up and touched her leg, and her face just went from angel to demon. She grabbed him by the ears and just slammed his head on the wood and said, 'Don't you ever touch me.' I just remember that was a bit of a buzz kill. You probably partied with her, and she was nicer after that. I was drinking, but I was not part of the cocaine contingent."

I never knew much about the provenance of the fish. As it turned out, Jim went to see a wildlife artist for a story he was doing on duck stamp fraud, and noticed that the artist had a muskie he posed to use as a model.

"I knew I was going to this muskie fishing thing, and I said, 'Are you done with the fish?'"

It was a great snow job, one that I remember admiring at the time, but even all these years later, Jim worried about how it had landed on me. "It's possible that you thought that I was doing the muskie thing to kind of spite you—not spite you, but just pull one over on you. It was never like that. I just thought this was a perfect opportunity."

I wondered why he was telling the story so gingerly, but he reminded me that it was not all fun and games between us back then. I had bumped into him at the office of the *Reader* and confronted him about something I had heard he said.

"You threatened to kill me, and I was kind of shaken, and then you said that you were going to punch me," he said. "There were a couple people there, and I was eyeing the exits, but you were like a linebacker back then. I feared a little bit for my health, and there were a couple people that overheard that tried to calm you down. I apologized profusely, and I couldn't quite understand what I had done wrong. I learned later that you had a cocaine problem."

So, a little bit of an anger management issue. And what I had always conjured as good, clean fun—a frolic—seemed darker and more portentous to fellow travelers many years later. But could I throw a party or what?

I was, in retrospect, a complicated asset as a friend: a guy who presented significant upsides—when it was fun, it was really fun—but in pushing people past their boundaries, I eventually lost track of my own.

Daniel, a pal of mine who is now a filmmaker in Los Angeles, recalled in an e-mail that the muskie weekend had its share of frolic, but there was some darkness on the edges.

"You had that drive back then; that need to find the lines and then cross them, or consume them in some cases," he said. "You also seemed to have the need to push others to cross those lines with or without you. That was your challenge, and it was constant and relentless and bold and even beautiful at times."

Ah, finally, someone recognized me as the crown prince of all clown princes. But then he wrote this:

"But it could also get pretty fucking ugly. Because as often as not, at the end of the day, when you and the rest of us were spent and sick from the drugs and the drinking and whatever other mischief we had gotten ourselves into, and there was nothing left, you were still pushing."

6

MY BROTHER'S ENABLER

The truth is rarely pure and never simple.

—OSCAR WILDE

It was assumed that I would go to Benilde High School, a suburban all-boys Catholic school where my older brothers had gone. We were expected to work summers and pay half the tuition. I caddied at a Jewish country club, came up with my share, and hated nearly every second of it. Benilde had the same triumvirate that existed in every high school at the time: jocks, nerds, and freaks. I self-assigned to the freaks.

In an all-male environment, worth is signified by athletic prowess and the ability to get in a girl's pants. I was a decent but indifferent athlete, and I had enough friends who were girls that I didn't feel comfortable talking about the ones I managed to sleep with. I smoked pot instead. Going to school on boy island, a place where idiosyncrasy was pathologized, made getting stoned every day seem like a reasonable activity. We listened to Queen, playing stoner air guitar, and smoked endless amounts of crappy Mexican reefer. Greg, Tim, Fred, John, and Dan. A few others. Every once in a while, we set down the bong and got into some trouble—I was questioned but never charged in the theft of a yellow Maverick from the car dealership across the highway from the high school. We were not stupid guys, we just did stupid things. In retrospect, getting chronically stoned, even in high school, was dumb, like driving through life with the parking brake on.

Fred was farther out in the weeds than most of us. He did not pretend that grades, discipline, and convention were of any special significance. Eventually he was kicked out or dropped out and hitchhiked to California. He came back on a glorious summer night just after school had let out junior year.

We made plans to meet later. He and Greg were at Shady Oak Beach in Hopkins, working through some serious downers while catching up, and I was at the other end of town, sitting drunk and stoned on the roof of somebody's parents' house who had left for the summer, looking up into the gorgeous night. Under those stars, I zoned out. And a few miles away, Fred went for a swim.

> Authorities said that [Fred], 16, died at Methodist Hospital Saturday following a swimming accident at Shady Oak Lake in Minnetonka. [Fred] had been in critical condition since the mishap occurred Wednesday.
>
> [Fred] and a friend attempted to swim about 50 yards from the dock to shore when [Fred] went under water, authorities said. He was pulled from the water by lifeguards and taken to the hospital.
>
> —*MINNEAPOLIS TRIBUNE,* JULY 1, 1973

The funeral was wretched. All those jocks whom I loathed, who never gave Fred the time of day, coming up wobbly with loss.

Fred's family was bereft, including his little brother Frank, who was about nine. In my family, we were taught to be of service. Middle-pew Catholic stuff. I told Fred's parents that I would try to fill in some of the gaps, and I did, taking Frank to the zoo, ball games, and playing Frisbee. I also dated Fred's sister, who had a musical, generous laugh.

Frank and I stayed in touch through the years, and by the time I came back from traveling out West, he was out of high school. Things had changed for us both. Frank knew this guy in his neighborhood who would put money out on the street for high interest. I was acquainted with someone at the University of Minnesota who knew coke people who had access to serious weight. Neither of us had any clear idea of what he was doing, but late at night at my house in Minneapolis, we scratched out numbers on a pad of paper that showed us getting high and making lots of money. It didn't factor in self-induced shrinkage, the good-guy discount to pals, the free coke to the willing girls—not to mention that one time we weighed up a quarter ounce in a dark little room in my basement, decided to do a taste first, and when it came time to weigh it, it was gone, scattered into the detritus of the cellar. Nobody copped to knocking it over. We were idiots, what did we know?

Our first big deal was more sitcom than criminal enterprise, and, as in all my dealings with Schedule 1 narcotics, it eventually went to shit. The girl who hooked it up, Julie—short and cute as bugs' ears, a tough little broad from northern Minnesota—took us over to an apartment in South Minneapolis with some pretty serious guys and then left, kissing me on the cheek as she went. There we sat, two suburban rubes with two older black dudes. The bigger one talked in a street patois for ten minutes straight about our various options for buying two ounces: rock versus powder, packaging, pricing, that kind of stuff. He may as well have been speaking Mandarin. Frank and I looked at each other nervously when he finished, not knowing what to say. The other dude, Bart, finally broke the ice and said to his partner, "These white boys have no idea what you are talking about. Slow down and talk straight." (Bart eventually became a friend, and I saw him years later. "Look at you now, all prosperous and shit. I knew you back when you couldn't count. You remember that." I do.)

But when we finally figured out what we wanted—"one bag pure, one powder"—we found out we had to go somewhere else. *This dope peddling stuff was full of surprises.* We went to the West Bank of Minneapolis, near the university, and up a set of stairs on the outside of the house to an old, nasty apartment. They took our money, went into another room, and we stared at each other, not knowing if they were going to come back through the door with the drugs or guns. Eventually they came back with the drugs, and we left, both of us relieved and happy that we had pulled it off. Given that I was the brains of our operation, such as they were, I felt somehow responsible and tender toward Frank even though I had opened up a door to serious, felony weight and the kind of crooks who went with it. After I sobered up, I had enduring shame about taking what had been a good gesture—being a big brother to a kid who had lost his real one—and morphing that relationship into something toxic.

After being out of touch for more than a decade, I found Frank on his hobby farm west of the Twin Cities. When I pulled up, he came rolling out the door with a little bit of a beer gut, but otherwise, same old Frankie. Like a lot of guys from the old days, he really only had one question. "Where you been?" Long story, I said. We caught up for a while. He's married after a fashion, with nice kids, and working hard as a printer. We walked out to a huge shed that was really his clubhouse, full of tools, a fridge, and a huge wooden boat he is going to fix up one day.

When the story of that first dope deal came up, we both found ourselves giggling and holding our stomachs. What dorks we were. The dope house was a scary-looking place, and as Frank remembers it, it got scarier when we opened the door. "Before we even entered the room, there was an older black guy sitting in the chair, rocking back and forth with a gun laying across his lap. I remember the barrel on it was about . . ."

I tell Frank I think that's total bullshit. A quirk of memory. He remains steadfast.

"He had a gun laying on his lap sideways with a barrel on it that was about eighteen inches long, and he was running his hand across it, and I immediately went, OK—I'm the guy with the two grand in my pocket, and I'm thinking, Hey, what's gonna happen?"

I remember that feeling, at least. How well did I really know Julie, anyway?

They came back with the stuff, just like they said. And more, Frankie remembers. "They said, 'Is this all you want? Oh, look what we got!' And they opened up a garbage bag full of pot. And then the guy whipped out a magazine full of pages of LSD, and I said, 'We came for the first thing right now; I think we'll just take that and go.'"

My junkie pride kicks in while he tells the story. I tell Frank it makes it sound like he ran the whole thing—at what, nineteen years old? True, I did not know my ass from a hole in the ground, but I was definitely the senior member of the team.

"Hey, man, I was there alongside you," Frank finally allows.

That's better.

We chat a bit about our partnership, and he mentions that I was always too fond of my own product to make any real money, especially after I started smoking it. "I believe I turned you on the first time," Frank said, his smile somewhere between shit eating and shame ridden.

So he was the one. "Shut up, man. Don't you think I felt guilty about that the rest of my life?" I am secretly thrilled. It sort of made us even, in a weird way. Guilt about Frank had rattled around behind me for years in sobriety. Some of the burdens we carry include false weight, perhaps to make up for all the horrible stuff we actually did and forgot.

As Frank tells it, when I found out that he knew how to freebase, something I had only heard about, I insisted he come over to my house during the day. I also invited Crazy Ken, a chess champion, nudge, and all-around freak who had access to coke that was a very rare level of purity.

"This guy pulled out a sack of shit—had to be a quarter pound, I ain't kidding," Frank recalled. While Crazy Ken and I watched anxiously, Frank spent time working two grams on the stove and took the first hit.

"All right, let me give it a test go here. And I fire up the blowtorch," Frankie said. "Holy shit, man! I could just—my knees were going weak. 'That's it, it's good, yeah, it's fine.' I remember Ken asking what it was like, and I told him it was kind of like snorting, only better."

Sort of. Unless you have the tiniest little gene or penchant for paranoia. Kenny did his first hit of crack. He stood up immediately. Before I even had a chance to do my hit, he was out my back door and picking up garbage can lids, peering down into the cans looking for, I dunno, federales or something. I watched with interest, but I was more concerned with getting my turn. "He'll be fine," I said, turning back to Frank.

Twenty years later Frank and I sat in the gloom of that shed, arguing and talking smack about the old days, the whole highlight reel: the time I took down a door-length mirror and put down a line of coke from one end to the other; or the time the bad guys were after us for real, and we had to find their money, like, right this goddamn minute; or the time when we wrestled and I broke his ribs. But the memory that I had corrupted him, led him down a path? Not so much.

As it turned out, *I* was the one who needed the big brother.

"Well, there was a time when I took you inside and said I was gonna lock you in my basement, and I'm gonna pull you out of it," he said. "It might be the time you broke my three ribs. That's I think what it was. I said, 'I don't like what I'm seeing anymore.' So that was my telling you you've got to get out of it. And you didn't like it at all. Take you home, lock you in my basement till you pull out of it. That would have been something, huh?

"I think you got pretty screwed up. I'm not gonna take responsibility for it," Frank said, hands on his knees. "We were kinda tit for tat, I guess."

7

MOBY DICK'S

The vigour necessary to prosecute two professions at the same time is not given to every one, and it was only lately that I had found the vigour necessary for one.

—ANTHONY TROLLOPE, *AUTOBIOGRAPHY*

I was at my parents' house one day in 1982 when my dad told me about his pal Peter, a guy who ran Catholic Charities. He watched as a couple of beefy cops pounded two black suspects already in custody. Peter stepped toward them to ask why they were beating up those guys and got a piece of same. It sounded outrageous.

"Somebody should do a story about this," I said to my dad.

Maybe, my dad said, it should be you. I called the editor of the *Twin Cities Reader*. He sounded interested, in a bored, yeah-sure kind of way, committing only to read what I came up with.

I pretended I knew what I was doing—isn't that what most of life rests on?—and fumbled my way through police reports, disciplinary records, and relevant witnesses. With my pal David over my shoulder, I wrote it up. When it came time to deliver, I found myself chattering away in front of Brian, the editor, unable to hand it over.

"Ah yes, the selling of the story," Brian said, sitting in his house in 2006 when I went to see him. " 'Yes, fine,' I said, 'just give me the goddamn story. Tell you what, what if I read it and decide?' It was a kind of spoken-word performance, I recalled. You were twenty-five years ahead of your time," Brian said, laughing.

It worked out, running on the cover of the weekly on February 4, 1982.

> He was a visitor from another part of town, and
> he had seen enough. He stepped out of the crowd
> and asked the police the wrong question. "Why
> did you have to do that?" That question bought
> [Peter] a trip downtown. A short stop at the jail
> for booking and then over to the hospital to get
> the answer to his question looked at.

The story was followed by many others. A person who hated to miss anything, I had found something where finding that last little thing was considered an asset. I was not a maniac; I was a journalist, a head case with a portfolio. The manic, grabby tyrant inside me had found expression in an activity that would bring me recognition, a measure of recompense, and a reason to do something besides trip from high to high.

"There was a higher energy level, a compulsion, obsessive compulsive— whatever it is that makes you do it and do it well, somewhere in there," Brian said. "There was a force of nature thing, which was a huge part of your appeal—to me, anyway, and I think to a lot of other people. You could roll in, ingratiate yourself immediately, and sustain it for long period."

Brian and I had adjoining cubicles, with a word processing machine that was shared in the window between us. "It's nine-thirty in the morning, which was rare for me to be there at all, and I'm typing away," Brian recalled. "I look up, and here comes Carr, who looks like he probably has not slept at all, or if he did, he slept in his clothes. 'Hey Dave, how are you doing?' 'Good, Lambert, good.' Sits down, and I continue to type, and rustling of papers here and there, drawer underneath the typing carousel on his side slides open, and I'm typing away, and the next thing I hear is a big hovering sound followed by an expression of satisfaction. It's now ten in the morning, and we got the sales crew walking by, and I said, 'David, are you OK?' 'Yeah, man, I'm fine, really good.' I don't remember where you had been the night before or how soon the morning had come upon you, but that was a vivid moment."

Our office was just off the grubby Block E, the home of Moby Dick's, a place that served "a whale of a drink." We often went there late, when the muse seemed in need of one more quick shove.

Moby's was one of the few places where the races mixed in a state where even most of the food was white: lutefisk, lefsa, endless seas of milk—skim, 2 percent, whole. Even the butter was white. The queen of the state fair was carved out of white butter. White like the paint factory in *The Invisible Man*. White like me.

Moby Dick's was not white. The butter queen did not hang there. Clarence worked the door and let me in no matter how trashed I was, because I always minded my manners and tipped like the former bartender I was. There were deals to be made in the corners, but the drug of choice there was booze. Separators, kamikazes, a rainbow of shots. It was long rumored that people who had been awarded medallions as tokens of their sobriety could plunk one on the counter and get started again on the house. I never tested that.

It was as close to a big city as I could get; like *Cheers,* only with pimps, working girls, and hustlers. I loved it there. Moby's was less slumming than slamming, big-time fun, a place that didn't observe the clock or weekend cycle of normal people. It always rocked.

"Anybody who was prepared to get in trouble on a given night would be there, and they all knew you by your first name," Brian said.

I spent many late nights bouncing between Moby's and work, the job and the Life, getting information and obtaining substances. My colleagues appreciated the work I did for the paper, but they had to notice the train wreck that came rolling down the track with it. One day I dropped off Mary Ellen, a colleague who constantly covered my ass at work, to pick up a movie schedule for the paper while I waited in the car.

"I came out, and the cops had you against the wall; the backseat of your vehicle had about three thousand parking tickets in it," she said.

For every working screw-up like me, there had to be a Mary Ellen, a pal who told me when my behavior was out of pocket, or that the boss was up to here, or made phone calls to patch over some fiasco I had created. When I went over to her house in North Minneapolis in the summer of 2006, she got out the T-shirt that said "I Am a Close Personal Friend of David Carr." She generally earned it, but as I recall, on that day with the parking tickets, she pretended not to know me.

"I actually did say, 'What's going on with my friend?' I did say that. 'Ma'am, go back and sit in the car.' It gave me a chance to hide the pot."

I was booked on warrants and then let back out. Two decades after she watched me get hauled away, I visited Mary Ellen, and she drank enough whiskey for both of us as we talked deep into the night, arguing and laughing the whole time. Her boyfriend Michael, a talented songwriter-musician, had been at that thirtieth birthday party, and we all recalled that he had come up with a song for the occasion, "You Might Be Surprised," which flicked at my tendency to disrupt best-laid plans. He grabbed a guitar and sang it note for note, with words that sort of captured my ethos at the time:

> So don't be chicken, about something that you never tried.
> You might feel like you might fail.
> That's just fear and foolish pride,
> So go ahead and give it a try.

Don't give up and don't be shy.
You might not succeed at first,
But you might be surprised.

Or horrified, or pulled over, or out a lot later than you had planned.

———

The clips in the basement from those days are stuck together and hard to read, but the profiles of politicians, cops, and a few robbers still read well enough. Still, any pride in the work is circumscribed by what a jerk I must have been while I put them together.

After Brian moved on to writing, Mark, the publisher, put his wife, Deb, in the editor's job. She had no journalism experience and was far too demure for the job, but she also had a very firm grip on what she did not know and set about quickly learning it. She was a woman who defined propriety, and I was a walking offense to it.

I was working for Deb in 1984 when I went to treatment at the urging of my first wife. Deb showed up for a meeting at the request of my counselor. She handed me a 6,200-word story I had written about Noam Chomsky the week before. It looked like a piñata at an eight-year-old's birthday party, a once-delicate thing that had been bashed by sticks.

We sat on the edge of Loring Park many years later, laughing about my ability to write something vastly more turgid than even Chomsky himself. I made an immediate amends for putting her through that hell and dozens of others. She would have none of it.

"We broke some great stuff. You had more access to the more interesting aspects of political life in the city than almost anyone else who was writing. You cultivated all those people, and even when you were revealing things that they maybe didn't want revealed, you had it right, and you didn't abuse them. The calls that I would take, inevitably, they would say you were a loose cannon, they didn't think you were very professional. But then I would say, 'Show me what is wrong in this thing. What's wrong about it?'"

In her rearview, she failed to recall the remnants of coke mixed with salt and mustard packets at the bottom of my desk drawer or the wreckage I made of the weekly news cycle.

"When you ask me about all the negative stuff, I so long ago flushed that away," she said. "That's not the parts that are remembered at all. Other than in a vague sort of interesting, colorful way. That's not the vivid stuff that I remember. I remember the good work."

8

SPOT REMOVER

In 2006 and 2007, as I looked for documentary evidence of my past, it became obvious that my timing was off by quite a few years. If I had started earlier, maybe my defense attorney would not have vanished after being disbarred, taking my files with him. Some of the criminal files—misdemeanor stuff, mostly; there's one felony narcotics charge—are still there, but there are significant gaps. Arrests that I remembered as epic were just a blip, and more bizarrely, I came across a document that seemed to be about the arrest of someone named David Michael Carr that I knew nothing about. He seemed like a piece of work:

CHARGES						
ASSAULT 385.190, DAS 171.24						
PRISONER'S NAME (First-Middle-Last)		CHECK IF HISPANIC ☐	D.O.B.	AGE	JUVENILE	
DAVID MICHAEL CARR			9/8/56	31		
HOME ADDRESS	HOME PHONE	BUSINESS ADDRESS		BUSI. PHONE		
▉ Oliver Ave. No.	▉▉▉					
ALIASES/NICKNAMES		OTHER KNOWN ADDRESSES		OTHER PHONE		

That's me.

NARRATIVE: *Give detailed account of offense and circumstances leading to arrest*
Squad was southbound on Hennepin Ave. when officers observed the above defendant remove the complainant a party I.D.'d as William Y. Mikhil from the yellow cab he was driving. Defendant then began punching the complainant for no apparent reason. Officers exited squads subsequently placing the above defendant under arrest for the above charge. Complainant wished to sign a Citizen's Arrest which was later completed. A D.L. check was run on the defendant with officers later being advised that the defendant was DAS. Defendant was advised he was under arrest for the above charges, his vehicle towed to the Police Impound Lot, and he was transported to HCJ and booked.

sdj-3/27/88

And that's me too.

No idea what the beef was and how I effected to "remove" the guy from his cab. Was he still rolling? And who is William Y. Mikhil? I couldn't find him, but DonJack, a reporter I hired to come behind me to further investigate what I could not find out for myself, traced Mikhil, actually Mikhail, to Melbourne, Australia, and then he disappears. So is he still mad, or did his citizen's arrest bring him a sense that justice had been done? I can't make amends or get other details of how we got into it. But the part about "no apparent reason," no driver's license, and, suddenly, no car? I have to admit that sounds like me. I was clearly out of my box when I began "punching the complainant," apparently right in front of a squad. I remember nothing, except that I'm pretty sure he must have started it.

9

THE LOST BOYS OF ELEVENTH AVE.

This is our island. It's a good island. Until the grown-ups come to fetch us, we'll have fun.

—RALPH, *LORD OF THE FLIES*

The onset of adulthood is an organic, creeping process. No one wakes up one day and decides, "Lo, on this day I shall forever put away childish things and begin clipping coupons to go to Wal-Mart." But in his or her own time, the person who was preoccupied by beer pong and doobie cruises begins to notice that life has other aspects—careers, families, homes—serious matters in need of tending. But being an addict means that you never stipulate to being an adult. You may, as the occasion requires, adopt the trade dress of a grown-up, showing responsibility and gravitas in spurts to get by, but the rest of the time, you do what you want when you want.

Keeping shame at a minimum while you fend off maturity requires that adult activities are seen as the province of goobers—squares whose idea of a night on the edge is playing quarter poker with the boys and drinking a six-pack of imported beer before catching some tube and hitting the sack. But as screens in bedrooms up and down the block begin to flicker, signaling another day is being tucked in, the addict will come alive.

There is value in that choice. Too many nights of Johnny Carson back then, and before you know it, you're watching *The Tonight Show* in a nursing home, and hey, who is this Leno guy anyway?

In 1977 I went on the road in the West. In Montana I saw my friend Dale, who was working the railroad; in Denver, a college friend named Sue; and I made some new friends in California. I moved around without purpose or urgency, hitchhiking and remaining unspecific when I got in a car. Where you going? Somewhere else, I'd say.

Eventually the challenges of sleeping alone wherever I found myself wore out. Under a bridge? Snakes. In the woods? Was that a bear or a bird I heard? A flophouse in Cheyenne? Um, that cowboy looks rough and tough, but he seems a little too friendly. I came back to Minneapolis later that year and enrolled at the University of Minnesota. It was less about a renewed sense of purpose than boredom from living without one. To finance my return to civil life, I ended up working at the Little Prince, where I met Kim, my first wife.

Kim won't talk to me about those days. "I am very happy to no longer be part of any of that, and I don't want to go back there." It is not that she does not wish me well. She is married to a friend of mine from college and their response to the excesses of those early days was to move toward church and God. They seem very happy. But when I drove out to see her, about an hour outside of Minneapolis, it was extremely awkward; the equivalent of a burglar stopping by to ask you what it felt like to have part of your life stolen. She had no intention of taking a walk down memory lane. She is a bright person, capable of cold-eyed assessment about all matters, including our time together, so it is a significant loss in the effort to find the truth of what I did and why. But I secretly admired her unwillingness to engage my needs, my narcissism, one more time.

No one can really explain why I married her, including me. Not that she wasn't pretty, and pretty fun. But she was the kind of girl who had started collecting ironing boards and vacuums at a young age. Talk of marriage came soon after we met. For all my rebellious posturing, I failed to be honest with this woman or myself. The picture of me arm in arm with my parents in the vestibule of the church on our wedding day tells the entire story: a portrait of a nervous young man who knows he is making a very grave mistake.

I was a completely immature twenty-three-year-old kid who was a hard worker but clearly under the sway of mood-altering chemicals. My family knew I was nowhere near being ready to be married, and her family, decent farming people and fundamentalist Christians, had no idea what to make of me. Everybody decided to smile and wear beige and sort of hope for the best.

She thought, as the cliché goes, I would change. And me? I didn't really have a tiny thought in my noggin. But it became clear as I got a job, as we bought a house, as we tuned in to Carson and got ready for bed, that yes, I had made a big mistake. You can't become normal by pretending you are.

When I was married to Kim and living in South Minneapolis, there was this guy across the street, "Ralph," who was small but powerfully built, with a voice that could knock you off a sofa. (Ralph is a pseudonym.) His hair was cut short, his arms were big; almost more like legs in their heft and power. He worked asphalt, but he was canny, street smart, and brutally handsome. By the time I was getting to know him, he had already been there and back with the coke—moving quarter pounds in and out of Florida, among other endeavors—and now was newly unmarried and on a bit of a tear. We would stay up night after night, talking shit and doing our coke.

Ralph was a fairly robust man in all of his endeavors, no more so than when he laid down a line of coke. If the piles he did had been flour, you could have made doughnuts with them. He did not mess around with little toots of this or that. At Ralph's house, it was more *Scarface* than Studio 54.

Ralph was a bit of a whack job, but he was not a loser. He went to work, no matter how little he slept, and kept himself in coke—no small task, that—with all kinds of gambits, some of which veered toward scams but were just this side of legit. But he could go dark in a heart-beat, an ambulatory mix of barely contained rage and atavism, so we had a couple of other things in common.

On any given night, one of us might have decided to take it easy, to give it a rest, and then the other would send some luminous fiber out over Eleventh Avenue in South Minneapolis. Just one, I'd say. Just a bump, he'd say. Then it was on.

It was not all darkness and pathology between us. There were cross-street bottle rocket fights, lots of very serious Frisbee (if there is such a thing), along with orphan Thanksgiving dinners and goofing with all the kids on the block. We had wonderful friends in common, put on lots of great barbecues, and looked after each other in the way good neighbors do.

This was the early eighties, and we both kept it together, sort of. One weekend somebody booked a cabin up in western Wisconsin on Lower Clam Lake, blew a whistle, and before you knew it, it was on. On the way up, we got nailed in Siren, Wisconsin, for shooting big rockets out of my convertible, but the sheriff was a good guy and said that if we promised to head straight to our rented cabin, he would not effectuate any arrests.

Ralph had already been on a three-day bender, working his way through a rock of coke the size of a baseball. By the time we got to the cabin, it was down to the size of a golf ball—still impressive, but sub-ject to ineluctable entropic forces.

Ralph was more than happy to share until it looked like he actually might run out and that time was nigh. We were all partying on the porch, and he sat in the corner with his golf ball, glowering and doing lines. We all worked on the little odds and ends we had, sweating him for more, but to no avail.

Ralph, who had done at least two grams of coke in the past two hours, nodded off like a common heroin junkie, with a mirror and a ball of coke on his lap. We knew what to do. I said his name a couple of times, louder as I went, and he did not wake up. I got a pair of tongs from the kitchen—Ralph had massive, ropey forearms, and I didn't want to get clipped if he woke up—and reached in with a surprising amount of dexterity and proceeded to remove said ball of coke. We took it into the kitchen and tee-hee'd as we carved it equally on all sides, taking a few grams off of its remaining girth so that it still looked like a nice ball of coke, only slightly smaller. I placed it back on the mirror in his lap.

Somebody had some quaaludes. I always had trouble with dosage around pills. They seemed so small, so edible, so why have just one? After two or four or whatever it was, I took Donald and a girl named Jennifer for a ride at sunrise. I saw what I felt was a nice hill to climb to see the sun come up, but it was more like a swamp. I buried my glorious Pontiac convertible up to the wheel wells.

We were walking on the road, and the same cop from the night before came by.

"Is that your car back in the swamp?"

Yes.

"Get in." He brought us to the cabin where we were staying and told the folks there to keep me inside for a while.

So I got away with, not murder, but some bonehead moves. And that shrinking golf ball, I got away with that too. I've always felt a little sheepish about it. I think the technical legal term for what I did was, um, stealing, but Ralph sort of had it coming. Still, I wondered if he knew.

All these years later, I was sitting at a picnic table in a small town in the midwest with Ralph, and even though we have long since parted company, we still have a lot in common. Both of us are off the coke, we each have a daughter about the same age, and both of us got hooked up with women who eventually went to jail. Ralph's wife got into the coke a little, and then, almost right away, it became the only thing.

Ralph looked good, but then he always did. I edged up to that night at Clam Lake.

"You fell asleep with that golf ball on your lap, and we, um, reshaped it," I finally stammered out.

"You did! I never knew! Twenty years later. Reshaped it, and it was a smaller golf ball?!" He sounded impressed, which I was relieved to hear.

You could scan Ralph's résumé and see the lifetime of pushing asphalt and people around, the multiple wives, the dealing in heavy weight, the booming full-of-shit voice, and think he was a knuckle-head. But he had buried a little dough along the way and bought a house in a nice town. He was now managing, at nearly sixty years old, to still hit the job every morning, dropping his daughter off at day care before sunup and then coming home after dark. In the winter he chilled out and took his daughter on little trips. His ex-wife was in prison again after several escapes.

Ralph knows his way around a story or two, and he told me a few I had forgotten. Like the time he came out with a woman to the Anchorage, a seafood restaurant in a hotel where I worked in the eighties. It was a nice joint. I have only the vaguest recollection of this story, but he tells it with a great deal of detail. His date was a madam, but she scanned as a pretty, normal woman. By prior arrangement, he was seated in my station, and I played it on the down-low for the whole dinner, never letting on that I knew him. We had curtained booths, so I gave them their privacy and would announce myself before poking my head in.

As Ralph tells it, after they had dinner, I parted the curtains with a dessert tray, which probably featured a flourless torte, a mousse, a liqueur pie, and a small plate that was domed in silver. I leaned into the booth and explained each of the desserts in vivid detail and then, with a flourish, removed the dome to reveal a giant rock of cocaine along with a gold razor and straw—an aperitif he had given me in advance to be presented thusly.

"This girl looked down at that and looked at me and looked at you and looked there and looked at me and looked at you—and I was, well, 'You know, that looks quite good; why don't we have that for the night, would that be OK with you?' And she was looking at me and looking at you and looking at me and going, ah, yes. And you just played the whole thing off, 'OK, very good, sir, that is a good selection and a good choice. I think you'll enjoy that.' And you closed the drapes up, and away you went."

For the record, I did not reshape *that* golf ball before I presented it as a dessert.

––––––––––

As we talk, supply—having lots and having none—becomes a motif in the recollection. During the early eighties, Donald, Ralph, and I were booked to serve as groomsmen in our buddy Orv's wedding, which was held in Grosse Pointe, Michigan, where his fiancée Patty's parents lived. My wife, Kim, sensing a high probability of mayhem, had declined to attend, and I can remember thinking with satisfaction that she had it all wrong, that she was missing a spectacular time. Our reputation preceded us, which meant that we would be tethered to some kind of Emily Post lady for the weekend. It was her job to keep us on schedule and prevent us from trashing the proceedings.

We flew to Chicago, rented a Lincoln Town Car, and drove to Detroit. We were pretty torn up by the time we got there. Knowing
Ralph's tendency to consume ungodly amounts of coke, I stashed a bit
in the car when he wasn't looking, so that when we ran out—a moment
that was bound to arrive—I'd have a bit in reserve.

Orv and Patty were fittingly happy and good-looking—they are
still very well married to this day—and we kept it between the rails for
the most part. The reception was held at a lovely high-end country
club, and as the band started to wind down, Ralph came up to me and
said he was out.

"What a coincidence, me too," I said, not letting either eyebrow
move.

"You have nothing?" Ralph asked. Technically it was almost true.
Whatever I had—not much really; a snootful that would last me awhile
but be gone in a single blaze of Ralph's voracious left nostril—was out
in the car.

After a few minutes, he asked me for the car keys. I handed
them over without worry. What I had was buried deep. He would
not find it.

The reception began to empty out, and Donald and I went out
front and looked for the car, which was gone. Minutes went by, and
then we saw Ralph driving back and forth out front, the interior lights
on so I could see his smile. He had taken the car hostage and was screw-

ing with me. He would veer in close and then split. Ralph's junkie radar told him I was holding, somehow, some way, and he just wanted to show me that he knew.

He finally tired of the game and pulled up with the window open. I got the jump on him, pulled him through the window, and before he knew what happened, he was facedown in the flower bed in front of the country club. Donald and I got in the Town Car and drove away.

Back at the hotel, Donald and I were having a few more laughs when there was a knock at the door. There was Ralph, chest heaving, dirt still on his tux, wielding a butter knife, of all things. He was no longer pissed about the coke or the beat-down. But friends don't leave friends facedown in a country club garden. (Sort of like Donald leaving me at the Cabooze.) By the time hotel security got there, Ralph was working me over, and I was upside down against an adjoining hotel room door. I did not fare well. My hand was fractured, my head was lolling to port, and I had a limp.

It was quiet in the Lincoln on the drive back to Chicago in the morning, and we sat in separate rows flying to Minneapolis. Kim picked us up, her anger mixed with the satisfaction of knowing that she had made a wise move staying home.

Both Ralph and I have our regrets, even some about that night. But not much by way of explanation.

"Well, drugs and alcohol," Ralph said through his shades, his arms resting on the picnic table. "I think it might have been the alcohol more than the drugs. Everybody's doing coke and drinking, and, you know, how much can you drink? How much can you drink?"

A bunch.

"So in that particular incident, you know, that's all vague to me—I remember it about the same way. Maybe not the particulars. I don't know, you're asking one guy who is drunk and stoned if his memory matches the other guy's who's drunk and stoned."

Donald is dim on the details of the weekend. He remembered ripping his tux to shreds rather than taking it off, he remembered we ran out of coke, and he remembered Ralph taking me apart at the hotel. And, oh yeah, he remembered that I had it coming.

Our friendship—the nascent journalist and the wizened asphalt guy hanging out—was one small expression of the pub theory of life, that we are all of a common fabric once we have a pint in our hands. Or, by extension, a line of coke between us. Even two decades later, I never understood how Ralph could get up and confront that roaring truck, the hot asphalt that needed to be shoveled around, the foreman who never seemed satisfied. I was managing to keep it together, but good God, he was doing real work. As it turns out, he was a lot more worried about me.

"When you would come over in the morning to get a cup of coffee, which you dearly needed, you would have crap on your tie, on your shirt—your breath would smell so bad of puke, David, it would be hard to talk to you across the room. I would often wonder, How are you gonna go out like that? and you didn't seem to know. And I would say, 'Geez, David, aren't you gonna clean up?' And you'd go, 'No, I gotta go, I gotta go.'

"You would leave, and I'd wish you good-bye, and I'd fill your coffee cup, and I'd just shake my head and think, Good God, how are you able to keep a job looking how you are?"

Ralph stayed out in the Life for a while, but here we were, handing creased wallet photos of our daughters back and forth, discussing the merits of day care, the perils of single parenting, and dating while being a single father. We were two former roughnecks now in a position of explaining to their daughters why their mothers weren't around and why our households were not like the other kids'.

The comedy of how things played out—the sheer, brutal irony— hung for a while. We were men who had ruined or nearly ruined the lives of every woman we had ever hooked up with. And then Ralph explained something that I probably knew but had never been able to articulate.

"In my other marriages and with my other kids, I justified what I was doing because they had their mothers," he said. "So I was not a good dad, but they still had a sound home, going to church on Sunday and everything else. But all of a sudden, I was *them*. I had a daughter. Now what do you do? I had to become them."

He became the one who rushes to get the daughter from day care, feeds her, tucks her in, and then flips on Leno and falls asleep before he finishes the monologue.

"I'll tell you what: After I saw my daughter, I became everybody else in my life," he said. I couldn't see his eyes behind the shades, but I knew we were sort of having a moment. "I became my former wives. I saw them. And what a fucking dick I must have been, because it's horrible to be married to a drug addict. It made me not want to do it. I didn't want to be what I was seeing someone else be. Does that make sense?"

10

FUTURE SHOCK

In the fall of 1978, some of the people around me grew concerned that I was headed beyond party boy into something more pathological. I went to see a hipster therapist, Peter, the kind of guy who would talk about the *amazing* Talking Heads show we'd both seen earlier in the week before exploring why I ended up with my head in a toilet many hours after the show. Peter developed some renown as a guy who did not buy into the whole disease concept of addiction. But if there was such a thing, he was pretty sure I had it.

PETER: Do you believe in the pathology of addiction?

DAVID: Yes.

PETER: Well, in my opinion, you have all the significant indicators.

DAVID: I've known that for a while, but I always thought I could knock around for ten more years.

PETER: You probably can.

I entered treatment for the final time ten years later.

I went looking for Peter to confirm the conversation, but he had lost his license and disappeared off the map. After I finished the book, DonJack, a reporter who helped me track down loose ends, found Peter's daughter in Chicago, and she promised to pass on a message. Peter called me back from Norway. As it turned out, there had been some fiasco with one of his patients, and he had left the country soon after. He remembered a great deal about my case: the fact that I was a cokehead, the fact that I was married to somebody I should not have been, and the fact that I remained employed and respected professionally despite my hobbies. He didn't remember the exact conversation that is so burned into my memory.

"I may have said something like that, that if you believed you were an addict, then you probably were," he said. "I remember there was a lot of alcoholism in your family and that you were having a lot of trouble in your marriage.

"Look, who knows what was going on with you? You were in a culture at the time that saw coke as nonproblematic, even though it was clearly creating problems for you. You were very young, and you were writing, like, half the paper at the time, like three thousand words a week. You were stressed and burning the candle on every end."

And the ten-years part?

"I wasn't trying to be prescient or anything. I just figured, at twenty-four, yeah, you could probably keep it up for a while, and eventually you would hit a wall. I guess you did."

11

A MAN IN FULL

If Tony Soprano never killed anyone, if he actually loved Carmela and treated her with respect, if all he ever did was drink and laugh and pull a few capers, he might be in the same zip code as Fast Eddie. Long retired from the bad old days and the bad old ways that went with them, Fast Eddie and his girlfriend Laurie run a restaurant in a refurbished old building in a cool little river town on the Wisconsin side of the Mississippi. He misses the old corners and the fools who worked them like a rock in his shoe—he feels the absence, and it feels good.

Not to make out like he is or was a pussycat. My old neighbor Ralph insists that Eddie came to collect one time with a sawed-off, but Eddie waves this off many years later. "He only *thought* I had one. There was no fucking gun." (It's funny how many of our stories include the specter of guns, but twenty years later I found that nobody ever owned one.)

Eddie is a good storyteller but not always great on the details, an infirmity we share. But he was around for most of it, the good and the bad, and I was happy for any excuse to be in his presence. He, Donald, and I had a bit of a reunion in the summer of 2007. I used a crowbar and a few imperatives to get Donald out of his little shack in Newport.

"Road trip, asshole!" I barked into the phone. "I'll be by at nine." Donald came out fully armed, with rods and tackle boxes, and we ripped down over the river to Eddie's joint. We took a boat out to an anchored fishing barge, and Donald immediately caught a walleye.

I continued to fish while Donald and Eddie ducked around a corner of the barge for a joint just to add to the sparkle of an early summer day. Donald, always concerned about supply, had brought along a half gallon of Old Grand-Dad. All these years later, did I wish I could help him along with the jug of whiskey? I did not. I'm the kind of guy who would have been even more worried about the amount on hand if I joined in, half gallon or not, trapped in the middle of the river. None for me, please.

Eddie is a man in all that noun means. He pays his bills, works his ass off, plays decent golf, and does not cheat on strokes, rules, or his girlfriend. I have seen him in some very tight corners, and he never pussed out, never blamed anybody without cause. He was happy when he was rolling and philosophical when he wasn't. Having Eddie as a friend—he is the godfather to my youngest and something of a father to my twins—makes all the mayhem from those days almost worth it. If I hadn't made a detour, if I hadn't bush-whacked my way to the darker side of town, I never would have met him.

He comes from a family that includes some real, actual hoods, people who were all smiles and hearty welcomes but were always looking for an angle. They ended up in jail on and off, whereas Eddie ended up owning a couple of nice restaurants. He worked the front of the house while Laurie spent her days and nights making it happen in the kitchen.

It has always been thus for him. While others acted like gangsters and used like junkies, Eddie took care of business. "Numbers always worked for me," he says now. There was a lot of pot—cross-country trips in cars jammed to the gunwales—and eventually quite a bit of coke. The rest of us ended up burning whatever money came our way, but more came his way, and Eddie managed to stash a few coffee cans here and there. His only small fault was his generosity. Eddie feels naked without big gobs of cash, and he tended to spill it around for the rest of us. "Coupons" is what he called money. I have seen him take out a wad the size of a ham sandwich in the meat-packing district of New York, a ski town in Colorado, a townie bar in Wisconsin, and half the joints in Minneapolis, and it was always the same. That fat wad evinced power, like a gun, only friendlier. People—strangers, even—gave respect to the guy with the pocket full of bills, the *ack-ack* laugh and the tendency to kiss his male friends. I've always been in that number. He taught me a lot. How to count, how to collect, how to shoot straight with crooked arrows. Eddie taught me manners.

One time we were at a stripper bar in St. Paul. I knew a girl there, an idiot cokehead but exquisite to behold. She used that physical gift to grind dollar tips out of goobers on sniffers' row. She was fascinated by me—actually, by the coke that was always in my pocket, but why put such a fine point on it? Let's call her Misty or some other stripper name . . . say, Cherri. I couldn't remember her name, real or stage, if it would end world hunger. She finished her set, gathered up the singles, and came bounding naked over to our table and plopped on my lap, which was all I was there for, really—that moment when I took custody of the fantasies of the other men in the room.

"Honey, you know that place across the street, like right over there?" she said, pointing out the door. "The place with the really nummy tacos? I am *sooooooooo* hungry, and I have to get ready for my next set. Will you just run over there and get me a couple of beef tacos?"

"Sure, cookie, no problem," I said, as she rushed backstage to put on a different costume that she would take off a minute and a half into the first song of her next set.

Eddie went quiet and then spoke. "If you fetch tacos for that cunt, I am never speaking to you again," he said, almost in a whisper. And then louder: "We do not fetch tacos for strippers."

We left. More than twenty years later, I ask Eddie about that night at the Green Lantern.

"Well, it was actually the Lamplighter, so you're close," he said, laughing.

Close was always good enough between Eddie and me. Back then he showed enormous patience for my wobbly skills when it came to business. "You did all right. We ended up at zero," he said, taking a sip off a nightcap. "The balance was zero at the end, so it worked out well, compared to a lot of people. A lot of 'em were negative."

Neither of us ever got smacked hard by the law. "Stone cold luck," Eddie says now, from a distance.

For much of the time when Eddie and I were ripping and running, I was dating Doolie, a gorgeous waitress-student who adored Eddie above all my friends. The three of us were doing some daytime drinking in 1987 with other pals at McCready's, our little clubhouse downtown. Somewhere in there, Doolie made a sign out of a coaster and a cocktail stick that said, "Just Kidding." Someone would say something patently outrageous, mean as hell, and then hold up the sign. It was more hilarious than it sounds, but then, we were pretty hammered. Flying down to Chicago for the night came up, one thing led to another, and we called Leaping Lenny, a pilot we knew. Eddie had met him while taking pilot lessons. Although Eddie had soloed, he was not licensed to fly other people around, and he could not rent a plane on his own. But Lenny, who was fully qualified, if not exactly a Mensa, was incredibly game.

"It was your idea," Eddie says now. "You were always full of ideas." It was a trait that went well with Eddie's pocket of cash.

We tore out to the airport, putting Lenny on standby for our arrival because we wanted to be on State Street by nightfall. Our luggage consisted of some Thai stick, several bottles of Dom Pérignon, Eddie's usual bankroll, a half ounce of mother-of-pearl coke in a grinder—and a "Just Kidding" sign. Locked and loaded.

"It wasn't Dom," Eddie corrects. "It was the one with the flowers on it."

I suggested that there were six of us on the trip, but Eddie corrects again. "It was a four-seater." (Doolie, upon reflection, recalled there were six people on the trip, including Belinda, Eddie's girlfriend at the time. Eddie later agreed that she was right.)

We flew in a Cessna, probably a 205, a kind of minivan with wings. We got drunk and high the whole way, Wisconsin unfurling below us as the sun set. We laughed at the schmucks who were stuck on the interstate and toasted our good fortune with the champagne. As I remember it, our pilot abstained until we landed.

"I can't imagine that Lenny ever would . . ." Eddie said with mock seriousness, and then said, "Of *course* he did!" For the length of the trip, Eddie, what with the flight school and all, sat in the front and lectured ceaselessly on the nuances of aviation. *Enough already with the lectures, Johnny Quest, will you pass the fucking grinder back, please?*

After two hours in the air, we all had to go to the bathroom. Eddie threaded a pee into one of the empty bottles of champagne and tried to hand the now warm bottle back. Doolie spoke: "Bad for team morale, Eddie."

When we finally got over downtown Chicago, it was dark, and we had trouble picking out Meigs Field jutting out into the blackness of Lake Michigan and had to make several passes. We landed just before the lights on the field went out for the night and tore into the city.

Chicago was a big deal for some guys from Minneapolis on a spontaneous holiday. We okeydoked our way past a huge line at the Limelight. ("We walked in, threw a few twenties on the floor, and then left," Eddie said.) We then drank ourselves silly at the Kingston Mines till four in the morning while Sugar Blue played harp, and we didn't have hotel rooms. ("Yes we did, at the Marriot; we just didn't use them," Eddie said.) We watched the sunrise on Lake Michigan and then ripped through the next day, with stops at the Billy Goat Tavern and a number of lesser-known bars.

By the following night, Eddie, no longer alert to the glories of private aviation, collapsed into the backseat and went to sleep. I sat in front next to Lenny, who was equally burnt. We flew under O'Hare's frantic traffic pattern, with me freaked out the whole way. "Two o'clock, Lenny, looks like a big one. Not that way, there's a bigger one over there." By the time we hit the inky black skies over Wisconsin, I had developed some resentments.

"Lenny, can we turn out the lights in here?"

Lenny understood immediately. "I can shut down the running lights too. And if you want, I can rough up the engine a little." Everything went black, and the engine began to sputter some as he eased out the choke.

"Eddie, wake up!" I shouted. "We got no electrical, no navigation, we've lost the horizon, and the engine doesn't sound so good!"

I repeated these facts several times while Eddie came to. It took him a few seconds to understand the apparent gravity of the situation. He sputtered as he leaned forward, and then Lenny flipped on the lights. Eddie stared down at the "Just Kidding" sign in my hand. A hoary old story, told many times, this time with a few factual emendations from Eddie. It ends the same way, though.

"You got me," Eddie said, slapping his knee and filling the room with *ack-ack-ack.*

—————

Sometime in the middle of 1987, I stumbled across a line, and Eddie's laughing stopped. I don't remember precisely how our enduring friendship hit a cul-de-sac, but Eddie does.

Taking a sip of his nightcap, he remembered that he had passed out at my apartment in South Minneapolis and woke up at dawn. I was standing in the kitchen with some other losers, going back at it one more time. "I see you and these two hollow-eyed junkies with a spoon cooking," he said. "I don't know what the hell was in there, but you had something going. All I remember is the three of you over this blue flame. It was early in the morning, like six o'clock, and I remember looking at it, and it just turned my stomach. And you were getting ready to shoot up, but I don't know what it was. I went to the bathroom, and I came out, and I remember looking at you, and I said, 'David, I gotta go home.' And I just left. I went home. It was shortly after that that we had that conversation."

That conversation?

"About if you're going to kill yourself, go ahead, but I can't be there anymore, I can't do it." The living room of his old place was suddenly quiet. He said he spoke to me man-to-man back then, all business aside, telling me that he could not abide me turning into one of those nitwits who lived to suck on a glass dick. And then he walked away.

I ended up with a whole new crop of running buddies, people who lived and breathed the coke life with little regard for other pursuits. One by one, my pals from the old days drifted away, checking on me every once in a while and, seeing that there was nothing to be done—I would not listen to anyone at the time, no matter what they said— eventually leaving me to my obsession.

When I finally sobered up, Eddie was the first one in line to help me glue the wheels back on, buying me Diet Cokes with the same gusto he exhibited setting me up with whiskey. If he missed the maniac version of me, he never said so and took more pride in my subsequent professional accomplishments than I ever did. Best man at my wedding, best man in my life.

12

PERP WALK

Only need a little, but you want a ton.
—THE REPLACEMENTS, "DOSE OF THUNDER"

On paper, specifically newsprint, the mideighties were very good years for me. I was breaking stories, winning some awards, and beginning to feel my range and strengths as a journalist. When I got on a story, I was a dog on a meat bone. There were stories that pulled back the blankets on a food bank that was better at feeding its executives than its clients, and a piece that received national attention about how a Minneapolis policeman had used a surveillance program, "Target 8," to go after a personal enemy. According to the Minneapolis *Star Tribune,* I won five Page One Awards during this period, but if I received a bunch of Lucite tchotchkes for my success, I can't find them now.

Street gangs, long a fixture of life in bigger cities, were pulling into Minneapolis and St. Paul, grabbing the drug corners, infiltrating nonprofits, and occasionally killing people. Nobody took much notice until a young white girl was killed. Christine Kreitz, a confused young girl who became an associate of the Gangster Disciples, had been mistaken for a snitch—she wasn't—and executed in a park near where I lived. Working at an alternative weekly and under the spell of the so-called New Journalism, I tended to render my reporting with a giant purple crayon. The story began this way:

Christine Kreitz died a loyal Disciple. She believed the Disciples were her family. She believed they meant what they said when they said they loved her. She believed way, way too much. Christine gave her life to the Black Gangster Disciple Nation. She kept her mouth shut, did what she was told, and in return the Disciples executed her.

—*TWIN CITIES READER*, JULY 16, 1986

I got clobbered from both sides when the story came out. The police chief at the time suggested that I was conjuring some nascent monster through overheated coverage and ridiculed me. And people in black organizations felt that I had pathologized and indicted a huge swath of the community. I was invited over to what I thought would be a nice little meeting sponsored by the St. Paul Urban League and showed up alone after a long night and not much sleep, figuring I could fake my way through it. There were over a hundred people in a very hot, dark basement, with the only lights turned on me. I was hammered by the crowd for ninety minutes straight, and people showed teeth as I left, including some gangbangers I recognized. I walked out real slow, not wanting to show that they had me going, but I was covered in sweat by the time I got to my car.

I found it all bracing in the main. But beyond the day job, all was not well. I was in trouble in my first marriage for draining our bank account, being MIA for days at a time, and for failing to act like either a husband or an adult. At my wife's request and my family's demand, I entered treatment in 1985. A model patient, I said and did all the right things while I was an inpatient and made gestures at sobriety when I came out, but I had no ongoing program of recovery and soon backslid into using. When I reentered treatment in 1986—this time as an outpatient—my marriage was all but over. Kim was more than through with me—me of the long nights, the ravaged bank accounts, the evasive answers to simple questions. A smart woman with plans that used

76

to include me, she wanted to get on with her life. And I left on a dead run. Scotty, a pal I worked with, let me flop at his house for a few months.

A few decades later, Scotty and I are sitting talking outside the same house. One of his lovely daughters now lives in the room where I was doing God knows what every night of the week. He doesn't say so, but I think they burned some sage before they moved her into the room. I was sure he regretted his generosity even though by my count I set the house on fire only once, but sitting in the backyard many years later, he said it was a fair trade.

"You supplied me with a social life by moving in," he said. "You brought the parties here and brought the people here. There were many wonderful times, often on week nights, school nights. That was always kind of a challenge."

Scotty liked my company just fine, but my lifestyle corrupted him osmotically. He'd plan on turning in early, reading a book, and I would come plowing in after the bars closed with a crew of rowdies and a pocket full of dry goods. The best intentions frequently met their match around me.

When I was living with Scotty in the winter and spring of 1986, some guys I knew had a commercial music company—jingles, stuff like that—and they hired me to write a brochure for them. Seemed like easy money, a layup. I pulled an all-nighter to make the copy deadline and brought it to one of the guys' house to get a final approval. On that cold March day, he sat with the check in his hands and said he was leaving for Sun Valley, Idaho, later and needed a little, *you know,* to take with him. "Well, I'm in the brochure writing business today, not the 'you know' business. Besides, I gotta go to work," I told him. "Where do you expect me to cop at nine-thirty in the morning? I'm fresh out."

"Just a gram," he pleaded. "I told the other guys you could make it happen." He still had my check, significant money, in his hands.

One call. I said I would make one call.

I called Phil.

Phil's coke, at least what he sold me, was not the best, but he was almost always open for business. A guy with long hair and a penchant for feathers, he could scan as a Sioux Indian or a Hell's Angel, depending on the day. We had family connections going all the way back, and his brother, Steve, was a pal who ran First Avenue, the rock palace downtown.

Phil was in the Life full-time, including having a kind of office/rec room near downtown in a festering hotel that was wobbling toward closure. Called the "Blue Room," as in "Meet me at the Blue Room," it could have been named for the paint on the wall or for the things that went on there.

Raised out in the cushy suburbs near Lake Minnetonka, Phil seemed as if he were born on a cellblock. His familiars, Monker and Red-eye, lacked the IQ of a box of doughnuts between them, but their smushed-in faces and large hands were plenty articulate when they came knocking. (They called my house one time when I was behind with Phil on a payment. I came home and Kim said, "Some guy named Red-eye called, and he said to meet him and Monker at the Sunshine Bar. What's that about?")

Phil was the real deal, although after three federal stints, he is both officially and unofficially retired. We scheduled for coffee, and he pulled up on a Harley Springer—nothing tricked out or silly, just a stock bike in mint condition.

Many years ago I told him I hated the name Dave, which was a mistake. He still calls me "Davey Dave" on greeting, perhaps to double the insult. He can be rugged company when he is feeling sideways and taking the whole boss-of-all-bosses thing seriously, but he is big hearted, never hurting anyone who doesn't have it coming. The girls—smart ones, pretty ones—liked him, maybe because he made them feel safe anywhere on the planet. (Judging by some rather awkward times I spent in the Blue Room, he got them deeply in touch with some other feelings as well.)

He could be fun as hell when he wasn't "conducting," which is what he called dealing, full of street lore, philosophy, and mind games. Some guys look tough. Some guys talk tough. Some guys are tough. Phil hit for the cycle. I lost many hands of poker to him, woke him up more than a few times because I had a need, and became sort of a hobby for him. Sitting there all those years gone, Phil said that he thought that at a certain point, I was frittering away whatever talents I had on the wrong endeavors.

"You asked if you were a good businessman. Nah, I don't think so."

But there was some fun on the way.

"Yeah, socializing, woman chasing," he said, not looking much worse for wear for taking both to epic lengths. "You kinda just did what you wanted, when you wanted, how you wanted it. It may sound glamorous, but it has consequences. Things catch up with you. You let things go, it will catch up with you. I did get worried with you, David."

Awww, he's giving me the David, not Davey Dave. Kind of chokes me up.

I told Phil I had this memory of a robbery at the Blue Room involving him, Red-eye, and me that seemed more like a dream—every bit of it unreal. I still had a hard time believing it, but then I saw all kinds of stuff in that room—it had the vibe of a Chinese opium den with a chaser of absinthe—and breaking it down into hard-and-fast data points does not reflect the reality that hung there.

"Were you there?" Phil asked at the coffee shop. Red-eye's dead, so no help there. Stories take on an apocryphal lilt, even when they describe specific events, like getting robbed at gunpoint in a dimly lit dope house. Some of it was just so profoundly weird that I had a hard time believing it really happened. I tell him exactly what I remember, and after awhile, we both decide I was there.

It was 1985, and I must have been doing a drive-by at the Blue Room to pick up something quick. I was standing there with Red-eye and Phil, talking about nothing special, when the rippled glass in the corner of the window in the locked door was suddenly broken. Could have been the cops, but instead a handgun, a big one, came through the hole, backed by one beady eye. "Stay put," the guy said, while his other hand snaked in and flicked the lock.

Before us stood two of the twitchiest heroin junkies I had ever seen. They were obviously in the throes of dope sickness. Phil and Red-eye did not back up, so I didn't either.

The junkies came closer, told us to empty out our pockets. They grabbed a quarter ounce of coke off the table. There's more, they said. They were right. Three feet to my left, there was a hole punched in the wall, and I knew that on the two-by-four just above it sat a quarter pound of coke.

"That's all there is, boys," Phil said, all friendly like. They argued for a while, and then the junkies said that if that's all there was, they would need his watch and necklace, a big chunky dope rope of gold.

"Naw, you don't want that, because you'll have to come over here and take it off me," Phil said evenly. "And you don't want to do that."

I looked at the twitches with the guns, all freaky and nervous as Phil menaced them with his voice, the only weapon he had handy.

"Phil, give them the fucking dope rope," I said.

"Naw, you don't want my jewelry," Phil repeated. "A couple hundred bucks, a quarter ounce of coke—I'd say that you boys had a pretty good day so far. I have some people coming by to see me, and they aren't going to be happy to see you here. You'd better go."

That was Phil in a nutshell, running the show while he was getting gun-robbed. The junkies keened and argued, backing up the whole time, and then they were gone. I heard that Red-eye and Phil found them within days—Minneapolis is a pretty small town—and fixed their hands so that they wouldn't be pointing guns at anybody else for a while.

Phil ran a pretty tight show with his customers as well. He grew tired of my antic phone calls, and when I called him on that morning in 1986, he was not happy to hear from me. Reluctantly, he picked up a beep I sent him about the guy going to Sun Valley who wanted some, you know.

"Naw, Davey Dave, I'm on a social. I'm at the Skyway. You should give it a rest anyway. It's nine-thirty in the morning. Go to work." As he gave me this lecture, he was sitting at the Skyway Lounge, a titty bar on Hennepin Avenue full of desiccated, worked-over girls dancing for an even more bored clientele. Phil always seemed more worried about my job than I was. I explained that it wasn't even for me, that it was for this guy I did other business with, and the errand was sitting between me and a big, legit check.

"Hurry up then, I ain't going to be here all day," he said.

I waved off a drink when I got there. It was two blocks away from work, and I had to be at police headquarters by eleven for an interview with a cop who knew stuff about street gangs. In the half-light of the bar, Phil palmed me a film canister jammed with coke.

"You know what a gram looks like, Davey Dave. Don't get greedy," he said, words that would ring for years afterward.

I already had a paper bindle folded. I went to the skanky bathroom at the back and locked myself into a stall. I tapped out the correct amount—I could eyeball a gram from ten feet away—and folded up the packet. I took the opportunity to take a pee, and it occurred to me in that thirty seconds that I might need a bump to get through the day. I'd been up most of the night. The bathroom door opened and closed, and from the stall I could see the heavy black shoes of the guy as he took a leak. I unfolded the paper, knocking a few more tenths into it. The shoes moved suddenly.

"You roll a noisy joint, pal!" the uniform cop said as he snapped open the door. I threw the canister in the toilet, but the bindle bounced off the rim. I was just reaching for it when his knee came so far up my ass I saw stars.

"Whaddayaknow, I got myself a felony narcotics!" he cried with joy. "It's my lucky day."

I was wearing a Lakeland leather coat with lots of pockets. Cops loved going through that coat, and this guy was no exception. Phil appeared behind him, giving me some kind of high sign. *Oh, I get it, you want us to jump an armed police officer. Great idea, Phil.* I must have shaken my head. The cop turned and barked Phil out of the bathroom.

All of this is etched in my memory, but cops tend to write with a bit more economy than either junkies or journalists. Here is how Officer Quinn described his good fortune:

> *While on foot patrol I observed the deft. with a white paper in his hand. When I confronted him he dropped the paper which when recovered appeared to be narcotics. Deft was placed under arrest and transported to HJC. Narcotics inventoried.*

He cuffed me, and we started walking toward the front, out into the cold, bright morning. People, including some I worked with, were on their way to work. We took a right on Hennepin Avenue, toward the City Center mall. My dad would be heading in right now to open up Liemandt's clothing store, which he managed. As we turned up Seventh Avenue, alongside the downtown mall, my head started to swivel in all directions.

"Calm down," Officer Quinn ordered. "I parked over on Nicollet. Didn't know I was going to have company."

He held me sideways, so I had to crabwalk the block of Seventh on the way to Nicollet, walking the length of the City Center. I was never so glad to get in the back of a squad. We drove to the cop shop, and I went to booking for printing and photo. On my way to the holding cell, I looked up at the clock. Eleven sharp. I should be one floor up, taking notes with Lieutenant Freddy, a detective in the auto division, about the criminal scourge overtaking our city. I spent the day in a holding cell with three guys who admired, then coveted, my sneakers. Mickey, a criminal attorney Phil had on retainer, got me out very late that night by signing for me, and in the ensuing months, we had to keep going back to court, shopping for the right judge until I was allowed to plead to a misdemeanor violation of the city's drug laws. I felt like—no, I clearly was—a moron, a greedy little two-tenths-of-a-gram-chipping moron. I was at large because I was white, employed, and Phil had hooked me up with his in-the-know attorney.

Phil, wiser, older, the guy who now lives to pull a lunker out of Lake Minnetonka, said you can't regret the past. But you can learn from it. Phil had one last thought about my choice on March 3, 1986. "You shoulda gone to work anyhow that morning, David."

I wanted to talk to Mickey, the attorney who made it all go away. Mickey caught a case of his own involving client funds and had been disbarred. Phil didn't know where he was, and no one else seemed to. DonJack, my reporting pal, eventually tracked him down in suburban Minneapolis. Mickey was more than happy to get the call—the files were now gone—and I was thrilled to have a chance to thank him. Because of Mickey, I went from one more jamoke in lockup getting the hairy eyeball from his cellies to a citizen back on the streets and breathing free air. Even another day in jail would have been hard to explain back at the paper. Why hadn't I called? It was one thing to be known as the hard-partying reporter who somehow managed to hit deadline and quite another to admit that I had been felony-charged by a police department that I often covered. Micket recalled I was in a bit of a jam.

"I do remember that when Phil called me—he would call me every once in a while with a friend of his, an associate of his, whatever, when they would get jammed up—and I do remember he said, you know, 'You gotta go down there and get him out; you gotta get him out right away.' I remember him telling me that. I was on a phone with a judge before I ever got to the jail to see you."

We had a nice chat, but at the time he was representing me, we seemed to be at cross-purposes. I was mortified and terrified to be in the Hennepin County Courthouse—a place where I had covered many stories—as a defendant. But he knew that if I were to step before the wrong judge on the wrong day, the carefully arranged plea would fall apart.

"I negotiated the case with the prosecuting attorney to get the charge reduced, but then we had to be concerned about what the judge was going to do to you after you entered your plea. You pled guilty to a reduced misdemeanor charge."

It was not a layup, Mickey said. I could have been stuck with the felony, which would have changed almost everything. "You could've done some substantial time in the Hennepin County Workhouse, and I was trying to avoid that. So we kind of delayed a little bit until I was comfortable with the judge we had, and then we went ahead and entered your plea."

The hard part, he explained, was managing his client.

"You were very embarrassed, and you did not want to keep having to go back to court. I kept telling you, 'David, it's for your own good. I know it's embarrassing for you, but we have to do this to make sure you get the best possible deal.' I don't think that you were ever convinced until after the case was over with."

He was happy that we got a good result but not sure back then that I had seen the error of my ways. "I saw that you were going down the wrong trail and that you did in fact have a lot to offer, and if you kept going the way you were going, you were gonna end up putting yourself into a situation that you wouldn't be able to dig yourself out of."

Like any good criminal defense attorney, he gave me some lectures at the time in addition to legal advice.

"You agreed with everything I said and [then] did what you wanted to. You were full of shit, like any junkie. Not a crook, a junkie. That's what I saw. I saw the chemicals, and I saw what you were doing to get yourself someplace where you wanted to be in your head, but it wasn't doing you any good as far as your career was concerned." He said he told me that as much as I cared about being a good reporter, about doing good stories, none of it meant anything as long as I spent my nights acting the fool.

But everything turned out, give or take. I remember back then being profoundly grateful and thinking that whatever I had paid him had been worth it. But like so much of my past, it pivoted when I made further inquiry.

"You stiffed me, but don't worry about it. It was a long time ago. Statute of limitations is run. I have no idea how much you owed me, but I do remember you did because I stopped by one time. Your office was, I think, on Excelsior Boulevard in St. Louis Park, and I came knocking on your door one day, and you weren't in. As a defense attorney, getting stiffed was not an unusual event."

13

NUNS PRAYED FOR ME

My father is a man who swears frequently, goes to church every day, and lives his towering faith. I am a man who swears frequently, goes to church every Sunday, and lives in search of faith. He is a man who believes that I am not dead because nuns prayed for me. I am a man who believes that is as good an explanation as any.

After three boys, in 1956 my parents were looking forward to having a baby girl. When my mother went into labor on September 8, the anniversary of the birth of the Blessed Virgin on the liturgical calendar, it was ordained that the baby's name would be Mary. I arrived instead. That same day, their car was stolen from the church parking lot. Plans, well laid, well prayed, were like that. They still loved me within an inch of my life. Always. Even later, when I got in jams, got divorced, got fired, slipped after treatment, my mother said the same thing: "You are mine. We choose you no matter what."

When I was little, I used to get up at the ass crack of dawn to go to church with my father. He was impressed by my burgeoning faith, but the truth of the matter was that I loved sitting in the pew with him. As one of seven children, I rarely had him all to myself. He was my higher power. (I look at my own children when we are in church and feel the corollary. I go there to stand next to them.)

In our family, we had money, or at least it seemed like we did. The nice house, good cars, vacations like anybody else. And then one day I came home from caddying, and the electrician was there shutting off the juice. Things got a little hairy after that. We had never wanted for a damn thing, it's just that with seven kids and my dad's bumpy career path, we were always just a little beyond our means. My dad always said, "Things don't matter, people do."

At a certain age, I suggested he said that because he had a lot of good friends and not much money. When my dad and mom got older, it was clear that they were going to be OK but limited in their retirement. And then one of my dad's dear old friends took care of a few financial things. Nothing crazy, but it took the heat off. Things don't matter, people do.

I was not the only guy in our family who worked for some rough cats. My dad grew up the son of a very successful clothing store owner in Minneapolis. In 1961 he went to one of those newfangled shopping malls in the suburbs and opened up Carr's Fashion for Men. It was just about the time chain stores moved in on retail, and his store failed. He never declared bankruptcy and paid back every nickel.

My dad was drinking at the time—he would soon quit for good— and the business setback left him at loose ends. He ended up stumbling along, hooking up with a variety of outfits that sold mutual funds. He eventually ended up working with Deil, a local banker with a lot on his plate, and a guy named Roger, his right-hand man. My dad was the nice Catholic boy they sent out to perform cashectomies on rich widows. But behind all the afternoon drinks, the talk of big deals down the pike, they screwed him. My dad sobered up, went back into the clothing business, working the floor as a salesman for Liemandt's, eventually running several stores for them. My dad was and is a success by any objective definition.

The same could not be said for Deil and Roger. "They were really bad guys," my dad says now, sitting on a deck above St. Alban's Bay on Lake Minnetonka. Long after my dad had stopped working for them and I had become a reporter, Deil ended up in a very serious jam. He had leveraged his banks into ownership of the Tropicana casino in Las Vegas and was riding high. But he extended credit to the Kansas City mob, a violation of federal law, and they ran up debt in the millions. When they said they couldn't pay what they owed, he said he would lose his casino. Then they told him the good news: They were his new partners. The skimming began immediately, and Deil started kiting checks at his banks back in the Twin Cities to stay solvent. After he was charged, it was thought he was going to roll on the Kansas City mob. Before trial, he went up north for a weekend of boating. There was an accident, and Deil lost his right hand. There was a lot of speculation about how that hand got severed, but he did not implicate others at his federal trial, which I covered with deep interest. Roger testified against Deil and he was convicted, spending forty months in prison. I remember that the prosecutors were impressed by my understanding of the nuances of the case, but I don't remember telling them how I knew what I knew.

When I was out in the weeds, my dad, sober, loving, and furious, came after me with the nets a couple of times, trying to shove me into treatment and pull me back from what he saw as certain doom. But I mostly eluded his efforts to get me into some puzzle factory to straighten out. In one memorable instance, he and my brother Jim broke down the door to my apartment and rushed in, only to find my pal Fast Eddie and a couple of girls hanging out and me nowhere in sight. Sensing that things were getting a little out of hand, I agreed to meet with Dad on neutral ground, at the Perkins restaurant out on Highway 100 in Edina. By this time, I was out of work, with no visible means of support, and had a new girlfriend named Anna, who was keeping me in drugs and money. I don't remember my specific mental state, but it could be narrowed down to: high, about to get high, or crashing. He was waiting in a booth by a window. I wasted no time telling him I did not want for anything, that all of my needs were being met by my new friend.

He returned the favor and got right to the point.

"You are a whore." In a more Christian spirit—Jesus loved prostitutes as God's children, after all—he added that his prayers, the prayers of my mother, the prayers of his friends, the prayers of nuns, were going to straighten me out. "Nuns are praying for you."

(My friend Nimmer reminded me that he put a word in with the nuns as well, so I had a lot of women with Godly connections dialed in on my behalf. And my dad has since explained that while nuns may have prayed for me, and he may have told me as much, a whole bunch of others did, too, including his lay fellowship group, Cursillo. "Petitions for your recovery were rampant.")

In our large family, someone is always the problem child, the hot potato, the one the others are talking about, worrying over, bitching about. I had my turn more than anybody. My sister Lisa said that the tug of the family—insistent, nagging, and never-ending—kept me from flying off the edge in irretrievable ways.

"We were raised with values of family and church and all that stuff, but mostly family," she said, the two of us sharing a cigarette at her kitchen table in the spring of 2007. "No matter how screwed up you were and how you screwed Mom and Dad over, there is always somebody calling you up on the phone, brothers or sisters, saying, 'What's going on?' There is always a good cop and a bad cop, but we always had each other." She said that even at my worst, when I would either be snorting coke in the bathroom of my parents' town house or passed out on the couch, no one gave up on me. Prayers, lectures, ultimatums, they all added up in their own way. "I think you're blessed," she added, smiling at me.

So nuns prayed for me?

"I think nuns prayed for you."

In September of 1988, my cousin Tommy died. Nice kid who came from the best kind of big, throbbing Irish family, with a father who was a political leader in his community and many very accomplished siblings whose shared characteristic was decency. Tommy was a little younger than me, married to a lovely woman with a bunch of nice kids and a bad, long-running thing with coke. He finally sobered up for some months and went to work selling cars. One day after a big sale, he went to a no-tell motel with some coke and pushed a chair up against the door. He died there.

I had been out of touch, but when I heard about how it ended for Tommy, I knew that I had to make an appearance at the wake at O'Halloran & Murphy. You don't skip wakes in our family. His family pulled together around this wound, but it was a miserable affair, full of sorrowful smiles and sobbing at the memory of Tommy. I straightened out as much as I could and came by for a quick toe-touch, avoiding the gaze of my family as I expressed my condolences. I tapped my father's arm on the way out as a good-bye. He leaned in and hissed, "Take a look around you. Is this what you have planned for us?"

14

TIME HEALS, TIME FORGETS

For all of the pharmacological foundations of his stories, Mr. Thompson was a reporter, taking to the task of finding out what other people knew with an avidity that earned the respect of even those who found his personal hobbies reprehensible.

—FROM A STORY I WROTE FOLLOWING HUNTER S. THOMPSON'S DEATH

Mornings for an addict involve waking up in a room where every-thing implicates him. Even if there is no piss or vomit—oh, blessed be the small wonders—there is the tipped-over bottle, the smashed phone, the bright midday light coming through the rip in the shade that says another day has started without you. Drunks and ad-dicts tend to build nests out of the detritus of their misbegotten lives.

It is that ecosystem, all there for the inventorying within twenty seconds of waking, which tends to make addiction a serial matter. Apart from the progression of the disease, if you wake up in that kind of hell, you might start looking for something to take the edge off. Nothing like the beer goggles and a nice bracing whiff of something to help you reframe your little disaster area. *Hmmm, just a second here. A little of the hair of the dog. Yep. Now, that's better. Everything is new again.*

But it was a very different morning at my apartment at 3208 Gar-field in the spring of 1986. Next to me, there was an arm, long and lan-guid. I followed the contour over a back marked only by tan lines, the kind of thing you see in classic, figurative sculpture. This gorgeous girl smiled when she slept, each tooth a greeting to the morning, to me, to the night before. Then I remembered: Doolie.

I had known her when I was about to get married and she was the chubby, nondescript baby sister of my dear college friend Kat. I barely noticed her, and she did not give me the time of day. A few years later, Donald and I—I was now about to be divorced—were at the bar she worked at downtown, and things had changed. She was just back from Europe and looked exquisite, with a bookish, wisecracking way that stayed with me. More remarkably, she found me charming and funny. I saw her again at the Uptown bar, celebrating her pal Tony's birthday. Tony, a cook she worked with, was leaving for the night, and Doolie seemed content with my company.

The moon was full. I suggested a trip to Cedar Lake, one of the gorgeous lakes decorating the city. We did some coke and stopped at her apartment at her request. She came out with a blanket and a bottle of wine. I was used to hustling women by talking all kinds of smack talk, overwhelming as much as seducing. Not this time.

That night I saw Doolie plain as day, her smile an array of little moons illuminated by the light of the larger moon above. The smile, the way it made me feel, was still there in the morning. I rolled back from her and the reverie she induced and glanced at the clock—and then it came to me that I was supposed to be somewhere else.

Dear. Mother. Of. God. It was ten-thirty. I had an appointment at the governor's office at eleven for a final interview on a story about discrepancies in public bonding in St. Paul. Big story. Big interview.

In a panic, I woke her as gently as I could and went into the bathroom, taking a quick shower and an even quicker snort of coke. I grabbed a sport coat that looked like it had been made out of asbestos and a hopeless tie. We walked out together, and then I ran for it, swearing and muttering to myself, but some part of me was still back on the beach with all those little moons.

The governor was running late, I was told when I got there. Sweat poured from my brow, into my hair, and then dripped down my neck to my back, pooling at my waistband and below. I ran to the bathroom and used fistfuls of paper towels to mop myself. I started to settle down. This would be OK.

Governor Rudy was from Minnesota's Iron Range, and whatever he lacked in finesse, he made up for in pure humanity and street smarts. A Democrat, both big D and small d, he was a good guy. But when I walked into his office, he stayed behind his desk, flanked by a couple of suits I didn't know. Lawyer-type guys. Before I got two questions in, they said that they knew I was just carrying water for the Republican state auditor; that he had surely slipped me the documents about the bonding.

Gee, this wasn't going so well. The fight-or-flight mechanism kicked in, and I started *schvitzing* anew. Especially above my lip.

"Are you all right?" the governor asked. He looked really concerned.

Fine, fine, just a little hot in here is all. No, he said, your nose, I mean.

I put my hand up under my nose, and it came away blood red. One of the lawyer guys slipped me a tissue, but it was not a one-tissue affair. I continued the interview with a huge wad up one nostril, my head filling with blood as I struggled to finish. If someone had lit a truth candle, and the governor asked me why my nose was bleeding, I would have said it was because I had been sticking things up it all night long. That would have thrown Governor Rudy, a meat-and-tatties guy, for a loop.

Why in the world would someone do that?

No special reason, I guess. It's just all the rage.

Soon after Doolie and I began dating, her roommate was raped by a stranger who creepy-crawled into their apartment. I was good in a crisis, perhaps because I had generated so many of them. I looked after her roommate in the near term, offering practical advice and soothing bromides. She eventually moved out of the apartment and did not come back. It then seemed like a good idea for Doolie to stay over a lot.

I needed no instigation. I found her riveting. Academically she was lost, floundering around in pursuit of a reason to be in college. But that didn't mean she didn't know a lot about a lot. She was raised in a family of bright sisters, with learned, successful parents, and it showed in both her manners and brawny range of knowledge. And not just book smart; she had just gotten back from living in Barcelona, Spain, and as someone who got on planes mostly to make short-hop drug runs or to party in crappy towns, I thought it sounded magical.

She was an epic dancer, my friends adored her, and, most importantly at the time, she did not see anything unusual about the fact that in between work assignments, I careened through all manner of drugs and alcohol. She had her own issue with substances—teeny compared to what I had going—and was, for a time, charmed by my excesses. We went to see Bob Dylan, Tom Petty, and the Grateful Dead all on the same bill at the Metrodome. I can still see her walking up Fifth Avenue in a sundress and cowboy boots, laughing with anticipation of the huge concert.

In the months that followed, there was a lot of bar hopping, and we both enjoyed the fact that I was a known commodity; that people seemed glad to see me and the coke that generally accompanied my arrival. But you know what they say: Everybody laughs and has a good time until someone gets an eye poked out. Or sticks a crack pipe in their mouth. Soon after we got together, I began disappearing. She became clingy. She swore something was wrong, that I was up to something. I told her she was a psycho. She said I was a liar. In truth, I had met Anna, who had oodles of coke and plenty of time for me. As Doolie became more accusatory, I became scarcer and, strangely, more possessive. We had epic fights. I began, and there is no nice way to say this, smacking her around.

I had always remembered that I hit her—my face hot each time that I did—but I told myself that it was always in response to some physical provocation from her. I knew when I saw her again, without even reconsidering, that that was a lie.

It is one thing to type those words, but quite another to be sitting on a park bench in Chicago with Doolie, talking about what happened two decades later. I had flown there to see her in the middle of the summer of 2006. I was incredibly nervous, less about seeing her than the prospect of talking about odious things that occurred. If my behavior ever tipped over from drug-induced pathology to something darker, more evil—the joy in the unhappiness of someone else—it was aimed at this woman.

There is electricity between us when we meet at a coffee shop, but it has very little to do with bygone romance. We are resuming a conversation that ended abruptly. Sure, we had talked about who did what to whom, but we never really talked about what *happened*. When we came together back then, we sped through joy, passion, conflict, hatred, and heartbreak in just a few short years, and eventually we each walked away. But more than once in those years, I have wondered, What was that? What happened to me to do those things to her? When I thought of Doolie, it was with fondness and deep, deep regret.

We walk to the park near the shore. She is still beautiful, but settled in a way she never was when she was with me. Married to a smart, very successful guy, she is writing plays and raising their son. It is immediately clear from Doolie's recollection that there were times when I hunted her down.

For a time, she lived at Thirty-eighth and Cedar, just down the street from the Relax-a-Lounge, a massage parlor/whorehouse where I had some customers. As she talked, I remember I had stopped there to drop something off and then went to Doolie's place, and we got in some kind of argument. She reminded me that we ended up out on the lawn, with me kneeling on her arms and hitting her.

"You hit me, and you somehow pushed me down. Do you mind if I do this?" she asked, as she put her hands on my shoulders. "It might be kind of pathetic, but you had me on each shoulder, and you were hitting me back and forth and were saying, 'I'm going to kill you.'"

The demonstration was not meant to shame, only to create a clear picture of what it felt like to be her, restrained and pummeled at the same time. The memory comes pouring back to me as she describes that day. Every word of it was true. I had done these things. More than once in those days, she walked away with a black eye and started to get thin and spooky from the long nights with me. Her parents tried to get her to come home to North Dakota, but she hung in, even after she found out about Anna.

"The smart girl would walk away," she said. "But no, I didn't. I stayed there and took it for another year." She is smiling when she says this, smiling at her own lack of self-regard. What easily could have hardened into hatred and blame, has, over the years, become something more complicated. There is a mutuality to our discussion—what I did, what she did—that I had neither expected nor really deserved. In the course of an interview, blank spots filled in and mysteries resolved themselves.

As we talk, it becomes clearer that she allowed me to drive her insane over time, coming and then leaving, loving her and then hitting her. She lost her bearings. She ended up taking over my apartment somewhere in there, but details are unclear here. On January 18, 1988, Doolie jumped me when I came into the apartment on Garfield. I say she had a knife that she was threatening to cut the phone line with, and, by inference, me. She says it was a cigarette that she put out on me. Whatever, it was a minuet of misery—once sensible, decent people now hanging in to hurt and maim each other. I tortured her, mentally, verbally, and, eventually, physically.

"Not without my permission. I tried to put a cigarette out on you. I had a cigarette in my hand. I think I have a streak of violence, though, too." We don't dwell on it, but I'm sure as I sit there that it was a part of herself she never would have known existed had she not known me.

It was a bad piece of reality television, replete with goofy neighbor.

"The neighbor down the stairs called the police. Remember?" Doolie said, finding room for a laugh. "She goes, 'I can't get through, I can't get through.' Turns out she's calling 411. So it was, like, this really weird, hilarious moment."

This is what the cops found when they got there:

> *Sqd 530 responded to a heavy domestic. Upon arrival off's were met by vic who was sitting with a neighbor in apt 2. Vic stated that her and def had just had an argument and that he had struck her with his open hand on the left side of the face. Vic stated they had had argument concerning his infidelity at which time he became upset and slapped her. Off walked upstairs to apt 4 and confronted def who stated they had had an argument and he admitted to slapping the vic. Def was searched for weapons, cuffed and escorted to rear of sqd. He was then transported to HCJ and booked for above offense.*

These many years later, I made the amends as I could, telling her that part of the reason I was so frantic, so brutal, was that I was obsessed with her. But then she asked a quiet, logical question, with no accusation attached: "Then why would you go away?"

The answer was the same as in every other aspect of my existence at the time: I chose coke above all. And there was a part of our relationship that was twisted beyond repair. She pointed out that when I finally sobered up, I came back, and I was so fat that I could hardly walk, but she let me in. For a time, we were addicted to each other's saliva, remaining together far past the point of reason or common sense.

She was acting at the time, and after I got out of treatment, I would wait for her outside auditions. "I was a terrible actor," she says now. I thought she had a good role as some hottie in a play I have now forgotten. "They put me in tight dresses, a lot of makeup and hats, a lot of things like that. I was tarted up a little bit."

When we began dating again after I sobered up, I had company: my twins from my relationship with Anna. We did our best to find what had brought us together with such ferocity, but crawling across all that wreckage was too exhausting. We met, as they say, in each other's weakness. I was a slow-motion kidnapper, and Doolie served a long, brutal stint in my custody. But now anybody walking by the park bench in Chicago would have seen two old friends, laughing, sharing stories, smiling at each other.

Doolie is a terrific storyteller, generous in her recollection—this is a person who gave up a kidney for her father, so it is in her nature—and a bear trap for dates and memories, noting the prominence of the full moon at all of the glorious and sordid inflection points in our relationship. She knows a thing or two about me, too.

"You had an admiration for the bad guy. You had an admiration for the wiseguy," she said, pulling her knees up under her chin. "I think you would have been a wiseguy if you weren't a nice guy. You wanted to be the catcher in the rye. When people were in trouble, you would catch them. Or if they weren't, you pushed them."

She said I liked to collect stories, my own most avidly. She had heard that long after I sobered up, quit the booze and the coke, that I tried drinking again. She was not surprised.

"That's part of the tale too. You knew no matter what happened that it would never get that bad again. So then that would be a real good story too. Is that insulting?"

I told her I did not have a lot of capacity for the received insult.

"That's because you have a very high opinion of yourself, and that's OK."

She bid me good-bye as an old friend. Nothing to it, she said. "You don't remember this, but we left it nice."

15

THE HOUSE OF MANY DOORS

Who by now could know where was what? Liars controlled the
locks.

—NORMAN MAILER, *THE ARMIES OF THE NIGHT*

No one who knew either of us would have been surprised to see
Patrick talking to me in a prison visiting room in the summer of
2007. Patrick, a political adept who helped invent the version of Paul
Wellstone that voters were willing to make their senator, was always in
my corner. When I was a young reporter, he was one of my best
sources, the hyperwired political consultant who gave me guidance and
helped me break news occasionally. He gave me work when I was tipping over into addiction and then did it again when I sobered up. Later,
when I got sick, he and his wife, Cathy, were the first people to stop by,
armed with reams of medical information about how I might proceed.
But people in our circle who watched our improbable friendship in the
eighties and nineties would have been surprised at the end of the visit,
when I got up and walked out into fresh air, and Patrick went back to
his cell.

Patrick had been such a moral beacon to me that once I sobered
up, I would never so much as smoke a cigarette in his presence. Although he was a few years younger than me, Patrick taught me much
about how to conduct business at the greasy intersection of politics,
media, and money. As a reporter and his source, our relationship had

always been on the up-and-up, with him exercising great deference for my position as a journalist. And later, when we worked on various communications contracts, he was a complete straight arrow, never cutting a corner or padding a bill. He rarely judged my relationship with chemicals, but he found my involvement in illicit narcotics reprehensible and stupid. A guy who came of professional age on the Iron Range of Minnesota, where a tradition of mine unionism was often matched by public corruption, he was the counterexample: a guy who got involved in politics for all the right reasons and was a consistent voice for rectitude and truth.

So did he make up that guy, and was he just waiting for his shot? I don't think so. It is a long story, but Patrick, who could be a bit of a hot dog, decided that he wanted to own a bunch of minor league hockey teams. He cut some bad deals to get started—the numbers were never going to work—and when it tumbled, he began bilking his friends and partners for reasons no one who knew him understands to this day. He ended up millions to the bad and earned a long prison sentence when he was finally caught. Patrick has some mental health issues that attenuated his relationship with reality once he was in the thick of things, but that explains everything and excuses nothing.

No matter. He was my friend then, and he is my friend now. By my reckoning, you are issued about a dozen friends in life, and if one of mine happens to be in a prison jumpsuit, well, better him than me, but that doesn't erase the bond. Patrick screwed up, he is in the midst of the consequence, and during our visit, we concentrate on the good stuff. His children and mine, his release date, the job he has as a baker. I asked prison officials for permission to interview Patrick, but after I told them it had nothing to do with my day job at *The New York Times*, they would not let me bring so much as a pencil into the visiting room. So after I visited, I asked him a few questions by mail.

Patrick said he learned back in those days that getting what he needed out of me as a reporter required some clock minding.

"I finally figured out at some point that if I wanted to give you political news, I really needed to do it between about 1:00 p.m. and 4:00

p.m.," he wrote in the summer of 2007. "You were always crashing in the morning and too fucking high at night to deal with." Once I had washed out of journalism, he tried to pull me in on the Minnesota effort for the 1988 Dukakis presidential campaign. Patrick liked my writing and recalled that I was "desperate for money" at the time, so he thought there might be a fit. It was not, he wrote, a wise strategic move for the campaign. "I spent the first week nicely trying to get you to come to meetings as part of your job—the earliest you ever showed was 12:30 p.m. I was finally ready to fire your ass, but you just quit showing up, a perfect ending."

We eventually patched things up and went out one night to watch the Twins. We went bar hopping and ended up at Stand Up Frank's, the kind of place where a screwdriver was a glass full of vodka that the bartender whispered the words "orange juice" over before handing it to you. He said that when I pushed two of the notoriously strong drinks on him, he went into the bathroom and hurled immediately. We moved on to B.J.'s, a nearby strip club. In the letter, he wrote that after he parked, he noticed I was "fiddling around with some white powdery substance inside of some tinfoil." For some reason, I believed that the state director of the Dukakis effort would be more than happy to share a car with narcotics. "I told you to get the fuck out of my car and left you there."

Later we bumped into each other at the airport. "I remember thinking how paranoid you looked. I saw you a few weeks later, and you told me you had smuggled in a ton of coke by taping it to your body that day." Hmmmm, mighta, coulda happened, but I can say for sure that if it did happen, it was a domestic flight and that I didn't say much about it. Now or then.

Every time I drop a letter in the mail to Patrick, I do a double take on his federal prison ID. He was too smart, too careful, too much of a do-gooder to get jammed up by some kind of hustle. But I've seen enough to know that we all carry a measure of guilt and innocence along with us. If someone is going to suggest he is eternally damned for what he did, it probably won't be me. We all contain multitudes.

16

THIS IS HOW WE ROLL

How many of us persist in a precipitate course which, but for a moment of heedlessness, we might never have entered upon, simply because we hate to "change our mind."

—WILLIAM JAMES, *THE PRINCIPLES OF PSYCHOLOGY, VOLUME 2*

There are moments in the party lifestyle when you know in your bones that you are at the epicenter of something spectacular; a moment that couldn't be replicated no matter how much cunning and planning came before it.

Walking into a ski bar near Breckenridge, Colorado, with Eddie, Scotty, and Dale, we meet the suspicion of the locals and the bartender with blunt force: cash and cocaine. Eddie made a three-foot pyramid of champagne glasses and poured bottle after bottle until they were filled. I walked away from the bar with a local I met and found the boys out on the black-diamond runs of Copper Mountain the next day.

Witnessing U2's first tour, as Bono came out and threw a glass of water up into the lights, the drops misting down and my sister Coo and I swim into the mosh pit at First Avenue until the tops of our shoes were black from getting stepped on.

Buying a party bag in Washington Square with Donald while he was doing some photo work in New York. It was filled with all manner of controlled substances, including some really epic acid. "How can street drugs be so good?" I asked Donald in wonder as we tripped and walked from deli to deli all night, buying cans of beer. "Because we will be back tomorrow." We were.

The great thing about sober life is that you can reliably plan for what might come next. That's also the bad thing. As a certified maniac, you have an expectation that almost anything can happen if certain forces align, and sometimes they do. A fight, a new friend, a road trip, or all three on the same night.

Sitting in New Orleans talking with Chris, the guy who fetched the gun I thought I never had, we talked about that moment of ignition. He remembered one night when we were at Stand Up Frank's, probably in the summer of 1987.

"We were drinking whiskey, and we were coked up," Chris said. "It was near closing time, and you became convinced that there was some guy down at the bar that was giving you a dirty look, and I kind of physically had restrained you from going over there and confronting him. You were talking loudly, and I was pretty sure things were gonna get ugly there.

"That was the night we ended up getting in my truck and driving to Detroit Lakes. It was just on a whim to see Waylon Jennings or Willie Nelson or some country music festival up there. You know, closing time at Stand Up Frank's."

Detroit Lakes was five hours away, near the Minnesota–North Dakota border. Anna was already up there, ensconced in a cabin, seeing music and attending to the consumer needs of the musicians.

"We stopped somewhere along the way—I don't even remember— stopped at a bar that was open inexplicably," he said. "We chatted up some girls and talked one of them into going with us. I still never could quite figure that out. That was you and not me."

For reasons he can't readily fetch at the moment, fatigue probably, he let me drive his giant GMC pickup. "All of a sudden you just swerved down into the ditch with it, slammed on the brakes, stopped in the ditch, jumped out, laid out some lines on the hood of the truck. We got out, snorted the lines on the hood, and then jumped right back in, and then back onto the road.

"And then we got all the way up there to the festival, and we're standing in line to get some hot dogs, and you got into it with some guy behind us in line. Somebody squirted mustard on somebody—I don't know if it was you or him—you got into this shoving match with this guy, and we got kicked out of the festival fifteen minutes after we bought the tickets and got in. So we drove all the way up there and never saw a single bit of music."

17

A CONFEDERACY OF JUNKIES

Moderation is a memory.

—LIZ PHAIR, "JOHNNY FEELGOOD"

The nomenclature of addiction, the nouns that go with it—junkie, drunk, crackhead, doper—would tend to suggest that all people involved in the life are the same. They are not. Neil Young was right about junkies being like setting suns, including coming to untimely, but not entirely unforeseen, ends. Speaking of which, we might pause for a moment of silence for those I knew or ran with who are no longer with us:

TOMMY—my cousin and familial doppelgänger, who died trying to go back at it one more time. The difference between my status above ground and his below is luck and nothing more.

AARON—the first person I advised in a program of recovery. A gorgeous kid with a fondness for heroin, he jumped off the Richard I. Bong Memorial Bridge connecting Duluth, Minnesota, and Superior, Wisconsin.

PHIL—not my dope dealer, but a former porn actor and member of our tribe whose girlfriend died when a car he was driving while impaired went off the road. The night before he was to be sentenced—he would have gone to county for a year at most, which ain't nothing but doable—Phil used a massive hypodermic to inject an eight ball while lying in the bathtub, with "Two out of Three Ain't Bad" by Meat Loaf playing in the background. Always with the drama, that one.

FRED—went for a short swim and never made it back.

BOB—the guitar player who could not stop the music or the dope.

But there are plenty who have made it. The heroin people, that's completely understandable. Heroin has a pickling effect. Heading out into the world once or at most twice a day to cop, heroin people spend most of their time on the nod, watching soaps and listening to Leonard Cohen. Not a lot of risk there, other than copping a bad batch.

Cokeheads, well, that's a different story. All that ripping and running sparks a kind of corrosion—no sleep, lots of booze to take the edge off—that wears even the hardiest souls down to a nub. It is a lifestyle that leaves marks: the scar from the casual swipe of the box cutter during some beef, the burned extremity because he or she went to sleep with the blowtorch on, and the eyes that saw too much because they did not close often enough.

Booze has a nice, fat track record, dating back to soldiers toasting their victories under Herodotus. Drink a little, no big deal. Drink a lot every once in a while, not a problem. Drink a lot all the time, and your innards will swell up, giving you the look of a pear with legs, and if organ failure doesn't get you, your esophagus might bleed out, or you could just pull a lamebrained move like blacking out and face-planting for good.

In a broader sense, addiction can be enormously simplifying. While other people worry about their 401(k)'s, getting their kids into the right nursery school and/or college, and keeping their plot to take over the world in good effect, a junkie or a drunk just has to worry about his next dose. It leads to a life that is, in a way, remarkably organized. What are we doing today? *Exactly what we did yesterday, give or take.*

A drunk or a junkie will end up finding fellow travelers in the course of things. If you are a drunk, the guy down the bar who falls off his stool and then gets up, sits down, and orders another is your friend. He may be a peckerwood who makes speeches about the Twins or the Vikings or the mayor, but he is, after a fashion, your guy. In the same way, an addict will find his or her own level and his or her tribe to go with it. As in a lot of cities in the mid-to-late eighties, coke was ubiquitous in Minneapolis. But while vast swathes of people did a line here or there, there was a self-selected tribe who did little else.

To be a daily user of cocaine is, by definition, to be part of the coke economy. Unless you are a trust-fund kid or are lucky enough to be hooked up with one, all that getting and using is generally accompanied by the buying and selling. I was always more interested in writing about crooks than becoming one, but I began dealing coke in service to my habit.

I had some experience in moving dry goods. During the end of college, I sold pot, mostly for Eddie. It was a simple, lucrative business, although it involved a lot of lifting. I would show up with a garbage bag of pot, maybe fifty pounds, and come away with a grocery bag of cash, $15,000 to $20,000. It was a sane, civilized activity with regular-guy clients.

Coke was more complicated, even in small amounts. I worked mostly with ounces or fractions thereof, stepping on it a bit by adding lactose powder and then parsing it out to friends and friends of friends, and, in a few reckless moments, people I did not know from a load of hay. On larger stuff, I took preorders and went to fetch, telling the connection I would be right back, and I usually was. I have middle-manned a kilo, making almost $10,000 walking from one room to the next. Of course, the person who had the kilo did not want to meet the person buying the kilo, so the risk, along with some of that money, was mine.

The drug business, like all commodities, runs on the twin rails of price and quality. The truism still attains: You get what you pay for. Anybody who oversold his product or stepped on it too much was soon out of the business. And with Schedule I narcotics, there is the added frisson of serious federal time if things go wrong. I was careful some of the time and lucky when I wasn't. When the Hennepin County sheriff moved on some of Eddie's storage spots that were jammed with all manner of whatnot, he was out of town, and I called him with the bad news, but that was as far as it went. When the feds nailed Phil, I hammered his beeper for a week while he was in custody, but they never came for me. I got involved in some deals with big numbers, but I never was more than a gofer with really good connections.

Everyone works for someone. The hooker is either working for the pimp or her two-year-old. The stripper works for the dope dealer or the no-good boyfriend. And the deeper I went into the drug economy, I found that everyone, even the person who managed big money and serious weight, was working for someone else. During most of this time, we were all probably working for Pablo Escobar in one form or another. And he probably worked for someone too.

I learned stuff in those days, a little of which helps me in my current life. I can do a threat assessment when I walk into a room, I know how a cop acts when he is trying not to act like one, and that the smoother a bad guy is, the more menacing he actually is. The big, clanky guys who sprayed menace in all directions were mostly profiling, and it was the quiet guys you had to watch out for. One time at Phil's apartment during a poker game with people in the racket, I got a little fresh with one of those quiet guys even though I hadn't intended any offense. He took my arms and legs off at the poker table and then, smiling quietly, told me he would be happy to finish the job if I wanted to take a walk. I did not feel like a walk.

In Minneapolis the coke business was pretty much divided along racial lines. I spent most of my time in the Life in rooms full of white boys, all of them talking friendly and nice—no guns, mostly—but everybody kept one eye on the scale and the other on his back.

I ran around a tidy little circle of supply that I could trace blindfolded. Phil was a gangster who knew his way around people and a transaction and was completely fearless. Kenny had an antic customer base, some solid connections, and the virtue of almost never being asleep, which is a fairly adaptive characteristic in a coke dealer. Tony the Hat was a force of nature, a big, scary guy who had all sorts of rules and a penchant for both generosity and ferociousness in equal measure.

The rest of us, well, we were merchants of necessity. And there were a lot of ways to stay in coke. Around this time, 1986 and 1987, there was a whole ring of wannabees: chippers, gram guys, penny-ante dealers, people who knew a guy who knew a guy. It was a movable feast that could be accessed all over town. Over the bar at McCready's; or the bathroom at the CC Club, a hipster bar in South Minneapolis; almost anywhere at First Avenue, the big rock club downtown. And then when they closed for the night, there was a series of houses, not officially dope houses, but more ad hoc copping spots.

We cokeheads would see one another out and about at the bars, clap hands, and maybe take a trip to the bathroom together, knowing full well that we would see one another later that night when everyone else went to sleep. It was a tribe that included some rockers and artists, but most of us were primarily skilled at eyeballing a gram or cooking coke with nothing more than a Rolaid, some spit, and a crappy spoon. We tried to make like it was just a little something we did on the side, but it became the main event for far too many of us.

Sarah was a fellow traveler who continued to stick in my memory long after those days ended. Sarah was about four-foot-nine and all of fifteen when I met her. Her remarkable figure was draped in Stevie Nicks–like finery, all gauze and spooky hats. Her parents were musicians, and her theatricality was manifest—she'd had a bit part in *Madame Butterfly* when she was five years old. That little girl could make an entrance and take over a room. She cultivated mystery and allure in a very gullible, mostly male crowd.

"She had this ritual of putting her possessions, her keys, her cigarettes, all the stuff she'd emptied out of her purse and put all around her," said Kenny, a dealer and friend of us both who now lives in Seattle. "It was almost like a way of putting out some kind of power. Just the way she did it, it was like she knew what she was doing. Like she was at least subconsciously doing some occult manipulations."

Dealers liked having her around when they went out, because she could hold their coke—as a minor, she would not be subject to any felony counts. Sarah and I knew each other a bunch of different ways. We were fellow cokeheads, did business together, and she helped look after my kids when they were born. Later, in sobriety—both of us were off the stuff, as I recall—we were close for a short time.

Back in the day, she did not conduct herself as a fifteen-year-old. More than once, I was sitting in a room with some knuckle-dragger who was holding court because he had coke, talking smack and parsing out a taste here and there, and then Sarah entered. Within minutes, the large baggie of coke would be in front of her, and she would be directing the proceedings, the jerk now all but licking her hands and wishing he could get his mouth on more.

I never told her, but I knew her from my other life as a reporter. In the 1980s there was a scandal at the Children's Theatre Company. John Clark Donahue, its founder and artistic director, was indicted for sexual activity with some of the older children at the school. And in the course of the investigation, they discovered that two girls in their early teens had slept with the lighting director. Sarah was one of them.

"I went into a SuperAmerica to buy some cigarettes, and he was working as a cashier. They ruined his life; he didn't deserve it," she said in a voice that was a mix of gravel and whiskey when we talked at a restaurant in suburban St. Paul twenty years later. "I knew what I was doing; it was my choice."

But you were in fact, like, fifteen?

"I was a very precocious fifteen," she said. "I was a smart cookie. I knew what I was up to." We both laughed. She often walked around with several males wrapped around her little fingers. She said it wasn't that complicated.

"Tits and ass," she said, with a wave of a cigarette after lunch. "I didn't know how good at it I was. But I knew I could do it. I could do whatever I chose to. Whatever I put my mind to, it didn't really surprise me." Despite the collateral damage she had suffered, she said, "There were lots of fun parts. I had a great time. I was young, I was getting whatever I wanted, I was doing whatever I wanted."

When we were running together in the Life, she was prone to doing huge lungfuls of crack and then flopping around on the floor like a caught fish in the bottom of a boat. "Seizures," she said, letting the word hang. "I was a monster."

There is something of her that I still carry with me. The ring finger of my right hand bears an anomalous bump on the second knuckle. It broke when she had a seizure, and in a panic, I stuck my finger in her mouth. She holds my hand and inspects the old break. She seems impressed.

"You do bite hard," I said.

"I know," she said. "When we started smoking, it was all downhill from there."

18

CRACK: A BRIEF TUTORIAL

I drank a second mouthful, in which I find nothing more than in the first, then a third, which gives me rather less than the second. It is time to stop; the potion is losing its magic.

—MARCEL PROUST, *REMEMBRANCE OF THINGS PAST*

Crackhead is an embarrassing line item to have on a résumé. If meth tweakers had not come along and made a grab for the crown—meth makes you crazy *and* toothless—crackheads would be at the bottom of the junkie org chart.

Racism, as displayed through the prism of the criminal justice system, plays a role. During the urban crack epidemic of the 1980s, both state and federal courts pathologized crack cocaine far beyond its powdered sibling. Black people did crack, white people did coke, so sentencing bifurcated, and Whitey, including me, generally skated.

To avoid both the guilt by association and legal distortions, my gang always purchased coke in its powdered form. We were not averse to snorting; portable, easy to use, and requiring no more equipment than a rolled-up dollar bill, we contented ourselves with sticking things up our nose for many nights of frolic. Lots of the people I knew who loved coke took a long, hard look at crack and demurred.

But not me. Here's the thing: If you snort a great deal of cocaine, eventually your nose gets full and your synapses get bored. Crack cocaine offers all the benefits of injectable drugs—a complete and immediate rush, the possibility of easing up to overdosing without actually having it befall you—without all those messy needles, track marks, or exposure to bloodborne contagions.

When smokable cocaine first came on the scene, it involved very complicated processing to produce what was then called freebase cocaine. Powdered cocaine was dissolved in a strong alkaloid solution such as ammonia. Then ether, or some other highly flammable solvent, was added to further refine the mixture and conjure a smokable substance. It yielded a purity that could be eye popping, but it had its pitfalls. Just ask Richard Pryor.

Crack, on the other hand, required just four elements: fire, water, coke, and baking soda. The mix is heated, and the impurities from manufacture boil away. The remaining solid bonds with the baking soda, or base, and a rock is formed. To wit:

$$\text{Coc-H}^+\text{Cl}^- + \text{NaHCO}_3 \longrightarrow \text{Coc} + \text{H}_2\text{O} + \text{CO}_2 + \text{NaCl.}$$

Different ratios of baking soda to coke yielded different outcomes. I preferred the very prosaic 1:1. Most crack ranged from 75 percent to 90 percent pure, based on seizures by the U.S. Drug Enforcement Administration. When the coke is cooked with the sodium bicarbonate and water, it tends to make a popping, crackling sound, hence the name *crack*.

Do anything enough times, and you become an adept. Although a lighter under a spoon could do the job, I preferred a gas kitchen range. I could, using decent coke and a common tablespoon, step up to the range, drop the coke and baking soda into some tap water, give it a few expert sautélike movements to get the good stuff to congeal, and then literally flip the rock into the air and grab it, all in fewer than thirty seconds. The midair grab gave it a flash of tension and drama.

The second stage of ingestion required just a little bit of equipment. Under ideal conditions, a long glass pipe with metal screens at the end would be heated from below. The rock would become a vapor that would cool on its way through the pipe and into the lungs and then, about ten seconds later, the ventral tegmental area of the brain. In a pinch, a soda can with holes poked in it and some cigarette ashes to serve as a screen were sufficient. Necessity is a mother.

Once in the noggin, coke calls its own frantic tune, with all the amps turned up to eleven. The drug, especially when smoked, releases dopamine, the lingua franca of the pleasure impulse. In a neat trick, it attaches to the dopamine transporter, and so the dopamine hangs around instead of reabsorbing, creating a lingering sensation of extreme euphoria. Dopamine rides between the nerve endings for ten to fifteen minutes, cycling the user through a range of pleasurable feelings.

It is, for want of a better metaphor, akin to scoring the winning touchdown in the final game of a championship season, and then reliving that moment of crossing the goal line over and over until the rush ebbs. And rather than the gradual ride up from powdered cocaine, crack makes it happen immediately and profoundly. Senses are more acute, pupils dilate, blood pressure and body temperature rise, and you feel like the lord of all you survey, even if it is a crappy couch and a nonworking television in a dope house.

And then it goes away. There is only one thing that appeals after a hit of crack, and it is not a brisk walk around the block to clear one's head. There is no such thing as a social crack user. Many normal people get a sense of its lurid ambush and walk away. Others take another hit. In this chronic scenario, the brain argues against the dopamine festival by becoming far less receptive. Higher doses lead to diminishing returns and a brutal cratering after ingestion. What seemed like a way to leave the gravitational pull of this ball of dirt becomes a shovel repetitively deployed to dig a hole that the user cannot crawl out of.

I have not smoked coke in two decades, but I remember its every aspect. A pre-high emerged even as the drug was being made: The heart would begin to race, and the pupils would flare in anticipation.

Bent over the stove with my confederates, we would be doing our little happy dance. *It's on. It is all about to happen right here, right now.* Once the awkwardness of who would get the first hit was dealt with, your turn would come. Crack does not just make a noise when it is made, it makes a noise when it is smoked. There is an eminently satisfying bubbling sound as the solid becomes liquid and, soon enough, vapor.

Unless you are on the streets going from rock to rock with burned fingers and a broken stem—I was never that guy—smoking crack is an indoor sport. There is only this one thing until all the coke is gone. The drinking, chatting, dancing that goes with snorting coke is not really part of the crack experience. Smoking crack is less of a party and more of a religious ceremony, with a group of people gathered around a central icon—in this instance, the very small campfire conjured by pipe and flame. People would sit quietly, rubbing their thighs with anticipation, maybe making an occasional observation about the robustness of a particular hit or how wrecked somebody looked. As long as the coke held out, it was mostly silence and goofy grins of satisfaction. The high would last fifteen or twenty minutes, and then the synapses would begin making a fuss—a head full of little baby birds with their beaks open, crying out for more.

When it comes to rendering the experience in written form, people tend toward the sexual metaphors, but I never found that sex, even good sex, reliably hit for the cycle like crack. Smokable cocaine initially taps into a childlike wonder, a feeling that the carnival had come to town and chosen your cranium as the venue for its next show. Nothing compares to the first hit of your life, the first hit of the night, the first hit of a new batch. The ensuing chase, the endless pursuit of that first time, provides a riddle that cannot be solved.

With nerve endings and dopamine levels in a natural state, inhaled cocaine vapor is the mallet that hits the spot and sends the ringer straight to the bell. Every time thereafter, it goes up a little less quickly, rises not so much. But it still feels better than not. A kind of group hypnosis settles in, with the ebb and flow of the activity—inhale/

exhale, your turn/my turn, cook it/smoke it—becoming the end in itself. I have never had any trouble understanding people who can play poker or the slots for days on end, long after anhedonia has set in, win or lose. To stop, to come to your senses, is to admit that it is over; that you have played and lost.

After two minutes, or two hours, or two days, supply dwindles and desperation sets in. The spoon is scraped, and if people are geeked enough, they fall to their knees and claw the carpet for a crumb that might have been dropped. As if. Crack cocaine had the power to reverse the polarity of the relationship between user and drug. All of the smoke in all those pipes was going both ways: The narcotic was being inhaled while my soul was exhaled. Before I started smoking cocaine, I spent a bit too much time on William Blake's road to excess, but I maintained. But smoking crack was a completely unmanageable activity from the beginning, the vehicle for my trip from party boy to junkie.

Sitting in his cabin in Newport, Donald told me that all my friends took notice immediately. "We hid from you. I can remember working at the bar at Tam's, and somebody said, 'Carr is on his way here.' I split."

Why?

"You smelled bad, you looked bad, you were sweating like a pig, you were smoking crack."

He paused.

"As good as friends as we were, as much as I loved you, you weren't you. I wasn't talking to my friend David, I was talking to a wild man. You were a creature. I was afraid."

I can't remember if that was before or after I came over to his house with a gun. Neither can he.

———

Donald ended up going for a ride with the crack after I got off, and a bunch of other people I knew lost years to the smoke. Beyond physiology and pharmacology, I'm at a loss to explain my two hard years of smoking it. Even now, as a recovering person, when I see kids in New York clubs sneaking off for a toot, I have no trouble understanding the attraction. A bump of coke in the bathroom, a shot of whiskey at the bar, no worries. But crack? It is a very refined bit of idiocy to get mixed up in that life and expect to remain functional.

By the time I went back to Minneapolis to look around, all of the detox records were gone, but I was able to talk to Bob Olander, the guy who ran Hennepin County's detox programs at the time. I had done a few stories involving him when I was a reporter, and I had always thought he was a no-bullshit guy. He ended up getting involved in my case when I came back as a client.

"It took awhile to get here, but crack moved into Minneapolis, but it was a whirlwind when it got there, and we were just overwhelmed with all kinds of people who were addicted to crack," he said. "Most of them were black, but it took out its share of white guys like you."

Several times when I tipped over, I would end up flopping into Bob's office, no longer employed and no longer employable. At least twice he got me wired into state-funded treatment. I had always thought that part of the reason that he took a strong personal interest in my case was that he thought I still had a good, strong shot at returning to civil society. But talking to Bob, it was clear that he felt I was not a real good bet by the time crack got done with me.

"It took more than once, I remember that. Your prognosis was not good. I never fooled myself about that," he said. "You had a well-established set of compulsions and a history of engaging those compulsions, and a downward spiral to show for it." My time at the end of the pipe managed to wipe the smirk off my face.

"Your physical affect was that of an over-the-hill rogue," he said. "There was a sadness to you, a guy who had been flying high and now was flat on his ass. You just looked beat up. After I saw you a few times, well, you were a pretty arrogant guy, and it gradually dawned on you that you could never be arrogant enough to pull off the life you were choosing."

He said the fact that I was a white male who possessed skills that made me employable, and that I had a supportive family, made my odds better. Not great, but better.

"You were a man of good intent. You had a sense of remorse of what you had done to the people around you. It is a soft piece of the statistical end of this business, but you had the ability to be hopeful. It was a steep hill you were walking back up—I sort of remember the odds as seventy-thirty against, but I thought, 'This guy might have a chance.' I thought it was worth pushing a few buttons for you."

He had to push those buttons more than once. I was not, as they say, a first-time winner in the program of recovery.

19

WHEN ELEPHANTS DANCE

Tommy and I are sitting in a hotel in midtown Manhattan. At the end of the summer in 2007, we are finally getting together after a number of false starts. He is in town to do *Letterman* for no particular reason, just because Dave has liked him ever since he was the ne'er-do-well husband of Roseanne. I was there the night they met in Minneapolis, a particularly debauched one, and I failed to notice that they were interested in trading something besides jokes. I had done a story or two about him when he was first taking off as a comedian, and we connected. He was the most outlandish, off-the-hook version of a drunk and addict I had ever seen. When Tommy was using, he made me look like Mister Rogers in a leather jacket.

That was a long time ago. Tommy has since moved on, landing a few good movie roles, along with a few television shows that did not pan out. He has been counted out so many times that he is something of a running joke, but he has been on a tear lately, working with talented directors in indie films.

In spite of his reputation as a buffoon among people who don't know him, he has played a substantial and steady role in my recovery. Because he's antic in manner—his leg is always bouncing—people think he's still a cokehead, but as I know him, he is coming up on almost twenty years of recovery. I sobered up before he did and helped him along a bit, and in turn, when I relapsed, he was very much a presence. I have been to meetings at his house, he has called friends of mine who were new in sobriety to help them along, and he is known as a go-to person in Hollywood for people who need a hand up with addiction issues.

Tommy is a loyalist. When he first went to Los Angeles, he dragged along a whole gang of knuckleheads, many of whom work in the entertainment business still. After I got custody of the girls, he gave me a *Roseanne* spec script to write, which was approved but never produced, and I used the money to buy our first decent car. I stood up at his weddings—two of them—and I continue to see him now when I get out to Los Angeles. The only time he ever lied to me was when he first started seeing Roseanne, but then again, he was selling information to the *National Enquirer* at the time to stay in coke money. He eventually moved out to Los Angeles and ended up going to the hospital with a massive nasal hemorrhage. I talked to him on the phone that day, as I did whenever he got out of his box. He wanted to know what he should do. And I would always tell him the same thing: If your nose hurts, quit sticking things up there. Tom sobered up, and he and Roseanne would have the girls over whenever they were in town.

When I arrive at his hotel, he is downstairs working out. While he showers up, I look around his room, which looks like it has been hit with several bombs. Suits, workout clothes, magazines, and several phones are in the mix. Hollywood people, regardless of who they are, never seem to travel light.

The day before I got fired in 1987, the day before the Night of the Gun, we had gone out on Saint Patrick's Day. It was huge, murderous fun, as it was almost every time I was with him, and it ended badly, as it usually did.

In his room, Tommy and I work to remember how it went down. Tommy was a rapacious, reflexively offensive comedian, the kind of not-always-jolly guy who lived for the presence of a ripe heckler. On that Saint Patrick's Day, there was a loudmouth there at the Knights of Columbus hall, a guy named Sarge, who sort of unofficially ran the joint. I told Tommy to lay off of him when he did his routine. Small tactical error on my part.

"You said to me, 'Don't fuck with Sarge,'" he said, the leg bouncing as he warmed to the task. "I started fucking with him immediately and for the whole act. It was death. First of all, the people at the Knights of Columbus hall, they weren't there to see me or my version of comedy, and it just got ugly. I threw beers at somebody's face, almost hit somebody in a wheelchair. I didn't know they were in a wheelchair, and I immediately apologized, but it was too late. It seems to me that the repercussions from it were mostly directed toward you."

That is my recollection. I also recall that we left quickly.

"Very quickly. It was a posse situation," he said.

We had become very skilled in the art of leaving quickly, or if cornered, fighting our way out. Tommy was 86'd from many of our regular haunts in Minneapolis, and it was rare for him to be out on the road doing shows and not end up getting booted out of the joint where he was appearing. He recalled that he was at McDonald's in Rochester, Minnesota, after a gig and got kicked out before he had a chance to go to the bathroom. He went in the parking lot instead. When the cops came, midstream, they asked what he was doing. Tommy told the cop he was making him a cocktail. All of that would have been pretty routine, except Tommy was due the following day in Los Angeles for Roseanne's first big HBO special. Calling in incarcerated would have been a profoundly bad career move.

He called me in a panic, contrite, but the Rochester cops were plenty pissed. I called Ron, the biggest criminal defense attorney in the state. He knew people, Tommy got sprung, made the late flight to L.A., and nobody was the wiser. "You saved my ass," he remembered.

We had a lot in common. Both large guys back then, we could take over a room or turn it against us with a flick of the wrist. In the summer of 1987, Tommy stiffed on a coke debt from the night before—he still denies this, but some things I do remember. Like a lot of us, Tommy was better at doing drugs than paying for them. He was not one of those guys who would steal your dope and then help you look for it, but he did what he needed to to stay high.

I will cop to hassling him a little bit too much about that. Then I remember him, out of nowhere, attempting to remove my left eye. In my mind, it had always been one more bit of tomfoolery gone bad, no big deal. We had joked about it many times, but when we really got down to cases and were talking about it at length, I realized Tommy felt bad about it.

He said it took place at Anna's house on Oliver Avenue, with a bunch of rockers from bands like the Replacements, Soul Asylum, and the Flaming Oh's. His girlfriend at the time, Melanie, was a gorgeous R & B singer who had a vocal in "Funkytown," the smash 1980 single out of Minneapolis.

"Honest to God, you were subtle at first, but you kept coming up to me, and you're fucked up. I told you that I didn't have the money on me but I'd give it to you; we could talk about it tomorrow, not now. Melanie is here, the guys from the band are here, I'm trying to get some work."

But I kept coming in close, hassling him, my voice growing from a whisper into something more menacing. I had a history of throwdowns in bars and backyards, but my win-loss record was grim, and even though I was tenacious, my pugilistic skills would not have been out of place on a *Bum Fights* video.

"Finally, I felt in my heart that this was one of those times where you just wanted to be punched out," he said. "I warned you though. I said, 'OK, seriously, the next time you do that, I'm gonna hurt you. I'm really gonna hurt you.' I just wanted you to really believe that."

He said I was embarrassing him, embarrassing myself in front of our gang.

"You're bitching, first of all. Everybody knows why you're mad; they think I owe you money or whatever, that I'm not paying my coke debts. You did a lot of people a lot of favors, people liked you, sometimes people didn't like me. You're coming over, and it was like, fuck, I had two choices: either hit you right in the throat, or I'm gonna get you and stick my fucking hand in your eye. You weren't a small guy. It's not easy when you're fucked up, so I feel my fingers so deep in your eyeball that it was—I don't know."

I remember what happened next, and so does he. I went down to the ground, slowly, making girly-man screams about him poking my eye out.

Later, in the cab ride downtown for dinner, he feels compelled to explain himself more even though I didn't lose my eye, and I really had something like it coming.

"It wasn't going to be easy. I would have just thrown you to the ground or something, but I have seen you be tough, and I didn't want to have to go there. I told people that you wanted to have your ass kicked, that I was doing you a favor," he said, not laughing.

It's odd. It hurt at the time, but I never gave it another thought, really, and here he is explaining himself to me. He might be a comic and an actor now, but back in those days, he was fresh out of the meat-packing plant. And although he is now much bigger than I am—cancer and some other things shrunk me back to life-size—back in those days, I was probably the kind of guy who could have made a problem. He still could have kicked my ass, but it would have been a long, painful event for both of us and for everyone watching it. Maybe he *did* do me a favor. Even with the occasional bit of combustion, we spent a fair amount of time together, including nighttime visits while I was working on stories.

"We were going to smoke some crack or something, but first you had to interview some kid that was living off the streets and write a poignant story, hard core, like a poignant, sweet story. Then after that, your dealer showed up," he said. "But you always treated everyone the same way. No different."

Unlike almost everyone I talk to about the old days, Tom thinks the reason that I sobered up had less to do with the twins and more to do with an ambition we had in common:

"I think your career means more to you than you would admit," he said. "I think you're like me. I pretend like I would be happy to be nowhere, but I don't want to fuck it up and go backward and go back down that far."

20

BAM BAM

In drug gangster movies, the kingpin is always some guy with a pock-marked face who brandishes money, women, and weapons as a kind of jewelry, worn or used for effect. They are loud, menacing figures—they are flanked by goombahs on the way into the restaurant, sit with their back against the wall, and always get the big piece of chicken.

But the most serious and successful person I did business with was just a touch over five feet, cute, with a full head of dyed-blonde hair, a little mouth, and a fondness for maniacs in matters of the heart, if not business.

When I met Anna, she was in full effect, moving a kilo a month from straight-up Colombian sources through a series of reliable associates who were also her pals. She worked dead drops in storage spots, safe deposit boxes, and mules to keep her at a remove from the nuts and bolts of the drug enterprise. That girl knew how to count—click, click, click went the bills, with an occasional swipe of the thumb to the lips to maintain traction. And when the piles were too big to hand-count, she had a digital scale that weighed piles of twenties. She had two kids in a nice house in North Minneapolis; the serious dope business was done elsewhere. We met at a bon voyage for my old connection Phil, who was going away to do some federal time, so the timing was inspired, or at least seemed so then.

In 1986 I was in the midst of a professional transition from the *Twin Cities Reader* to *Corporate Report Minnesota*, an excellent business monthly owned by the same company. The idea of working as a business reporter had never occurred to me, but it represented a step into new subject matter and additional money. Doolie had moved in with me on Garfield Avenue in South Minneapolis, and we were in our usual cycle of intense romance mixed with incendiary arguments. I loved her, as much as I cared about anything besides myself, but she required maintenance and reassurance that I had little time for.

Over the course of the fall of 1986, I began seeing more and more of Anna, under the guise of doing business for a while, and then it became clear to Doolie and others that something other than dry goods was being exchanged. As a consumptive, grabby four-year-old in the body of a grown man, I wanted to hang onto everything simultaneously. I lied to Doolie about Anna and to Anna about Doolie, keeping each off balance and me in the middle. The meretriciousness of my life was etched on slips of paper in the wastebasket, traces of perfume on my collar, missing underwear, and newly acquired T-shirts. Everything implicated me except my mouth, which was in a constant state of explanation.

Anna and I came together slowly at first, with our first date at a Minnesota North Stars hockey game followed by dinner. We were both still only snorting at the time, and we mowed through the eight ball—3.5 grams—of indifferent coke that I had. I had no idea that Anna was anything but an enthusiast like me.

We were in her room at her house at the end of the night, and when the coke ran out, she sent me to the safe under the third step down to fetch some more. I came back empty-handed, telling her that there was only a large white brick in there. "That's it, you nitwit," she said. "Just break off a corner and bring it."

Decades later, we are talking outside a hotel in Tucson, and she still has no trouble recalling the dimensions of a pressed kilo of coke.

"It was about as big as a book, about this big," she said, framing the air with her hands. "It still had a snake seal; I mean, it was right from the Medellin cartel.

"I sold a kilo a month for seven years," she said. "It cost me twenty-five cents a gram. It was twenty-five thousand dollars a kilo and there's a thousand grams. And I turned around and sold that for one hundred grand."

Anna was plenty sharp in business matters, and for a dope dealer she was on the girly side, with lots of alluring frocks and a good, deep laugh. When I first met her, she had a beefed-up Nissan Maxima, a nice family, and a very successful wholesale coke business. Anna liked me because I had a real job and did not let her boss me around. All the men in her life, including her ex-husband, worked for her. I liked her because she was her own damn thing from some backwater Minnesota town who took shit from no one and had an unlimited supply of pure coke.

Chris, my pal in New Orleans, remembers Anna as a "good-hearted, stand-up person. When I first met her, she was a smart, tough woman doing well for herself, you know, in a difficult and illegal enterprise and something that is generally male-dominated. You don't see a lot of women at that level conducting that kind of a business. And, you know, she owned a house, she had kids she was taking care of."

For Anna and me, no moment was unalloyed by drugs. Chemicals define a vast swath of intimate relationships in the modern world. The doleful, uninvolved husband who works through a twelve-pack in front of the TV and side trips to the garage to visit a pint of vodka. The wife whose headaches require a steady stream of Klonopin. The fifth-grade daughter who is wired on Adderal. The teenager who sustains himself with one-hitters in his bedroom. Ships passing in a mood-altered murk, each regarding the other through the lens of pharmacology.

For a time, we were both riding high. I had friends all over the city, and Anna was treated as royalty whenever she went out, which was not that often. She had been married to Steve, a good guy who ran the coke business until he got in trouble by doing the product. He ended up in a deep hole, and when Anna flew to meet the Colombians he owed tall money to, they agreed to work out a plan with her. She became one of the most respectable sources of serious weight in the city.

In her version, everything was going swimmingly until I came along (which is sort of true), and then I seduced her into smoking cocaine (more or less true). In my version, I lumbered into her life, succumbed to abundant blandishments, and tipped over into a violent, destructive mania, a drug-induced psychosis. Which is sort of true, but only as far as it goes.

In every city, even a smallish one like Minneapolis, there is someone like Anna, the respectable person doing the disreputable work of dealing to the various elites. She had lawyers, medical doctors, and serious business people on her client list. By dealing with someone like Anna, who had a home, kids, and real friends, they could keep their dirty secret from seeming dirty, not really acknowledging that they were involved in consuming serious narcotics. It wasn't like they were out copping on some street corner.

She was an especially handy person to have around when there was visiting rock royalty. If some Major Name was playing a big gig, you would find Anna backstage, looking for all the world like just one more rock chick, but with a purse in tow that contained enough coke to fell an elephant. People looked after her, made sure she was comfortable and happy, because she had the goods, was not a crook, and did not look like a gangster. When I met her, Anna's approach to running her business made all sorts of sense to me. Never mind that it was, in legal terms, an ongoing RICO, it was still an impressive achievement. She recalled that the professional regard was mutual.

"I had a lot of money when I first met you, and I felt that you had a lot of good connections, you worked, I admired your job, what you did for a living," she said, lighting up a cigarette. "I was just impressed, and I thought, Well, maybe between the two of us, we can go somewhere."

Anna introduced me around to her pals as her trusted associate, but they all knew precisely what I represented: the guy who would fuck up a good thing. As a business person, she probably sensed the same thing, but she still wanted me to wear the pants every once in a while.

"Steve, my first husband, I kind of emasculated him, and I learned a lesson that I never wanted to do that to anyone else," she said. "Well, by giving you drugs and money and making you run around, that was by no means making you masculine, either. It never worked. You never had the money, you never had the shit—once in a while it might work, but rarely. Rarely did it come back."

Apart from an inability to execute what were really errand-boy duties, I would disappear for long stretches for other reasons: I was still very much involved with Doolie.

"You lied to me completely for months about that," she said, just stating it as fact, without a wisp of accusation. I had forgotten how she actually came to know the truth. "She called me and threatened to kill me," Anna said. Again, very matter-of-fact. I do not know that to be true, but I asked if she took the threat seriously.

"Not really. 'Cause at the time I was winning. I was rolling," she said. "Things were going good for me, I had a beautiful home, and I had two beautiful children, and I had a sports car. And I just thought, I wanted you, and this woman was just not gonna have you, you know, and whatever happens, we're gonna—not duke it out physically—but she was going to have a fight on her hands."

So the sense of possession, of entitlement, was not just mine. She was a girl who had gotten used to getting exactly what she wanted.

"I was not an addict yet," she said. "Because I didn't like it that much. I liked money more. I liked to travel, I liked nice things, I adored my children, I just really didn't have a clue what it was like to be an addict. I looked at people around me and could not understand what was wrong with them; why they were making the decisions they were making. It wasn't until I became an addict that I understood at all."

Certainly she got a primer from her adjacency to me. As someone in the supply business, she had observed that the difference between snorting and smoking coke was vast. But after a time, she decided to see what all the fuss was about. "We fought for about six months about it, and then I joined you." She tipped over almost immediately. "The person who invented crack is so evil," she suggested. Someone walking by our table at the hotel did a double take when she said that, but she continued. "You have to be really self-destructive to stick a needle in your arm, do all of the preparation, where it's so easy to stick this pipe in your mouth, suck in some smoke, and the next thing you know, you're in hell.

"At one point I was so in love with you that I was willing to give up, basically, my soul, you know? I don't know exactly why," she said. "You're funny, you're gregarious, you can be an extremely charming guy. You also were the first man I felt wanted to protect me—if anybody did or said anything to me, you made sure that they knew who I was and you were my boyfriend, and you said, 'Don't do it, or you're gonna be in trouble.' You were my protector—*you* could say bad things about me, but nobody else could. I never had a father who stuck up for me; it was the first time I ever had an old man that would go to the line for me."

It was, she recalled, a strength occasionally taken to weakness.

"You had a tad of paranoia," she said, letting the understatement hang. "I can remember we were at a party one time, and somebody took a picture of me. I said I didn't like that, and you grabbed that person by the neck, took the camera, crunched it, made this huge scene, and I was like, well, I didn't want *that* either."

By the fall of 1987, her business was in disarray, I had lost my job, and then, oh yeah, she was pregnant. Her friends begged her to have an abortion. We were fulminating crackheads, and her ex-husband, who came by to take care of her two kids, was the only semiresponsible person in the house. Anna locked herself in her room for hours on end and would occasionally insist that Doolie was actually roaming around the rafters of her home. I explained to her how that was sort of impossible from a practical perspective, but there had been so many lies by that point, she had no idea what to believe. Both of us were chronically, psychotically high, and I was spending all of my time lifting the blinds and peeking out at a world that I was increasingly scared to venture out into.

"I can remember before I knew what was going on, you were always peeking out windows," she said. "I said, 'Motherfucker, if you don't get away from that window, I'm gonna kill you.' I didn't think I was really aware of what was going on, but you had yourself planted at my front door, and you would not leave. You were looking out those little windows, and that was all there was to it. You weren't budging."

And there was a really bad Fourth of July, her birthday, in 1988. Anna was set up as the supplier at a country music festival in Detroit Lakes, and I was coming over from my cabin in Wisconsin. Halfway there, I was speeding around a bend and came very close to plowing into a station wagon full of kids. I can still see their faces in the back window. I grabbed a ditch to avoid an accident. I ended up in the Brainerd, Minnesota, jail, celebrating our nation's independence by arcing lighted matches across the darkened cell. When I finally got out and arrived in Detroit Lakes, I found out that as a birthday gift, her friends had surprised her with a naked young man hanging from the ceiling of her cabin. I was livid.

"I can remember being at my cabin, and you giving me a black eye and breaking my rib and throwing me off the dock," she said. I had not remembered that last part, but as soon as she said it, I knew it had to be true.

I did not so much move in with Anna as suddenly become someone who did not leave. Regardless of who is doing the remembering, some nasty, ineluctable truths lie between us. She was in the habit of slamming doors in my face—I called her "Bam Bam" in part because of that—and I was in the habit of coming right through those doors and choking her. She was using crack when her water broke, signaling that the twins had arrived two and a half months early. I was the one who had brought her those drugs. I treated her as an ATM, using her drugs and money almost at will, while she seemed more than willing to make the trade. In spite of the fact that I was the one who stepped up and raised our children, who shook off the Life, there are times when the moral high ground rests with her. I hit her, for one thing. For another, whatever she did, she did out of a kind of love. My presence in her life was far more mercenary.

When I went to see Anna, it had been ten years since we had seen each other. There was very little context for our meeting other than the children we shared. Of all the trips I had taken in pursuit of the past, this was the one in which a common truth was unlikely to emerge. Each of us has a need to find someplace to put our time together that does not leave either of us immobilized with shame. Very separate narratives had been constructed in that time away from each other. (As Daniel L. Schacter wrote in *The Seven Sins of Memory,* "We often edit or entirely rewrite our previous experiences—unknowingly or unconsciously—in light of what we now know or believe.")

Anna is now living in a trailer in Tucson. A series of bad choices involving men, including me, some heavy legal stuff, and health matters had left her in a diminished state. Her life had become one long, punishing tumble, the kind of thing you see in dark indie movies. She once called me and said that she had missed a court date because her front tooth had fallen out and the dog had eaten it. She said she was sober now, but years of use meant that some of her five children—including the twins we had together—had been scattered. Her oldest daughter, stunningly beautiful and congenitally optimistic, was still around, looking after a baby she'd had recently and, sometimes, her mom.

We should hate each other, and sometimes we do, but not today. I was speaking at the Biltmore in Phoenix in 2006, and I drove down to Tucson to see her. At a certain point, she had gone her way and I went mine. The twins stayed with me. Anna has always been very vocal about the good job I did raising them—in between reminding me that I stole them in the first place—and I made it a habit never to speak ill of her in the presence of her daughters.

For a time, I sent them down to Arizona or Mexico, wherever Anna was, but it became clear that she was involved in a lifestyle that put them at risk after she had been beat up, gun robbed, and arrested. I stopped sending the girls. We stayed in touch sporadically after that.

Anna, who never had much of a career besides the drug life, was now working with other people who have drug problems as an intake person at a social service program. She has a car, a house, and a paycheck, but is just living month to month. She has gained weight and lost ground; there is very little evidence of the diminutive kingpin I knew back in the day. We did not belong together, then or now, but something profound knit us together and brought us to this day, this table, this conversation.

"I went to the doctor, and there were two heartbeats," Anna recalled of a day late in 1987. "You heard that over the phone. I said, 'I've got something to tell you,' and you said, 'What!?' I said, 'I want you home,' and you said, 'No, no, no! Tell me, tell me, tell me!' and as usual I caved, and I told you, and I think that probably sent you off on a three-day bender."

Do I recall that? Of course not. The bender is safely assumed. But what did I think? Did I actually attempt to process the implications of bringing not one but two new sentient beings into the Valley of Death I was walking through? Did I look in the mirror and say, "You have no business inflicting yourself on anybody small, dependent, defenseless"?

I did not.

In that year, I got fed up every other day and quit smoking crack, sending the pipe wheeling into the dark night air, finding some small, idiotic satisfaction in the crunch when it landed. Well, that oughta do it. Even while I was filling the pipe with another hit, with Anna mostly, the conversation was always the same: "We gotta knock this shit off."

And then the pregnancy. Together Anna and I drew many lines in the sand and then stepped across them, usually with me leading the way.

The friends we had left had no idea what to say. My twins were gestated in an environment that was akin to Baghdad, with IEDs going off all over the place. My friends tended to blame Anna, and her friends tended to blame me.

I tracked down LeAnn, a pal of Anna's at the time, to ask her what it was like to watch that pregnancy proceed. She and her sister Cheryl had known and loved Anna for many years, but they were speechless at the prospect of her carrying to term, especially with me standing there and enabling her. Like a lot of people who are still around from those days, LeAnn is sober. We sat in a booth at Archie's Bunker, a joint where I used to hang.

"She went downhill pretty quickly. I remember Cheryl coming over to my house once and going, 'I don't know what to do, I'm really concerned, I just don't know what to do.' I said, 'Well, we could have him hurt,' talking about you.

"Just to get rid of you," she clarified. "I don't mean dead."

21

DIAGNOSIS: NARCISSISTIC ASSHOLE

It was a running conceit of mine that even though I did not tend to prosper after treatment, I was a star pupil in the various programs I went through. Blessed with a gift for both blarney and psychological jargon, I often felt as if I had served in an unpaid consulting role while working my way through some institution. Although I failed to get the hang of some of the fundamental tenets of recovery, I believed I was an asset to every treatment center I wheeled through. A highly verbal person who still tested well for intelligence in spite of a punishing history of chemical abuse, I took a keen interest in the well-being of my fellow patients and was always willing to give an assist to the counselor when he or she seemed stuck. Some of those counselors were hard on me, but I always secretly believed that they were struck by my intuition and synthetic medical insights.

But then in the course of researching my medical records, I found one from a treatment at St. Mary's Rehabilitation Center from the start of 1988, the beginning of the end. (I also found that I had entered and left a rehab at Hennepin County Medical Center a month before, which would give me a grand total of five trips through treatment, when I had always thought the number was four, but who's counting besides me?) Anna was pregnant, I was jobless, so this time I really needed to get and stay sober. The record reflects that I had no real understanding of the stakes at hand.

COUNSELOR'S DISCHARGE SUMMARY

ADM:	1-25-88
DIS:	2-20-88
PATIENT'S DOCTOR:	Dr. Routt
PATIENT'S COUNSELOR:	Cal Scheidegger
PATIENT'S ADDRESS:	3208 Garfield Avenue South, Minneapolis, Minnesota 55408
TELEPHONE NUMBER:	825-9110
STATISTICS:	Age 33, Single, Male

PRESENTING PROBLEMS:

The patient entered treatment in need of detoxification and also suffering with the flu. He reported prior treatment followed by relapse. He also admitted symptoms sufficient to support the ongoing diagnostic impression of substance dependence. Specifics included daily use exceeding one month, compulsive use to intoxication, and increased tolerance. Areas of the patient's life that had been affected by his usage included vocational, physical, financial, emotional/psychological, spiritual, and familial. Impression: Substance Dependence.

COURSE OF TREATMENT:

The patient attended most unit functions of lecture, group, and adjunct therapies, including relaxation therapy, spiritual care, and individual counseling. The patient presented himself as considerably passive/aggressive and somewhat narcissistic. He tended to victimize group members and attempted to be a junior counseling [sic]. He was challenged repeatedly by his group for behavior involving two women, with whom he had relationships.

The patient was instructed in the preparation of a personal character inventory (AA Fourth Step). He verbalized that inventory to a Spiritual Care Counselor (AA Fifth Step) prior to discharge. At discharge, the patient had still not taken responsibility regarding relationship issues. He was seen as manipulative, victimizing, and apparently unwilling to make decisions. He did superficially verbalize an understanding of the recovery processes within the framework of the Twelve Step Program and verbalized the need to enter a supervised living facility after treatment.

PROBLEMS PRESENT UPON DISCHARGE:

The patient continues to need work on his passive/aggressive personality style and his self-centeredness, as well as issues of honesty and commitment.

AFTERCARE PLAN:

There is to be no further use of any mood-changing substances. It is recommended that the patient immediately enter Progress Valley (an intermediate care facility) and complete their 90-day program. The patient is to regularly attend AA in the community where he lives (two to three times weekly), as well as NA groups. He is to have follow-up psychiatric consultations with Dr. Routt. It was also recommended that the patient attend a domestic abuse group. Al-Anon was recommended for family members. In the event of relapse, it is recommended that the patient enter long-term care in either a therapeutic community (such as Eden House) or perhaps a state institution, such as Moose Lake, Fergus Falls, or Willmar.
Prognosis: Poor.

Poor? No shit. I began using two days after I left.

22

BONGO, TONY THE HAT, AND STEVE

If memory is fungible, then time is its wingman, stretching and compressing to conjure a coherent story. In restrospection, I've always thought of my career, both as a journalist and an addict, as a series of rapid ascents and declines. Sort of like this:

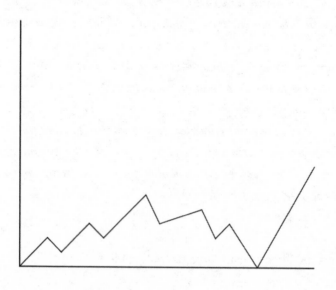

But after a year of investigating my past, it became clear that I had been chugging along pretty nicely until 1986, and then dropped off the face of the earth in 1987 when I started smoking cocaine. What I had remembered as four years of struggle had actually been about eighteen months. Documents, interviews, and pictures suggest that I kept all of the balls in the air until I didn't. Sort of more like this:

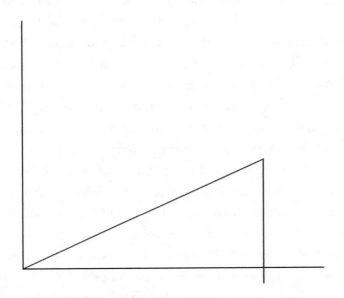

Who knew? I lost my job in March of 1987, and by the end of the next year, I had multiple arrests, and I was in long-term treatment at Eden House. In the recollection and the telling, I had always thought I washed out of journalism for many years, but it was more like a single year, counting the time I spent in the booby hatch, and even in there, I wrote stories. Regardless of what happened to me, I rarely stopped typing. Perhaps I was worried I would disappear altogether if I did.

———

At the start of 1987, the components of my jerry-rigged life started flying off in all directions. The longer deadlines at the monthly business magazine created more room for mischief and unaccountability. Everything I did was somehow transformed into an adjunct to my addiction. In the final months of my employment at *Corporate Report,* it was decided that I would do a story about Roger, a prep-school teacher turned bookie turned "sports betting consultant." It was a match: We were both guys with some history of professional accomplishment and smarts who were now in a barrel heading over the falls.

Roger was brilliant and mordantly funny. He was romantically involved on and off with Rebecca, the city's chief madam, who ran a bunch of massage parlors. She was a source and subject I had covered on and off. The story about Roger was supposed to be about a guy who had found a way to make a living off of what he was good at even though it was not technically legal. The assignment quickly became a story about addiction—his jones written through the prism of mine. In a series of conversations at the marginal office spaces he rented and frequently slept in, he schooled me in gambling, which I did not know much about. Those daytime reporting trips morphed into late-night conversations with lots of booze and coke, which continued even after I was fired and the story had been published.

The profile, entitled "Playing the Game within the Game," was a weave of his wiseguy and academic philosophies. Roger had been a highly respected teacher at the St. Paul Academy. He had a nice touch for betting pro football, and his wins eventually tipped over a St. Paul bookie, who handed him the business to pay him off. He ended up out of teaching, caught a couple of federal cases, and did some prison time. The sports information service hosted a phone bank that gave out tips to subscribers, but Roger was no longer living on the vig, and his betting touch had soured. He was in debt—six figures, probably more— and had tapped his girlfriend Rebecca for some of his losses. He was increasingly dependent on a madam for money, while I was leaning on a drug dealer to help me get by. We made quite a pair.

Roger had a good mouth, even though he hated guys who made speeches and was laconic in the extreme.

"In the stock market, it can take six months to find out if you made the right decisions. With betting, you lay down a bet, and you know that you made a mistake three hours later when a shot by some jerk you'll never know rolls off the rim," he told me during an interview in 1987. I sat next to him in front of the television a few times when that happened, a bad bounce taking tens of thousands with it, and he always smiled, laughing at the absurdity of his disenfranchisement. Roger—his pals called him Bongo—made above-average picks for the sports information service, but that did not prevent him from heading steadily south as a gambler.

"It is very important for you to understand that handicapping and gambling are two separate things," he told me for the story. "Gambling is money management. I have never had much success managing money. I was successful enough in the beginning to get away with being reckless, but I just continued to gamble more until I got in trouble. I had trouble with the downside."

Don't we all? It is the stopping, the quitting, the walking away that we cannot abide because the ceaseless activity keeps the accounting at bay. The mania of addiction, as expressed by anything—coke, booze, betting, sex—finds renewed traction every time it halts because once the perpetrator stops and sees how deeply and truly his life now sucks, there is only one thing that will make him feel better: more of same. Often the only thing that imposes limits on someone who is hooked on his own endorphins is money.

"I don't care about money until I run out of it," Roger said, speaking for me and many, many others. "Then I have to crawl around and beg people to borrow me some. Then it becomes very important." Roger had over a million bucks when he was going good. I asked him if it would have made any difference if another zero had been added to that first big winning streak.

"Now you are beginning to understand. It wouldn't have mattered how much I won. Eventually I would have bet until it was gone. I would be in exactly the same position I am right now."

Listening to him, I began to hear the parallels in our narratives. I had gotten started with a good job, no huge financial burdens, and eventually had Anna's kilos more or less at my disposal. Now I was headlong on my way to nothing. All addicts are gamblers working with a bad hand. The chance that you will pick up a substance that had kicked your ass before and somehow manage to walk away whole are so low as to be immeasurable.

"I seem to be living a cliché," he said finally. "The one about all gamblers dying broke. There's a lot of truth in those clichés. Things like how you don't pick your passions, they pick you. I think that's true."

So there, poised on what would be my final run, I had all I needed to know about how it would end. I was fired before the story came out, but reading it two decades later, it was a manual that foretold all that followed. Roger knew the score, he just couldn't bet it correctly. And neither could I.

After Anna found out she was pregnant, she went into treatment at the end of 1987. I watched her kids with the help of her family. When she got back, she seemed to have some new friends from treatment and began disappearing. One night I confronted her at the front door and began fishing around in her pockets, not precisely sure what I was looking for. My index finger came out of her shirt's front pocket stuck to a needle. I raged, lectured, talking about the dangers of overdose, but probably sat down with her and began shooting cocaine later that same day. It was a dangerous, bloody activity. I feel a profound sense of shame even typing about it. No one can really describe how lost you have to be to get on the treadmill of sticking a needle in your arm, leg, foot, or hand every twenty minutes.

By the spring of 1988, both Anna and I had been through treatment and relapsed, both of us in an intense state of cocaine dependency. Things became more unpredictable still. I was in and out of Anna's place, and in and out of work at a weekly football paper where I had landed.

One of the few people who was present during those days was Steve, Anna's ex-husband. He came over to take care of the two kids she already had. He chipped a bit when it came to the coke, but many times he was the only one sober enough to function. Oddly enough, Steve and I always got along very well. After I met with Anna, I called him in Colorado, where he now lives with Anna's son. I asked him about those months before the twins were born, in part because I had almost zero recollection of those murky, chaotic times.

"You were drunk every day," he said. "You would slug a pint on the way to work. Those were rough days, weren't they? Very tough times. You beat yourself to death. I'd say that you are lucky to be alive at all. You didn't give a shit one way or another. You were on a monthslong bender. The jobs weren't going good, you had all the powder you could use and all of the alcohol you could drink, and that's what you did."

He had a front row seat, so I had to ask him: Did I take Anna with me as I headed into the ditch?

"The trouble for her was inevitable," he said. "You didn't cause it. You certainly didn't help it, but you didn't cause it. You end up losing it with that shit anyway. It is pretty hard for anybody to keep it together.

"People would come over, and you guys would start cooking that shit up. It wouldn't be five minutes into the deal, and somebody would lose something or drop something. Everybody would be crawling around on the floor looking for something, and other people would be standing there with a piece of lint in their hand, thinking they had found something. It was all so crazy. I smoked it a few times, but who in their right mind would want to get like that?

"You guys were completely, completely off your rocker. I was in no great shape, but I could not do what you guys were doing. No one could for long."

Anna and I were as far out there as you can get. Anna's business was crumbling. A shipment came in, and we took a kilo to a suburban hotel to break it up. In addition to the newly arrived merch, we brought an elaborate glass pipe, a box full of fresh screens, and a blowtorch. We planned on staying one night to prep the goods and make deliveries the following morning. We stayed in that room for three days, sliding $100s under the door to pay for another night when housekeeping came by.

Somewhere in there, I passed out, and I can remember waking up and seeing Anna at the table in the room, her face covered in soot from the pipe, going back at it. The phone rang constantly, each time an insistent voice saying a lot of people were waiting on us. No matter. We did what we did. When we finally left, geeked and spent, we got out to the car and realized we had left thousands of dollars in the couch. Anna told me to go get it. I fetched the money at her command.

When you are so far gone that you spend time only with people who are enmeshed in the drug lifestyle, it falls to the only people you see—dealers, fellow hypes, and drunks—to tell you that your shit is out of pocket. Tony the Hat was on my case almost constantly. Tony was a full-on gangster who talked with an accent straight from the mining towns of northern Minnesota; he was a joyful piece of work in his own way. He was wrapped in his particular dialect and folkways. To do business was to "wrang," as in wrangle; a full-on sweat was called a "lath," for lather; and he always, always called me "Fridge." He always marveled at my ability to do all sorts of cocaine and still stay fat. Boys liked Tony, girls did not, except his sister Dee, who was devoted to him.

Tony was a talented athlete and had been on his way to pro hockey, but a catastrophic knee injury ended that. He would have made a fine goon—even with a blown knee, he skated with a great deal of finesse. He and Dee had a pretty serious retail drug business in South Minneapolis. You didn't just bring anybody by—he was a moody dude—but if the stars were aligned, it could be off-the-hook, buck-wild fun. One night a huge rain created a flash flood by the creek down the hill from his house. The rest of the cokeheads stayed bent over the mirror, but Tony and I went outside and swam out into the rushing water overflowing the creek. A car came floating by, and Tony jumped on it and pulled me up. We rode it for blocks, shouting like loons.

Nobody ever sat in Tony's chair; more of a throne, really, with a cooler for coke on one side and sometimes a big handgun on the other.

144

He wasn't one to wave it around, but he was a guy who just felt more comfortable with a piece. One night right before my friend John was leaving for Central America, where he worked as a reporter, we stopped at Tony's, and Tony bought John's car right off him for cash.

I called John in Bogotá, Colombia, in the summer of 2007 to ask him about his recollections of Tony the Hat. "He was a very menacing guy, even compared to some of the narcotrafficantes I had covered. He offered me, like, one hundred dollars for this crappy VW Rabbit I had, and it sort of seemed like the kind of offer you couldn't refuse."

Everyone in the Life loves to talk about how old-school he is, but Tony lived it. He had his own code about what it meant to be a man. One night in 1988, the Minnesota Bureau of Criminal Apprehension came in—riot gear, forced entry, all get-the-fuck-down and keep-yer-hands-where-we-can-see-'em. Luck of the draw I was not there, but some of the guys went all girly-man when it happened, freaking out and crying. Not Tony. True enough, it was his place, but Dee was really the boss, which is not how he put it to the cops. He protected his sister and caught a significant county sentence followed by probation.

Tony had some other ticks. He loved Warren Zevon—too much—and hated crack and the people who did it. Bad for business, a bunch of twitchy fucking paranoids in the basement messing up the wrang, made it unpleasant. Sometimes when he sold me coke, he made me snort it right in front of him. "Don't be sneaking off and making crack balls out of that, Fridge," he'd say.

I pretended I wouldn't, and he pretended not to notice when I did. One night before he got busted, I called him very late. He sounded happy to hear from me. When I got there, the usual mopes were not hanging around the basement. I got the sense that Tony had dismissed them. He was not what I would describe as a public intellectual, but he respected the fact that I was a writer; that I did something besides knucklehead stuff. And he surmised correctly that I was in the process of screwing that up.

"Fridge," he said, setting out a line, "I hear stuff about you. Bad stuff."

"It's probably true," I said. I liked Tony enough not to bullshit him now that it was man-to-man.

Both hands went to the arms of the chair, and the knuckles went white.

"You know what I could do to you?" he said. "Don't fucking lie to me. You are deep into the crack shit. I hear you're shooting up too."

Yes to all, I said. He looked like he might jump out of his chair and choke the living shit out of me. His nostrils flared, he tugged at his long hockey hair, and then he softened and looked at me. "You see what it does, you see who is doing it, you know how it goes. That is not a way for you to go, Fridge. Do you hear me?"

That's how I recall it and it will have to suffice. Tony sobered me up and became a hockey coach, but that big, scary heart gave out in 2000.

23

MUGGED:
A COMIC TRAGEDY IN THREE ACTS

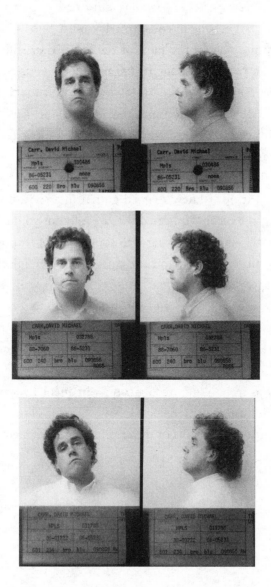

When I was very little, my dad would tell me stories about "Billy the Lucky Pup." Billy's doggie buddies were constantly getting in jams, careening toward the brink of something, and Billy would always, always come charging over the hill. With no more than a "ruff, ruff," he would signal that the cavalry had arrived—that Billy was on the case, and disaster had once again been avoided. In those months of relentless havoc, I'd arrive at an odd moment of consideration, and I would think, *Where the fuck is that dog, anyway?*

Once you start getting in jams, you develop a halo of flies. The cops smell fear or, more likely, the taint of the loser. They sniff the out-of-date plates, the missing headlight, the wobble in your step, and they decide to take a look. And then they find the detritus that lies at the feet of every addict: the two-month-old warrant, the bag of pot, or the glass tube with cocaine residue on it. In eighteen months of 1987 and 1988, I was arrested at least nine times—not a felony among them—but a lot of trips through booking. I was stunned by the number when I finally tallied it up. I knew that I'd gotten in a spot of trouble here and there, but the record indicated that I could not go down the street to buy a six-pack without getting into some kind of trouble. I ran out of people to call to bail me, and the cops ran out of adjectives for the reports. My speech was "regional" and "obscene," I was "married" and "single," my eyes were "blue" and "brown," I was "stocky" and "obese," I lived on "Garfield," no "Oliver," no, I was homeless. At the time, I was surprised that the cops and the turnkeys were so indifferent, so bored by me. "Lemme guess, lurking with intent to mope, right?" said one of the cops in booking, recognizing a frequent flyer when he saw one. I became just one more part of the human chum that courses through the creaky apparatus of the criminal justice system.

24

INCOMING

If in a shimmering room the babies came,
Drawn close by dreams of fledgling wing,
It was because night nursed them in its fold.

—WALLACE STEVENS

M an, them are little babies, where'd you get 'em?"

The kid, about eight, saw me coming out of the University of Minnesota hospital with a twin in each arm in May of 1988, Anna walking behind me. I was speechless. How could a kid this small, this unknowing, tell at a glance that these children had landed on me from a very great distance?

They had been patients in the NICU, the Neonatal Intensive Care Unit, for a month. Born at 2.7 and 2.9 pounds, and each just over fifteen inches, Erin and Meagan were born two and a half months premature. They weighed a bit more than a kilo, a term of art in our current context. They were infinitely more valuable, of course, and far less commodifiable. Both girls had to be intubated immediately because they could not breathe on their own. According to medical records, Erin "cried spontaneously, but each time her crying stopped, her heart rate decreased and her respiratory effort became poor. She was intubated in the delivery room . . ." Meagan "had umbilical, artery, and venous catheters placed on 4/16/88 for blood pressure and arterial blood-gas monitoring and for delivery of emergency medications." Once the jaundice of their early birth wore off, they were pink spots surrounded by tubes and machines. Meagan was a tad bigger, but only relative to her even tinier sister. They were the organic part of the apparatus, but all of it seemed to throb with life.

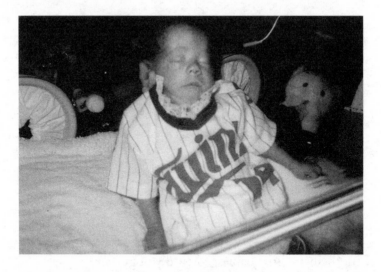

That would be Meagan. By now, I know her by heart.

But at the time, none of it—not their early birth, not my part in it, not their existence—was real to me until we left the hospital, respiration and heart monitors in tow. They were so, so tiny. My mind wandered to bath time, something I had heard that you did with babies. What would we use, a teacup?

When Anna's water broke in her living room on Oliver Avenue, I had just handed her a crack pipe. We stared at each other, each of us running the numbers in our head. She had just entered her third trimester. It was hard to tell whether we were in the midst of giving birth or participating in a kind of neonatal homicide. The water beneath her became a puddle of implication. *Now look what we did.*

When we got to the hospital, we were honest about what we had been doing prior to our arrival, which meant that the twins got the benefit of informed, exceptional medical care. And it also meant we became "those people," the ones all the staff knew about. And even if we hadn't confessed, they would have surmised what they needed to know. I was a complete mess every time I came in to see Anna or the girls.

Sitting outside my hotel in Tucson, nineteen years after the twins were born, Anna suggested that I had, on one occasion, smoked crack in her hospital room. There is no personal recollection of doing so, but I have no reason to doubt her. Anna had made efforts, significant ones, to stay off her drug of choice while pregnant. And then every once in a while—or maybe more often; who can remember through all that shame?—she would use. I was completely unsupportive, save for not joining the chorus of people chanting at her to have an abortion. Otherwise I slipped in and out of her life, staying for a time and then disappearing. Once the twins were born, I started hanging around more often, for all the good it did.

Once we got the girls home, the heart and respiration monitors seemed specifically designed to terrorize us. One of them would shift positions or spit up a bit, and the alarms would go off. *Shit! Fuck!* It was less the interruption than a panic that it might be meaningful, that while they had survived a hostile prenatal environment, something terrible would happen now that they were out in the world.

In my memory, in my soul, I remember this as a very short time. A couple of months max. I always thought that I came to my senses fairly quickly and made changes to ensure that my kids were out of harm's way.

Anna and I kept thinking it would get better. In spite of our shared pathology, we had the biological attachments that all new parents develop. The twins were loved, just not in a way that meant much of anything.

My parents heard the news and came by the hospital, did their best to be polite and not reveal the full extent of their repulsion, but once we took the girls home, they were no longer invited to visit. Friends who cared about us would come by to see the kids, but they rarely came back. Others hung around and did what they could. "We were never out of touch for that long, I don't think, primarily because of the twins, and I was around quite a bit, and that's when I spent time with Anna," my friend Chris remembered when I went to see him in New Orleans. "One winter night you called me late and said 'We're out of diapers, we don't have diapers,' and you thought somebody was watching the house. You guys were paranoid and getting high, and you said, 'I think the cops are watching the house, I can't leave,' and so I went to the convenience store, got some diapers, drove over with diapers and milk or something.

"The girls were back there in their cribs, and we took care of them—changed their diapers and got them put to bed—and then sat around the dining room table. There was literally a pile of coke sitting in the middle of the table. So I was always conflicted about it."

Fast Eddie recalled getting invited over for dinner, but dinner never arrived.

"There were friends of Anna's that were there, and the babies were being kind of tossed around, and everyone was holding them, and it was kind of scary," he said. "You were going at it pretty strong. Eight o'clock, nine o'clock, ten o'clock rolls around. We haven't eaten yet. Lots of vodka. We got really, really drunk, it was eleven-thirty, twelve o'clock, and we left without ever eating.

"We left your house, we drove home—we were too drunk to drive; we never should have been behind the wheel—but we got home, and we said, 'That is the scariest thing in the world. Can you believe those babies in that environment?'

"And what do we do? How do you respond to that? You were my friend; what am I gonna do, call child protection on you?"

Actually, they were already on the case.

25

WELCOME TO THE FAMILY OF MAN

UNIVERSITY OF MINNESOTA
TWIN CITIES

The University of Minnesota Hospital and Clinic
Harvard Street at East River Road
Minneapolis, Minnesota 55455

1600564-9

April 22, 1988

Hennepin County Child Protection Intake
300 South 6th Street
Minneapolis, MN 55487

Re: Carr, Meagan
     UH# 16005706
     Carr, Erin
     UH# 16005649

Dear Child Protection Intake:

This letter is meant as a follow-up to our phone referral on 4/20/88 concerning the parents of newborn twins, Meagan and Erin Carr. These babies were born prematurely on 4/15/88 at 30 weeks gestation and are now on the Neonatal Intensive Care Unit at University of Minnesota Hospital and Clinic. The parents are Anna ███████ and David Carr; they reside at ███ Oliver Ave. No., Minneapolis. Phone number is ████████. ██████████ children, ████████████, age 5, and ██████████████, age 2, also live in the home.

On 4/13/88, the day of admission, the mother stated she smoked ½ gram of "crack" on the evening before. (Mother was admitted for premature rupture of membranes.) Upon further questioning, mother stated that she had smoked cocaine "12 times" during the pregnancy and also used marijuana daily. It is our understanding that father also abuses alcohol and has recently been treated for chemical dependency. The mother's urine screen was positive for cocaine and nicotine. She was discharged from the hospital on 4/21/88.

The babies each suffered from respiratory distress syndrome, a common disorder of premature babies. Otherwise, they appeared healthy with appropriate weights for their gestational age with no morphologic or metabolic sequelae of maternal substance abuse. Analysis of the babies' urine demonstrated no cocaine or other drugs in their systems. The anticipated length of hospital stay for the infants is 6-7 weeks based on their degree of prematurity. We have informed the parents that we are making a referral to you based on the drug use during pregnancy. They have given every indication that they will cooperate with you, as they have with us. A chemical dependency consult was done on the mother here with a recommendation that she attend chemical dependency treatment. She states that she cannot afford to pay for treatment.

The parents have appeared to be open about their drug use. They have stated their intention to attend AA meetings and provide a chemically free environment for their children. This may be difficult without intervention considering the long reported history of drug use.

153

Hennepin County Child Protection Intake
Re: Carr, Meagan
     UH# 16005706
     Carr, Erin
     UH# 16005649

In order to make a safe and effective discharge plan for the twins (about June 1), we would appreciate information from you regarding your assessment and planning for this family.

Please feel free to contact us with any further questions.

Sincerely,

Dr. Michael Georgieff, M.D.
NICU - 626-3032

Stephanie Koehler, ACSW
NICU Social Worker - 626-3366

Harold Williamson, MSW
OB Social Worker - 626-3366

rp

26

HAIL MARY

The sewer ran only by night. The days were the same as they
had ever been.

—WILLIAM FAULKNER, *LIGHT IN AUGUST*

In the summer of 2006, I made my first trip back to Minnesota to
start setting up interviews and gathering personal and public records.
I was filled with immediate regret about the undertaking. It is one
thing to talk about how back in the day you were a narcissistic, abusive
loser. It is another to show up two decades later in apparent sound
mind and body and proceed to engage in reporting on your own life, a
vainglorious endeavor that is presumptuous in the extreme. It would
make sense that when people washed their hands of me, they wiped off
the memory while drying their hands. Who is to say that they ever gave
me another thought, let alone wanted to share any of them with me?

And yet there I was, poised to come rolling back into their lives.
The fact that I had gone on to good things was less important to many
of them than that I had gone. Reporting can be obnoxious no matter
who is asking the questions about what, but all this was the more so because the reporter wanted to ask deep, probing questions about himself. Even for me, it was a new level of solipsism. Fact-checking what I
remembered is a fine idea in the abstract, but as a practical matter, it
made me feel like a golem of my own abasement. The process conceits
of the book—all interviews videotaped and audio-recorded—made it

seem both more conscientious and frivolous at the same time. After I taped some interviews, I watched some of the subjects staring at the camera and then staring at me, wondering what precisely I was up to.

The journalism was meant as a fig leaf, enough of a gimmick so that I wouldn't have to confront the fact that I was adding to a growing pile of junkie memoirs. But now, when I landed in Minneapolis with a list of reporting stops, some of them fairly toxic, I fervently wished that I had stayed in my basement office in New Jersey to crank it out. People could love it or hate it or ignore it, say I lied with great ease or showed tremendous personal courage, that I was an inspiration or a remorseless, entitled thug, but I wouldn't be present when they did. The process I had chosen managed to seem cloying and reckless at the same time.

As I walked to the luggage carousel, I wondered what it would be like to plop myself in front of women I had dated, friends I had endangered, bosses I had screwed. I didn't have to wonder very long. While I waited for my luggage, I stepped outside to have a smoke. A guy pulled the door open for me.

Todd. The last guy I had worked for as a fulminating addict. Here was a man whom I had inarguably put through hell. Nice, smart, sweet Todd, the kind of manager who didn't even need pom-poms, he was so enthusiastic. I took it as a sign that he was the first person I bumped into. Whether it was meant to be or not, it was on. Todd, genetically gracious, agreed to see me later that week.

When we sat down, he recalled that he heard at the end of the summer of 1988 that I was out of work. He asked me out to lunch to talk about a weekly paper about the Minnesota Vikings that he was publishing along with Tommy, the team's quarterback. We had worked together at the *Reader*, and I always admired Todd's unalloyed optimism. I proceeded to take his faith in me and trash it, creating enormous havoc in a little office he had put together. He found out soon enough that I was unemployed because I was unemployable.

I had always assumed that back in the fall of 1988—I had been out of work for months—that I talked him into giving me a job, no doubt reassuring him that all the trouble was behind me. My take, my memory, was not even close.

"No, you actually said, 'I don't think we should have lunch; I don't think I'm your person.' I persisted because you were MIA," Todd recalled, sitting in his downtown office. "You had shown a great talent and had good energy in the publishing setting, and I thought here is a weekly job where you can be the editor and control what happens with this publication, and it should be an exciting way for you to step back in. I went to sell you on doing this, and you reluctantly agreed to have lunch. At lunch you came around to say, 'I do need to get back in, and I can do this. Thanks for getting me out of my shell, and let's go do this.'"

In retrospect, you could say that Todd got what was coming to him, but it was not like that. Normal folk cannot be blamed for expecting that someone, even someone with a history of chemical abuse, will eventually decide to act in his own self-interest. A rational person would look at me, look at my professional history, and figure I might want to get back in the game. But Todd had the misfortune of extending a friendly hand at precisely the moment when I was destined to break every bone in it. Nothing personal—when we got back together, I told him I was sorry, deeply sorry—but at the time, I was firing on all cylinders of addiction: clinically alcoholic, a volatile coke user who had graduated to intravenous use, with two newborn twins and two women I was trying to keep on the hook. I was like Fat Elvis without a wisp of the talent or legacy.

Viking Update was a weekly fan paper, meant for people who spent the off-season reviewing the last one and plotting the next. During the season, it would offer deep game analysis and lots of face time with the players. As a matter of necessity, the publication had a very high metabolism. The final paper was put together a few hours after game day and then shipped quickly to the waiting stalwarts. I have no fear of deadline writing—my first thought is often my best—so in theory, there was a fit.

In practice, I was drinking when I got up and shooting all the coke

I could find. Just sharing a drink with me could be a drama, let alone trying to work with me. I can remember vividly one day when I was feeling pretty ragged, but I dug out a nice pressed white shirt, a rarity for me. But after I put it on, I noticed the crimson blood stain in the crook of my left arm.

"You would go to your desk, and we would be working, and we would come back, and you might be asleep at the keyboard," Todd recalled. "We had to get it out and printed and out on the street by Monday morning because it's timely. So we would fuss about it, and we would keep doing our part, and then all of a sudden you would say, 'OK, it's all done.' The writing would be great. Maybe not by your standards now, but it was lucid and had energy, and we would go, whew.

"You were just lost to us—except for the salient moments when you would kick it out so that we could do it, and then you would be lost again. It unraveled. Part of me wondered if—again, trying to put a good face on it—I got you up in the game, and you just realized you're just in big trouble."

Well, sort of. That and a hundred other things big and small. The Vikings ended up going to the NFC divisional playoffs that season, but by that time, I was in the booby hatch, watching it on television. Todd ended up with a good editor, my friend David, and the little weekly became another success in a career that had its share. Todd was right about one thing: It would have been a perfect way to get back in the game. Instead it became one more horribly broken play.

27

GOD SEES EVERYTHING, INCLUDING THE BLIND

Where does a junkie's time go? I know how it goes: in fifteen-minute increments, like a bug-eyed Tarzan, swinging from hit to hit. For months on end in 1988, I sat inside Anna's house, doing her coke and listening to Tracy Chapman's "Fast Car" over and over. "Any place is better. Starting from zero, got nothing to lose," she sang. I sang along. I would shoot a large dose of coke or smoke some crack, start tweaking, and then go to the front window and pull up a corner of one of the blinds to look for the squads, which I always expected would be forthcoming. All day. All night. A frantic kind of boring. After awhile I noticed that the blinds on the upper duplex kitty-corner from Anna's house were doing the same thing. The light would leak through a corner and disappear. I began to think of the rise and fall of the blinds as a kind of Morse code, sent back and forth across the street in winking increments that said the same thing over and over.

W-e a-r-e g-e-t-t-i-n-g h-i-g-h t-o-o.

They rarely came out, and neither did I, so I never made their acquaintance to discuss our shared hobby. End-stage addiction is mostly about waiting for the police, or someone, to come and bury you in your shame.

One night I was there with all of the kids, and Anna was out some-where. I was working on a particularly remarkable batch of coke. I had a new pipe, clean screens, a fresh blowtorch, and the kids were asleep. It was just me and Barley, a Corgi mix I'd had since college. When I was alone with Barley, I'd ask her random questions. Barley didn't talk back per se, but I saw the answers by staring into her large brown eyes.

Am I a lunatic? *Yes.* When am I going to cut this shit out? *Apparently never.* Does God see me right now? *Yes. God sees everything.*

I began to think of the police as God's emissaries, arriving not to seek vengeance but a cease-fire, a truce that would put me up against a wall and well-deserved consequences, and the noncombatants, the children, out of harm's way. On this night—it was near the end—I was on highest alert, my subcortex sounding out the alarm.

The massive hit I took to quiet my vibrating synapses put a mega-phone to them instead. If the cops were coming—Any. Minute. Now—I thought, I should be sitting out in front of the house. That way I could tell them that yes, there were drugs in the house and enough paraphernalia to start a recycling center, but there were no guns. And there were children. Four blameless, harmless children. They could put the bracelets on me, and I would solemnly lead them to the drugs, to the needles, to the pipes, to what was left of the money, while some sweet-faced matrons would magically appear and scoop up those babies and take them to that safe, happy place. I had it all planned out.

Barley and I walked out and sat on the steps. My eyes, my heart, the veins in my forehead were pulsing against the stillness of the night. And then they came. Six unmarked cars riding in formation with lights off, no cherries, just like I pictured. It's on. A mix of uniforms and plainclothes got out, and in the weak light of the street, I could see long guns held at 45-degree angles. I was proud of myself. I had made the right move after endless wrong ones.

And then they turned and went to the house kitty-corner. Much yelling. "Face down! Hug the fucking carpet! No sudden movements!" A guy dropped out of the second floor window in just gym shorts, but they were waiting. More yelling and then quiet. I went back inside the house and watched the rest of it play out through the corner of the blind. Their work done, the cops loaded several cuffed people into a van that had been called in. I let go of the blind and got back down to business. It wasn't my turn.

Of all my memories, this one seemed the most fantastic. I waited for the cops, and then they came, but it wasn't for me. But there are no records to support the recollection. The Minneapolis cops did not begin indexing crimes by address until the 1990s, and I received no hits in the database on the names of the people that may have lived across the street. DonJack, the reporter that I hired to come behind me, worked the back copies of community papers that covered the area, but no luck. We were able to establish that the house had been a longtime problem property with a history of drug sales, but there was no specific incident to go with my memory.

I sat outside that house on Oliver Avenue on a hot summer day in 2006, staring long and hard to make sense of what had and had not happened there. The neighborhood had turned over from white to black, but it was pretty much the same. Nice lawns, lots of kids, no evidence of the mayhem that had gone on inside. Sitting there, in a rental car with a suit on, with those little babies now on their way to college, I almost would have thought I'd made it up. But I don't think I did. While I sat there staring at the place, someone lifted up the corner of the blind in the living room window. It was time to go.

28

SNOWSUITS

Fierce as ten furies, terrible as hell,
And shook a dreadful dart; what seem'd his head
The likeness of a kingly crown had on.
Satan was now at hand.

—JOHN MILTON, *PARADISE LOST*

I remember driving to a dark spot in between the streetlights at the rounded-off corner of Thirty-second and Garfield. Right here, I thought. This would be fine.

The Nova, a shitbox with a bad paint job my brother bought me out of pity, shuddered to a stop, and I checked the rearview. I saw two sleeping children, the fringe of their hoods emerging in outline against the backseat as my eyes adjusted to the light. Teeny, tiny, itty-bitty, the girls were swallowed by the snowsuits. We should not have been there. Their mother was off somewhere, and I had been home looking after them. But I was fresh out. I had nothing. I called Kenny, but he was plenty busy. "Come over," he said. "I'll hook you right up." In that moment of need, I decided to make the trip from North Minneapolis to South, from Anna's house to his.

I could not bear to leave them home, but I was equally unable to stay put, to do the right thing. So here we were, one big, happy family, parked outside the dope house. It was late, past midnight.

Then came the junkie math; addled moral calculation woven with towering need. If I went inside the house, I could get what I needed, or

162

very much wanted. Five minutes, ten minutes tops. They would sleep, dreaming their little baby dreams where their dad is a nice man, where the car rides end at a playground.

The people inside would be busy, working mostly in pairs. Serious coke shooting is something best done together. The objective is to walk right up to the edge of an overdose, to get as high as humanly possible without actually dying. The technique was to push the plunger in slow but push it in large. One would be pushing, watching as the other listened to his insides—to the sound of blood and nerves brought to a boil. Push the plunger in until the ears ring and then back off. Are you good? *Yes. No . . . Just, um . . . ah . . . that's perfect.*

As shooting galleries go, the house had much to commend it. Kenny, the guy who ran the place, brought a touch of the mad professor to his retail coke business. With weak eyes behind thick glasses, he was a straight shooter and always seemed to be in a good, if amped, mood. He and I traded credit, depending on which one of us was flush or on a run. Kenny's lip-licking coke rap was more ornate, somehow more satisfying, than that of most of the losers I dealt with. His worldview was all black helicopters and white noise—the whispering, unseen others who would one day come for us. It kept me on my toes.

Back when business was good, Kenny refurbished the sound studio in the place, an old musician's house, now decorated with various out-of-tune guitars and a trashed drum kit. That way the people who came and went, mostly white-boy crackheads and girls who lived for a hit, could pretend they were there to jam or to listen to the real musicians who were part of the client base. But it was plain as the pile on the scale what we were all there for.

When Kenny was tweaking, which was often, he would insist that we were being monitored by tiny video cameras in the holes of the acoustic tile that covered the room, a studio where only the needs were amplified. One night Kenny was particularly frantic about surveillance issues, and in a gesture of junkie solidarity, we each claimed a panel and peered into hundreds of holes looking for tiny cameras. Ironically but diligently, we marked the ones we had checked with the slash of a pencil. Kenny clearly appreciated our efforts and spilled more coke to assist in finishing the task. We ran out of coke before we ran out of holes.

But tonight I had company. I certainly couldn't bring the twins in. Coming through the doors of the dope house swinging two occupied baby buckets was not done. Children did not mesh with a house full of skanky people sitting around with rigs full of blood and coke hanging off their arms. Not pretty. Not done.

Sitting there in the gloom of the front seat, the car making settling noises against the chill, the math still loomed. Need. Danger. A sudden tumbling? Naw. Nothing to it, really. In that pool of darkness, I decided that my teeny twin girls would be safe. It was cold, but not *really* cold. Surely God would look after them while I did not.

I got out, locked the door, and walked away, pushed from behind, pulled by what was inside. I clearly remember solving the math out in the car, but not much of the rest of it. Just a bit of a pick-me-up while I am here, I probably said, glancing at the door as I did. Of course, I told no one in that forlorn circle in the studio that I had, um, friends waiting in the car. There were no windows in the place, and the outside likely disappeared in a flurry of consumption. My kids may or may not have been safe, but inside, a transformation—almost a kidnapping—was under way. The guilty father was replaced by a junkie, no different from the others sitting there. Time passed, one thing begot another, the machine bucked, whistles blew, smoke came out, and eventually I was thrown clear.

Leaving, I remember that. Out the metal door and then out the front door with its three bolts onto the porch and the hollow sound of my boots on the wood floor. A pause. How long had it been, really? It had not been ten minutes tops. Ten minutes times ten, probably, if not more. Hours not minutes. I walked toward the darkened car with drugs in my pocket and a cold dread in all corners of my being.

I cracked the front door, reached around, unlocked the back, and leaned in.

I could see their breath.

God had looked after the twins, and by proxy me, but I realized at that moment that I had made a mistake He could not easily forgive. I made a decision at that instant never to be that man again.

I went to see Kenny. He was out of the Life and living near Seattle. We drove a long way to his house, chitchatting our way through the people we both knew, and then I broached the topic of that night, which was a huge inflection point for me, but a night like any other for him. I stopped, I copped, maybe paused to do some shooting, and then on to next. He never knew the twins were parked out there that night. A multiple felon, but a good-hearted man in his own way, he would have talked me into leaving had he known. He wouldn't have gotten all judgmental about it, but he would have nudged me out the door.

Everyone I talked to—from Anna, to Sarah, to Donald—was filled with regret when talking about the old days, always the bad old days. But not Kenny. Now in a good job in a helping profession, he regrets none of it. As a coke dealer, he ran with comedians, rock stars, gorgeous women, and although he ended up going to jail a few times, he would not change a thing. Kenny actually has a lot of fondness—in clinical terms, it would be called "euphoric recall"—for those days.

We talked about the room in his house where all the action was.

"Totally soundproof. It had a big, heavy locked door, central air-conditioning, the floor was multitiered levels, with yellow pegboard throughout."

Check.

We talked about what went on there.

"There was, like, lots of interesting, talented people, beautiful women. And oh yeah: People went to excess there, definitely."

Check.

We talked about trading all our marbles for coke.

"When Freud did coke, he wrote about how when you reached a level of toxicity with the drug, it brought out your innermost paranoias, so that's not a new thing. After you've done enough of that drug, there comes a point where you have to stop because it just brings out the negativity."

Check.

I told him about what happened that night.

"Yeah, that's the downside of it—you can tend to lose your responsibilities and your sensibilities, and I read about that kind of thing in the paper once in a while, where people do that, leaving their kids in their car. Yeah, it takes over."

Check.

We talked about having newborns while still in the Life.

"That situation at your house there, things really fell apart. The house looked like hell. People were concerned about the girls, their welfare."

Check.

So me and mine were a source of pity and concern from one of the most active coke dealers in town. Even given who I was talking to, my face was hot with shame.

In Minneapolis nineteen years later, I stood on the spot outside Kenny's where I had parked that night. The car was, according to my brother Jim, aka Savage, a Chevy Nova. He sent me the title: '79 Chevy Nova with 89,950 miles on it, plate number NHS 091, reminding me that later I had literally lost that car on the streets of Minneapolis, never to be found again. I remember standing by the car, I remember looking back. I remember the math. And I remember the snowsuits.

But that's where the plot thickens and the facts collide. Erin and Meagan were born on April 15, 1988. Whenever I felt compelled to explain myself and the cold facts of our history, that night outside Kenny's was the necessary moment, the bottom of the Aristotelian tragic fall.

In the story that has been told through the years, that horrible night occurred very soon after they were born. I thought I quickly went to treatment because even though I had been an unreliable employee, a conniving friend, a duplicitous husband, nothing in my upbringing allowed me to proceed as a bad father. The twins then were whisked into temporary foster care soon after their birth. After that, it's a Joseph Campbell monomyth in which our hero embraces his road of trials, begins to attain his new goals, and hotfoots it back to the normal world. In that paradigm, my recovery was not just an act of self-indulgence followed by self-realization, but a kind of mitzvah to the world.

Nice story if you can live it. Or prove it. For one thing, the snowsuits made no sense.

If the girls were born in April, and I went into treatment a few months afterward, as I have always said, where did the snowsuits come from? Minnesota is cold, but not *that* cold.

Perhaps in owning my behavior in all its abject glory, I needed my choice to be even worse than it actually was. Apparently it was not enough that the twins were left alone in a car in a bad neighborhood while I was in a house doing drugs. As a natural storyteller, perhaps I knew that the threat of the cold would add drama and horror to the narrative I told myself and very few others. Still, I remember the snowsuits best of all. When I started making calls for the book and wondering aloud about why the most vivid detail in the story rang false, the past changed. In my recollection, I was a drug-addicted new parent who quickly recognized the error of his ways and went to treatment. But when I was talking to my brother about the make of the car and mentioned the snowsuits, he said, "That's easy. You didn't go to treatment until sometime in December, like eight months after they were born."

He's almost right. I did not enter Eden House, a six-month inpatient treatment program in Minneapolis, until November 25, 1988. So the presence of snowsuits on a cold November night were undoubtedly real. That part about me straightening out right after they were born? A fantasy. Total bullshit, a myth, but not the kind Joseph Campbell had in mind.

29

THE LAST WORST NIGHT

Yeah but except so how can I answer just yes or no to do I want
to stop coke? Do I think I want to absolutely I think I want to. I
don't have a septum no more. My septum's been like fucking
dissolved by coke. See? You see anything like a septum when I
lift up like that? I've absolutely with my whole heart thought I
wanted to stop and so forth. Ever since with the septum. So but
so since I've been wanting to stop this whole time, why couldn't
I stop? See what I'm saying? Isn't it all about wanting to and so
on? And so forth? How can living here and going to meetings
and all do anything except make me want to stop? But I think I already want to stop. How come I'd even be here if I didn't want to
stop? Isn't being here proof I want to stop? But then so how
come I can't stop, if I want to stop, is the thing.

—DAVID FOSTER WALLACE, *INFINITE JEST*

Sometime soon after that night at Kenny's—it could have been
days or weeks—I became convinced that something brutal and
unspeakable was about to land on all of us, including the kids. The
twins were being neglected, along with Anna's other two kids, and her
customers were leaving in droves because we were reliably unreliable.

I had been fired from the football paper and was not even pretending to work on various freelance projects. In the journalism community, the word was out—stay far, far away—and even some of my
wildest running buddies wanted nothing to do with me. My family,
which had long worked to tug me back from the edge of the abyss, had
pretty much given up. Anna's situation was no better. Her Colombian

amigo shut her down for nonpayment, so absent the amazing connection and sales, we became just a couple of day-to-day addicts. And each of us had graduated from smoking crack to shooting cocaine.

As hobbies go, shooting coke is the worst. At least with heroin, people nod out for hours. With IV coke use, the addict has to reload every twenty minutes, find a new way in. That's a lot of equipment, a lot of blood, a lot of mayhem. After awhile it was needles, blood, babies, and piles of dirty clothes. High or not, it was hellish to behold. I just wanted a moment's peace, a respite from the chronic waking thought—drunk or sober, drugged or not—that I was perhaps the lowliest bastard who ever lived. A couple of days in detox with microwave macaroni and cheese, mooched ciggies, and sleep—blessed, elusive sleep—sounded like the beach in St. Bart's.

Just before Thanksgiving in 1988—on November 18, 1988, as I later found out—I called my parents and told them that the twins were not safe, and I needed to bring them by. "You told us that there were no adults in the house, that it was a dangerous place for children to be," my dad recalled. He said I promised to enter detox right away.

I drove in Anna's Maxima to Hopkins and carried the girls up the narrow stairs of my parents' townhouse—first Meagan and then Erin. (Funny what you do remember. Meagan could not abide being left alone for even a moment, so she always was the first in the door.) The girls sat cooing in their baby buckets, making friendly noises and faces at their grandma and taking in my dad behind her. We all just looked at them, their innocence of the matter at hand a comfort to us all.

No one knew what to say. My parents were speechless, in part because it was hard to say what came next, a bold new world having been opened up by my abasement. Poised in the moment between hitting a new kind of bottom and, perhaps, going into detox, I was a walking bundle of loose ends.

Did I say good-bye to the girls? I can't remember, and neither can my dad. My mom, who would have been running the show, is gone now, so no help there. Did I tell them I'd be back, um, someday? Yeah, probably. And then I left. Having benchmarked a new kind of bottom, I needed gas and a boost, so I stopped at the station just up the street from their house. The attendant noticed I was getting busy in the car and called the cops, but I was none the wiser. I drove down Excelsior Boulevard and turned left to go north on Highway 169 with a cop trailing me all the way. The drugs, the booze, the shame, all of it overtook me, and I gunned it to eighty and fishtailed onto the highway. The cop had seen enough and flipped his lights. The jig was not only up, it was about to be placed in bracelets. I pulled over so fast that he went into a ditch. He was pissed when he walked up, breathing real hard and fast. I knew I had a problem, so I came to my own defense and spoke up.

"I have a suspended license, sir. This," I said, indicating the glass of vodka in the console, "is an open bottle. I know I am going to jail, and I don't want to make a problem."

His face relaxed. He nearly apologized as he cuffed me and said he would put them on loose for the short ride to the station. He put me in the back of the car and went rummaging around through the bottles, marijuana roaches, and other detritus in the Maxima.

When we got to the station, he saw me in the bright light and stared at the welter of needle marks on my arms. He immediately asked me where the drugs were. I said nothing. He went out to his car and came back red faced. He tapped a packet containing what seemed to be several grams of coke in the palm of his hand.

"I found this under my backseat," he said. "You put it there."

"I can't help you with that, officer," I said as politely as I could manage.

He put me in the cell and told me to think it over, telling me to keep in mind that I was not leaving until we got that package of cocaine straightened out. Three cops wheeled through my cell. Good cop, bad cop, medium cop. I told all of them that I was happy to cooperate, but I couldn't help them with that package. As the night ticked on, that last hit in the car wore off, and just when my resolve slipped and I thought I might do something stupid, they kicked me loose.

The compounding of consequence, the meager ends, the bad luck of my own making followed by worse, all seemed too pathetic to be true. Had I really been so feckless as to give up my children and get thrown in a jail in the space of the same hour? I spent a great deal of time searching for records that would back up my memory, but the Hopkins police did not keep records going back that far, and there was nothing in the court files other than some bare-bones charges. I began to think that the last worst night was a figment of my darker imaginings. But as I dug deeper, I realized that when I eventually entered treatment, those charges must have been extant. Someone had to have helped me put that case to rest. I had a dim memory of my cousin Steve, a lawyer, helping me out at some point. In the fall of 2007, I called him and asked if he had represented me some point. "I certainly did," he said. "I still have the files."

| DEPT 0900 | OFFENSE/INCIDENT ATL Warrants, Open Bottle, DAR VICTIM Def Carr, David Michael | CONTINUATION REPORT | SUP APR PAGE 2 OF 4 |

32 year old male is arrested for warrants, open bottle and driving after revocation after he is stopped for erratic driving.

HPD received a complainant of a possible drunk driver eastbound on Co Rd 3 from 11th Av. Vehicle was described as a dark Nissan or Datsun Maxima lic#NPH 128. Suspect had been in the Amoco service station and the attendant felt he was intoxicated because he was having a hard time with his balance. I caught up to the vehicle as it was making a left turn onto NB Hwy 169 from EB Co Rd 3. I followed as the vehicle pulled onto Hwy 169 without using a signal. The vehicle then began to swerve abruptly back and forth. It swerved to the left and crossed over the lane deviding line and then drove half over that line. I activated my red lights to iniciate a stopp The vehicle "slammed" on the brakes and came to a quick skidding stop. I approached the driver on foot and opened the drivers door. I asked for his drivers license and he told me that it was suspended because of a prior DWI. He admitted that he knew that his license was not valid, but he was driving anyways. I verbally identified the defendant as David Michael Carr, DOB/9-8-56. The defendant did have a slight smell of an alcoholic beverage but did pass a PBT test. When I had approached the vehicle I noticed a glass in the middle console area of front seat. The glass contained a liquid that smelled of an alcoholic beverage. The defendant admitted that it was alcohol and thta he had taken a few sips of it. The glass and contents was confiscated and marked and placed in property room A binC-5.
A routine check with the MN Bepartment of Public Saftey showed that the defendant's license was REVOKED. It had been revoked because of a prior DWI and Driving after Withdrawl. A routine warrant check showed a active Misdemeanor warrant out of Crow Wing County for DWI. The defendant was placed under arrest and transported to the station for booking. Officer Stumpf impounded the vehicle to Dick's Towing.

Officer Wilentz goes on to say that I had outstanding warrants from an incident in Crow Wing County and that I was released to a friend—that would probably be Anna—for bail in the amount of $613. He does not mention the back-and-forth over the package of cocaine, but then he wouldn't because it was left unresolved.

Steve was yet another relative who I ended up getting flopped on, probably through my dad. He said I was engaging in a pattern of conduct, however misdemeanor, that the court would not look kindly on.

"You're a DAR, driving after revocation, there were some alcohol-related incidents. I think there were two or three of them, so you were looking at a potential license revocation. You were inimical to public safety to the point where they could pull it for good."

Steve also sent along another charge he handled that stemmed from an incident on March 2, 1988, at 2:20 a.m. It made for interesting reading because I had zero recollection of the events described. According to the Minneapolis police report Steve sent, I was parked in the Maxima with two other males behind a house at 1801 Third Avenue. The cops flipped their lights. They said that when I got out of the car, they observed the "defendant's balance to be very unstead [sic], his breath smelled of an alcoholic beverage, and his eyes were watery and bloodshot." I failed field sobriety tests, had a revoked license, and was placed in the squad. But I was not charged with DWI, only careless driving and driving after revocation. Given the facts described, it made no sense, but deeper in the file, I found a letter I had written to Steve:

"Enclosed please find info you requested. Note that I was not charged with DWI, although there is more than a little indication that such a charge would have been appropriate." The break, I wrote, came because the cop who pulled me over was someone I knew from my reporting days.

It was a surprise that cut many ways. Not only did I come across one more jam I didn't remember, but I had skated on part of it because I knew the cop. I had always steadfastly maintained that I had observed a bright line between my job as a reporter and my career as a screwup, but here was hard evidence that I had cut at least one corner because after many nocturnal interactions with the Minneapolis police, I had finally come across an officer I knew. I wonder what I said when I was in the back of that squad.

It was a nice gesture on the cop's part, so I'll leave his name out of it, even though it rings no bells. But if his intent was to put a scare into me and help me get back on the straight and narrow, it didn't help. I spent the next nine months in and out of handcuffs, in and out of jail, until it all ended on Highway 169 near Hopkins in November. I got out of jail and went to detox three days later at a suburban facility near my parents' house.

Right after I got admitted, they walked me to a table in the middle of the room. Detoxes are really human aquariums, a place where large, Librium-infused humans bob here and there, watched by the staff through thick plate glass in case one of them freaks out or starts flopping around. My job, as it turned out, was to settle my arms up to my biceps in a large tub of Dreft detergent, a nice low-tech way of disinfecting my track marks without involving a lot of hands-on work by the staff. I had become a white trash untouchable, all festering pus and contagion. They dropped pills into my mouth from a few inches away while I waited like a baby penguin, open-mouthed and expectant.

Did I have an epiphany in that suburban aquarium? No, I had a moment with the macaroni and cheese. It had been awhile since I had eaten. I did what I was told. I ate the macaroni and cheese. I ate the pills.

A few days later, my parents had Thanksgiving dinner, and I came straight from detox. My babies were there. I drank the nonalcoholic grape juice and shared in the family ritual of saying what I was thankful for. I have no idea what I came up with.

After dinner, my parents spoke to me quietly, off to the side. They were too old to handle the twins and had a lot of other things going on in their life. They had spoken to my older brother John, a guy who worked in leadership for the Catholic Church, and he had wired up temporary foster care through Catholic Charities. Erin and Meagan would be placed with a family, safe and warm, while I went "to deal with things." It was decided that I would go straight to Eden House the following morning.

So that was it. Only it wasn't. When I was in New Orleans talking to Chris about that time, he reminded me that the night before I went in to Eden House, I had to go back at it one more time.

"You had called me and wanted me to pick you up some rocks, 'cause you were going in the next day, and you wanted to get high one more time. And I did. I think it was the only time I'd been to your parents' house, but we were in your basement or first floor, the bedroom down there. I had to open up the car door for you because your hands were all swollen up, your arms were all bruised up from—"

Um, shooting coke?

"Yeah, I think it was kind of a moment for me," he said.

Me too. A new day was upon me, give or take one more flail at getting high. The last rung was in view, and the fullness of my dispossession was at hand. I was a treatment washout going in for another stint, the twins' mother was headed off to a different facility, and my children, both of them cooing away in their baby buckets upstairs while I sat in my parents' basement—the last stop of all losers—getting high.

Job? Gone. Girlfriend? History. Dignity? Please. Money? As if. Children? Orphans.

The math had been solved. I was at zero times zero.

INTERMISSION

Gonna rise up
Turning mistakes into gold

—EDDIE VEDDER, "RISE"

Y ou should write a book about all that."

I heard that a lot whenever my stumblebum history came up. I always said it was a bad idea. Why go back to hell if you somehow slipped out a side door? And beyond the grime that is bound to accrue from a trip through the gutters of one's past, what is the value in one more addiction memoir to me or anyone else?

Let's say, for the sake of argument, that a guy threw himself under a crosstown bus and lived to tell the tale. Is that a book you'd like to read? Yet pop literature is alive with the chemical doppelgänger of that same choice. Even within the frame of the disease concept of addiction, there is room for choice. Regardless of predispositions, no one had a shotgun to anybody's head when that shot glass or needle reared into view.

At bottom, recovery stories go down a very familiar track:

I had a beer with friends.

Then I shot dope into my neck.

I got in trouble.

I saw *the error of my ways.*

I found Jesus or twelve steps or Bhakti yoga.

Now everything is new again.

I have sat in rooms full of like minds, telling and listening to those stories to very good effect: I've got years of sobriety to show for it. But to weave that self with my writing self is a far more complicated matter. I stay alive by telling my story in those rooms. I have prospered professionally by telling other people's stories.

Even if I am endlessly grateful—I am, by the way—that the war within has quieted and I now have a place to stand, why not shut up about it and enjoy my nice suburban profile on Cooper Avenue where I live? I fit right in, give or take. Just ask my neighbors. *Carr? He lives down the block. Drives a late-model Ford Explorer, nice family, goes to work like everybody else. His lawn seems to be a problem—grubs, I think— but otherwise he seems OK.*

Certainly there is ownership in the telling, but there are other, less ennobling imperatives, commercial ones. Because most of the reporting went off in Minnesota, people were unfailingly polite, but I could almost hear the conversations behind me as I left. "What the heck was that about?"

At the precise moment I was deciding to roll around in the bad old days, Erin and Meagan wrote essays for college that centered on their backstory, and I noticed that they were remarkably different than the story I thought we had lived together. They had their own take, and it did not directly comport with my trope of mortification followed by a crowning triumph.

Suddenly, writing about the idea of self-fashioning, of coming up with a history that allows you to make your way in the present, began to seem like a worthy intellectual pursuit. At the same time, one of the most successful hood ornaments of the genre—James Frey's *A Million Little Pieces*—was coming apart in very plain view, a story I covered. I began to think that there might be room for another memoir from a lost-and-found soul, a work of recollection that was based on reporting and fact-finding.

Still, I don't like talking to strangers about intimate aspects of my life. It's embarrassing, and it's not like many will respond in kind. And if they do, well, who really wants to know about all that?

Most stories about one's past could fairly and adequately be told in a single sentence, and a short one at that: Everyone did the best they could.

I always thought that people who spent endless amounts of time drilling into their personal history looking for meaning or causality were fundamentally unhappy in their lives, and I'm not. I'm ecstatic in my own dark, morbid way, thrilled to be out the other end, and do not have a lot of pride or hubris about the things I have done. In the end, I didn't so much decide it was my turn as give in to reporting out a story I thought I knew.

But when I went down into the basement and began rummaging around in folders, one of the first things I found was this:

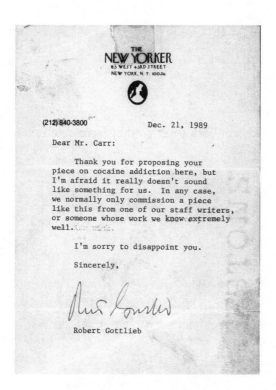

THE
NEW YORKER
25 WEST 43RD STREET
NEW YORK, N. Y. 10036

(212) 840-3800   Dec. 21, 1989

Dear Mr. Carr:

   Thank you for proposing your piece on cocaine addiction here, but I'm afraid it really doesn't sound like something for us. In any case, we normally only commission a piece like this from one of our staff writers, or someone whose work we know extremely well.

   I'm sorry to disappoint you.

   Sincerely,

   Robert Gottlieb

There I was, less than a year sober, pitching my tale of woe. At the time, I was jobless and had a couple of kids to feed, but my belief that I had always been above such a crass exercise collapsed the minute I began considering it. And there were more. *Esquire:*

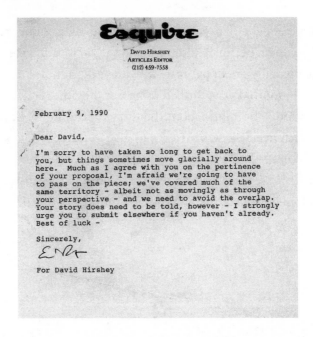

Playboy was a big deal back then, so they were definitely worth a try:

The *Washington Post:*

Thank you for letting us see the enclosed
article. I am afraid we are not going to be
able to use it at this time. We do appreciate
your sending it for our consideration, however

Meg Greenfield
Editorial Page Editor

Parade:

PARADE
PUBLICATIONS, INC.

Fran Carpentier
Articles Editor

January 17, 1990

David Carr
123 N. 3rd Street, Suite 203
Minniapolis, Minn 55401

Dear Mr. Carr:

We were pleased to receive your recent
article proposal. Though the idea has
merit, we find that it does not meet
PARADE's present needs.

Thank you for your interest in PARADE,
and all best wishes in placing your
story elsewhere.

Sincerely,

Fran Carpentier

750 Third Avenue, New York, New York 10017 (212) 573-7177

And a year later, I was still pushing it to *Detroit Monthly*, for reasons I still can't recall:

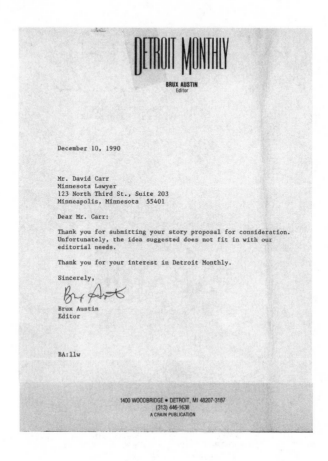

And so, even though I had sobered up and supposedly never looked back, early in my recovery I was walking around with a sandwich board, telling people to step right up and see the man who ruined his life. A junkie, a drunk, and now, many years later, a grown-up, sober writer, I was about to live out the cliché. As a friend of mine put it, "Sure, it's all been said, but it hasn't been said by *you*."

Memory is the one part of the brain's capacity that seems to be able to bring time to heel, make it pause for examination, and, in many cases, be reconfigured to suit the needs of that new moment. Long before TiVo, humans have been prone to selecting, editing, and fast-forwarding the highlights of their lives. Even if every good intention is on hand, it is difficult if not impossible to convey the emotional content of past events because of their ineffability. Even in an arch me-as-told-to-me paradigm, the past recedes, inexorably supplanted by the present.

Memory remains an act of perception, albeit perception dulled by time, but it is also about making a little movie. Remembering is an affirmative act—recalling those events that made you *you* is saying who you are. I am not this book, but this book is me.

Episodic and semantic memory each lie in different ways, but each is eventually deployed in service of completing a story. Stories are how we explain ourselves to each other with the remorseless truth always somewhere between the lines of what is told. In this way, memory becomes not a faculty but a coconspirator, a tool for constructing the self that we show the world.

In *Midnight's Children,* Salman Rushdie writes about the "special kind" of truth that memory conjures. "It selects, eliminates, alters, exaggerates, minimizes, glorifies, and vilifies also. But in the end it creates its own reality, its own heterogenous but usually coherent version of events, and no sane human being ever trusts someone else's version more than his own."

I get his gist, but I'm not sure I give any more credence to my memories than to the recollections of others.

When I committed to write a reported memoir about my past, I proceeded on a few assumptions:

1. Every person's story has value, including my own.

2. My life is the one thing in the world I am the leading expert on.

3. If I am truthful, no real harm can come to me.

4. Keeping careful video and audio records of everyone I talk to will give the memoir a verisimilitude born of transparency.

5. I am a good man who did bad things, but I'm better now.

I had no understanding of the fundamental audacity of writing a memoir. I do now. It presumes a level of interest in my life that I had not historically displayed and also has an embedded promise that something will be learned.

Even with the gimmick of reporting, my addiction narrative arrives at some very common lessons. Too much of a bad thing is bad. Everybody laughs and has fun until they don't. If you don't sleep and eat, but drink and drug instead, you will lose jobs, spouses, and dignity.

And the lessons of the recovery narrative are important, but even more prosaic. In the ensuing chapters, you will be unsurprised to learn that once I stopped doing narcotics and alcohol, things improved. I got jobs, remarried, had a baby, and, of course, learned to love myself.

Junkies and drunks frequently end up putting a megaphone to their own pratfalls because they need to believe that all of the time they spent with their lips wrapped around glass, whether it was a bottle of vodka or a crack pipe, actually meant something. That impulse suggests that I don't regret the past—it brought me here to this nice, happy place—but I'd also like to squeeze something more from it.

Even if the conception of the memoir is venal, or commercial, or flawed, there is intrinsic value in reporting. For instance, in spite of what I believed, it was probably me who had the gun, not Donald. I can't say with certainty, but that picture began to cohere after some reporting. I called Joseph, a professor at New York University, who knows a great deal about the mechanism of human recollection, to ask him how I could have gotten such a signal event in my life so completely wrong.

"Well, the drugged state you were in is going to alter the way you formed memories," he suggested. "You could probably have misattribution. You have lots of pieces that are recorded and stick together by that experience. Perhaps in that situation the sticking mechanism was not working well, and so all the pieces were there, but it wasn't put together quite right.

"Especially under the conditions you were in, you could have faulty mechanisms of various kinds. Because those little pieces are there, when you retrieve the memory, you put them back together, and for whatever reason, the gun ends up in his hand. You can get Freudian about that or not." He added that so-called flashbulb memory of the kind that I had can be incredibly vivid and still be very wrong. "The other thing that may be relevant is something called state-dependent learning, where certain memories are processed only when you go back into the state in which they were formed."

I'd do almost anything to remember what happened on The Night of the Gun or the snowsuits, but that is a state I don't plan on visiting anytime soon.

Each time I would return from a reporting trip, I would go through a ritual. On-site notes would be transcribed, interviews logged, and then I would empty the digital audio and video onto my computer. In order to make sure that the accumulated data of my life did not tip over my computer, I would transfer the large audio and video files to an external hard drive. As the data accumulated, I began to think of that hard drive as all-knowing, a digital oracle that knew more about my life than I did, a device that told the truth because that was all it contained.

Even so, my past is a phantom limb, something I feel the presence of but cannot touch. John Updike called it part of our "dead, unrecoverable selves." When the past is shifted to the present moment, it is infected by a consistency bias that requires that all things fit together, whether they do or not. Examine your own family history and folklore if you don't buy it. How many of those stories are literally, exactly true?

Memoir is a very personal form of creation myth. Whether it is in the form of a book or something told across the intimacy of first date candlelight, the this-is-me, this-is-who-I-am story is a myth in the classic sense, a tale with personal gods and touchstones. It becomes more and more sacred as it is told. And perhaps less and less truthful.

Going back over my history has been like crawling over broken glass in the dark. I hit women, scared children, assaulted strangers, and chronically lied and gamed to stay high. I read about That Guy with the same sense of disgust that almost anyone would. What. An. Asshole. Here, safe in an Adirondack redoubt where I am piecing together the history of That Guy, I often feel I have very little in common with him. And that distance will keep me typing until he turns into this guy.

PART TWO

30

RX FOR GARBAGE HEADS

Sobriety checklist (tear out and use as needed, but never as a coaster for beverage alcohol):

1. It helps to crater in Minnesota. Apart from the whole "Land of 10,000 Treatment Centers" trope, it is a state that still has a functioning health-care system, even for a ~~four~~ five-time treatment loser.

2. Accept the gift of time. A low-bottom drunk or junkie will take months just to remember who he or she is or was.

3. Enter the booby hatch. Preferably a place you never, ever want to go back to. Avoid treatment centers with duck ponds, good food, or a record of admitting Britney Spears or Lindsay Lohan.

4. Form alliances with the lame and infirm. Consort with others who have smashed their lives to bits and are humbly looking around for the pieces.

5. Don't date people in recovery. Every transaction will take on a therapeutic lilt: "That's not what I hear you saying . . ." "Oh really? What I said is what I meant, you twit. *Did I just say that aloud, honey?*" Date civilians. Don't expect them to "get" you. Expect them to love you.

6. Take on new responsibilities: making coffee at the meetings you attend, helping others who are new in recovery, or obtaining sole custody of infant twin daughters. If you are thinking about sailing into the abyss, you'll probably consider others that will fly off the cliff with you. To do for others is to do for self.

7. Respect the power of mood-altering chemicals, but allow for hope. When the inner pirate in your subcortex is seeking permission to come aboard, consider that if you get through that day, there may be many others. Trust God, not the pirate.

8. Develop new obsessions. Nineteenth-century literature. Bonsai. Ping-pong. Flourless tortes. Extreme skipping.

9. Avoid writing or reading junkie memoirs. The line between prurience and pratfall is razor thin. Nothing doing here, nothing but triggers, keep moving.

10. Party but don't use. A drunk alone with himself is in a terrible neighborhood. Resume life in civil society and go out, but always plan your own escape route just in case a glass of whiskey begins whispering your name.

11. The problem with your life is behavior, not disclosure. Secrets are what addiction calls foreplay. If you want to live a life that you can be honest about, live one that is worthy. The answer to life is learning to live.

12. Don't drink. Go to meetings.

31

A FEARSOME GOODNESS

All angels bring terror.

—RAINER MARIA RILKE

About a month after arriving at Eden House, I was surprised to see John, a Pulitzer Prize–winning columnist for the *St. Paul Pioneer Press*, walking through the joint with a staff member. He was taking a tour because he wanted to see for himself where some of the casualties of the crack epidemic were washing up.

I stopped him and said hello. Obviously surprised to see another journalist, he asked, "What are you doing here?"

"I'm one of the knuckleheads, John," I said. "I live here."

"Ohhhhhh, undercover, huh? Smart move," he said.

Not exactly. In the last month of 1988, and for the first five months of 1989, this was my place, and these were my people. And while it is one thing to find yourself in a place full of lunatics, crackheads, and career losers, it is quite another to notice that you fit right in.

When I called John in the fall of 2007—he's now a big-time fiction writer—he remembered bumping into me.

"It was kind of strange to see you there that way," he reflected. "You were a well-known journalist, and suddenly you walked up to me in this place. It was very helpful for me because I had talked to a number of people, and they were really stupid, just sort of dumb and clueless.

They were lost souls. But in talking to you, your mind was clear, and you were obviously smart. You had a real serious appreciation of your problem and everything that you had lost. And yet you were not sure that you could stay off cocaine. It was clear that it was tearing you up, but you couldn't just turn your back and walk away. You said that it wasn't that simple. That was useful to me because it gave me an under-standing of the complexity of the problem."

The place where I gave John a tutorial on the wages of crack had long been known as a last stop. Eden House, at 1025 Portland Avenue South in Minneapolis, was a therapeutic community be-cause the nuts ran the nuthouse. The other clinical term would be shithole. It wasn't dirty, it wasn't really dangerous, but there were enough skeevy guys there to make it seem like a holding cell on some days. Petty beefs would blow up and occasionally get physical, there were rats in the kitchen, and the counseling staff—mostly people who had seen their share of bad times—was unaffected by the keening and neediness of the clientele. It was a no-bullshit place packed to the rafters with bullshitters. Dan, who ran it, knew every scam in the book and had run a few of them himself. Its clinical motor suggested that the population was not in need of rehabilita-tion but habilitation. Eden House was brimming with slogans. This was the main one: "The answer to life is learning to live." We would say that, loudly and with a great deal of emotion, at the conclusion of each group meeting.

This is the point where the knowing, irony-infused author laughs along with his readers about his time among the aphorisms, how he was once so gullible and needy that he drank deeply of such weak and fruity Kool-Aid. That's some other book. Slogans saved my life. All of them—the dumb ones, the preachy ones, the impera-tives, the clichés, the injunctives, the gooey, Godly ones, the shame-less, witless ones.

I lustily chanted some of those slogans and lived by others. There is nothing ironic about being a crackhead and a drunk, or recovery from same. Low-bottom addiction is its own burlesque, a theater of the absurd that needs no snarky annotation. Unless a person is willing to be terminally, frantically earnest, all hope is lost.

It is what it is, which is a slogan we used to say a lot at Eden House. Most of the clients were criminal justice referrals, guys who had either gotten early release or avoided jail time by agreeing to go there. I came with trial dates for a bunch of misdemeanor stuff hanging over me, which in the aggregate might have added up to some jail time, but I flopped into Eden House primarily because it was the only place the county was willing to fund me. When the guys there complained that they were in on a bum charge, that someone had ratted them out for something they didn't do, Jerry, one of the counselors, would say, "OK, so stipulated. Let's say that's true. And then let's just say that you are here for all the other stuff you got away with."

The place had some talented, intuitive counselors and leadership, but its remarkable efficacy in treating the untreatable had more to do with the passage of time. Eden House was a six-month residential treatment program, which would seem like an extravagance, but for most of us, it was the bare minimum. A year before, I had gone through a twenty-eight-day program at St. Mary's, my fourth crack, and the counselor predicted I would land at either Eden House or a state mental hospital.

At the time, I dismissed state institutions as beyond the pale. As a reporter, I had been in and out of those places to do stories, and left on a dead run every time. People either had wild, feral looks or were so heavily medicated that they needed bibs to catch the drool. And Eden House? It was in a neighborhood I knew well for all the wrong reasons. Before I moved in, I would see the clients coming and going looking like nothing so much as a bunch of corner boys who were between opportunities. I had been to enough recovery meetings in town to see them arrive as a group and leave the same way. They might as well have been tied together with a piece of fucking yarn. I mean, good on them and all, but David Carr just did not roll like that.

Except there I was—for six months, no less. I could have done twenty-eight days standing on my head, gaming and grinning, but this was twenty-eight times six and then some. I can remember sitting on the skinny little mattress the first few nights, sketching out a calendar and staring at my distant discharge date. But once I jacked into the place, time roared by—it seemed like I had just gotten my wits about me when it was time to hit the street and use them.

In that time, I did not accept Jesus Christ as my lord and savior. I did not have a moment of clarity. I did not have a therapeutic break-through. Instead, slowly, somewhere along in there, I remembered who I used to be. In the fullness of time, I had walked away from the life of a normal person—in small increments at first, and then at a breakneck pace—and it took a long time to conjure a map to find my way back. Every day of that six months was important to me. It took a full month for the vestigial, drug-induced psychosis to wear off. I came in so addled that I could not even take in any new information. As the program required, I made my bed, went to the meetings, and avoided getting into any jackpots.

And I ate. Jesus, did I eat. Eden House sent out a van at the end of the day to various bakeries to pick up the unsold surplus. Doughnuts, crullers, and coffee cake; every night the bounty was laid out on tables in the kitchen. After years of sticking things in my mouth—ciggies, bottles of brown liquor, other people's body parts, and crack pipes—I was somewhat orally fixated. My addiction found expression in white flour and sugar. I ended up running the kitchen while I was there, which was less an expression of my background than a manifestation of my preoccupation with all five food groups and any of their cousins that might go down with a glass of sugary purple juice.

I had been a bit of a foodie during my years in the restaurant busi-ness, but I quickly dropped the pretension for a far more catholic range of edible interests. While instant mashed potatoes may not be an in-trinsically interesting food, I discovered that they were a highly effective medium for conveying gobs of surplus butter down my throat. By my math, I gained 90 pounds, give or take, which would mean that on each day of the 180 I was there, I put on a half pound. That sounds a little far-fetched, so let's be more judicious and say I gained 60 pounds. (I can't find relevant medical records for that period.) That's still a very impressive one-third of a pound a day. Photos suggest I was pushing 300 pounds by the time I was released, and that much is corroborated by Doolie, who began dating me again after I left. "You were sooo fat," she recalled, "you could hardly walk."

Um, gee, that was sort of mean. All the more so because it was clinically true. I was a man about my groceries when I was at Eden House.

Eden House was a place of what are called "trips," which had nothing to do with acid and everything to do with consequences. Someone who slipped out in the dead of night and came crawling back in the morning would have to sit on a bench in a hall for days on end—it was called The Bench—and beg for readmittance.

Getting into something physical with another client might have you scrubbing the stairs from the first through third floors with a toothbrush. My trips came from my tendency to stick my beak in where it did not belong. For a week, I wore a huge metal kitchen spoon around my neck, a totem of my propensity for spoon-feeding other clients. I also got to carry around a crappy vinyl briefcase for a few days, a symbol of my inclination to lawyer on behalf of other clients.

All the assets I had—an ability to verbalize, intellectualize, and filibuster—got no play at Eden House. In at least a few other treatments, I was often seen as baby Jesus, a counselor's pet who knew all the jargon and the right buttons to push—or at least I thought so. At Eden House, I was seen as a fool, and a pretty soft one at that. Early on, I got crossways with a guy named Tad—some silly stuff about the television—and I had to show teeth and a willingness to take an ass-kicking to find a place to stand. It wasn't Abu Ghraib, but it wasn't the treatment place with the elliptical machine and a staff nutritionist, either.

Eden House was a complicated place. Some of the people who were there were straight-up jailing it. No thought of recovery, just trying to do their time quicker and easier. Rick, one of my running buddies there, had no real issues with chemicals. He was just a gangster. Great cook, quick with a funny story, but a guy who pulled well-planned jobs on occasion—ornate affairs with lookouts and cash box extrications. I stuck by him because he was a man of honor in almost all regards, and although he was not much over five-foot-five, he weighed about 250, much of it angry muscle that could be brought to bear on any kind of situation.

Many of the guys there were so-called dual diagnosis, MI-CD, which stood for mentally incompetent, chemically dependent. I can remember having a conversation with a kid named Brett one night about the angels that were all around us, even as we spoke, and how they would look after both of us going forward if we said a prayer right then and there. I mumbled along.

One of the people who grabbed recovery with both hands lived a few doors down. Dave was on his second tour of Eden House. He was a smart guy who had done tough stuff and had a long, checkered résumé as a drunk and an addict. He had thirteen DWIs, among other credentials. But he had made a palpable decision that he was through. David was a giant man, with a booming voice and a real sense of justice. He talked of all the things he would do when he left there, and he went out and did all of them. But at the time, we were both so far back on our heels, we had nothing. My doughnut habit had pretty much reduced me to sweatpants from the swag pile, and near the end of our time at Eden House, we were tasked with going out into the world to look for work and attend recovery groups. Dave had a single pair of navy blue pants that still fit him even though he had put on a few, but I had borrowing rights. I can still remember standing at his room door and asking, "Are you wearing the pants tonight?" I'm sure some of the guys within earshot thought we had a little more going on than a strong recovery-based friendship.

There were no clanging bars there, but it was a noisy place, with a PA system that was constantly paging clients. With a lot of the clients raised on the corners and jails beyond, nobody ever spoke below a shout unless he was planning a caper. And there were plenty of those. Early in my tenure, Craig, the so-called "chief elder," the big cheese, not only went out and copped heroin and whiskey but brought it back to his room and got caught upstairs with a bunch of other guys having a big old time. The place had it all: drama, stakes, and conflict.

Things were actually going fine for me until I got my first pass on Christmas Day, a month into treatment. Anna had the babies on loan from foster care, and I was allowed to pick them up and take them to my parents' place. Except that when I was in Anna's back room, getting the twins ready to go, I noticed, tucked into the corner, a juice can filled with ashes that had obviously been used to smoke crack, with a lighter laying next to it. I made no conscious decision; I put a lighter to the can in a kind of see-and-smoke reflex baked in over the years. There was nothing there, not even a remnant, and I put down the can and went back to the business at hand. It was a moment of temporary possession, and it passed.

When I got back to Eden House the following day, there was an all-house meeting. It was the kind of free-for-all where grievances got aired, and anybody who had something on his chest was encouraged to unload. I shared what had happened at Anna's, thinking how impressed they would all be that I had made it back without taking the next giant step.

My admission had precisely the opposite effect. No one believed that I had made a failed attempt to use and then left it at that. The clients who were postured in leadership allowed that my story was not plausible. Empty can, yeah, sure, they said, empty suit. Nate, a giant black guy I grew to love, would mime smoking an empty can when I walked by. (I saw him on the streets a year later, skinny as hell, and he still had it in 'im to give me the empty-can salute.)

Derision aside, I took that Christmas Day as my new sobriety date, one that would stand for almost fourteen years. Somewhere in those days, I developed a belief that if I could make it through a given day sober, no matter what, there might be other days to follow. Hope, in other words. The chronicity of addiction is really a kind of fatalism writ large. If an addict knows in his heart he is going to use someday, why not today? But if a thin reed of hope appears, the possibility that it will not always be thus, things change. You live another day and then get up and do it again. Hope is oxygen to someone who is suffocating on despair.

The implications of a misstep arrived every weekend. My parents would come by with the twins after having picked them up from the foster care family. Zelda and Patrick, a middle-aged couple who took the girls in through Catholic Charities, were incredibly gracious, easy to deal with, and they clearly adored the twins. I adored them too, but I'm not entirely sure that they knew who I was as they toddled toward their first birthdays. Erin and Meagan responded well to me, but then they were happy with everybody. In between the times that I saw them on the weekends, both in foster care and Anna's care, they learned to walk, they learned to talk. They grew from an abstract notion of potential responsibility and/or shame and became small people whom we would set in the middle of the visiting room at Eden House and watch in wonder as they spun and bounced off each other.

I can remember one of the women counselors—Beth, maybe—coming in and marveling at Erin and Meagan and asking no one in particular who they belonged to. It took me just a second to realize the answer.

"That would be me."

She seemed surprised, and deep down, so was I.

While I was at Eden House, I wrote a horrid first-person account of being in the place for the *St. Paul Pioneer Press*. John, the columnist who'd seen me there, had wired up with Deborah, the editor. It had practical value in that it let every editor in town know with some certainty why I had constantly screwed up. The downside was that all of the people I owed money to knew where to find me. I was sufficiently addled to think there was value in a big tub of written claptrap. Suffice it to say that I don't include this piece in my clip file of greatest hits, with its odd combination of prissiness and sanctimony:

> There is no more grateful recovering person than someone who has come off years of cocaine abuse. The financial and emotional burden of maintaining the addiction is so corrosive that it is initially just a pleasure not to have to fight to live. Recovering cocaine addicts experience a particularly powerful treatment high, a sense of well-being, and a wish to share it with everyone. Unfortunately for the user and society as a whole, this state of bliss and this commitment to wellness evaporates when the user is exposed to cocaine.

Truthfully, I was less grateful than terrified by my last bounce along the bottom, just trying to stop the hemorrhage that was pumping the life out of me. Conventional wisdom suggests that recovery begins with submitting to a higher power. I have always had trouble getting the hang of that—less about a spiritual deficit than a tendency to overintellectualize things—but I found a pretty handy substitute in Marion.

Marion was not a girl. Marion was/is a man, a man of fearsome goodness. I hated his guts the moment I met him, he of the constant sunglasses, the Cheshire-Cat smile without a trace of friendliness, a person with a taste for whimsy who treated his clients as toys. A black man with the forearms of Hercules and the tactical aggression of Machiavelli, he cultivated mystery in a way that I found preposterous. He would say nothing for long stretches during group sessions, and I would step in and provide brilliant, synthetic analysis of what was being said. He would smile and say, "Whenever you get done bebomping your gee-whompers, you might want to take a look at your own shit."

Well, there's always that. Because he was as inscrutable as Buddha and a lot less talkative, clients began to assign superpowers to him, aided in no small part by the constant mirrored sunglasses. He may have been sitting in group thinking about things like whether he should barbecue chicken or hamburgers that night, but behind the mirrors, it all seemed very deep and portentous. And the rumors about the murky past helped. He killed a client. No, he *almost* killed him. No, he threatened to kill a client, and the client killed himself. I decided that it was all bullshit, just a matter of trade dress and a cultivated image. Except that he did seem to have mystical powers when it came to me.

A big part of the routine at Eden House involved the domestic arts. Our beds had to be made army style and our rooms kept spotless. Marion was the counselor in charge one weekend, doing inspections, and he took an interest in the stack of reading I had on my headboard. With a kind of delicacy I can still recall, he went three-quarters of the way down the stack and teased out two pages from a girlie magazine that I had ripped out and stashed deep inside a book. Another time, there was a public event in the basement with speakers and graduating residents. One of the women in attendance was pretty and very turned out. I stole glances when I could. The next day, Marion had me in for a one-on-one, never a happy circumstance. He got right to the point.

"My *wife* said that you took quite a bit of interest in her at yesterday's event."

Gee.

But Marion landed with the most weight the weekend my sister Lisa was going to be married. It was about three months in, and I had been out on passes before and made it back safely. I had all approvals in order, and my family was planning on coming to get me on Saturday morning. It would be the first family wedding I would ever attend sober. On the Friday morning before I was to leave, Marion had me paged down to his office.

"You're not going to your sister's wedding," he said plainly.

I went ballistic, whining that everything was good to go, that I had the pass coming, that my family was expecting me, that I was taking my twins, that it was all set. "Blah, blah, blah," Marion said, as he often did. "I am telling you no. You can go, but don't think you are coming back here. You leave, you leave."

Why?

"Because you need to hear that word: no. Call it a therapeutic no."

I phoned my family, and they agreed that I should leave the place; that it was a totally unfair and inappropriate decision. Even some of the counselors agreed that the decision seemed hasty and whimsical. I remember I went at the end of the day to tell Marion that I was leaving and to let him know what a pompous fucking asshole he was. And I planned on adding how I didn't buy into any of his silent Buddha ju-jitsu bullshit.

Marion pulled up on a motorcycle outside a coffee shop in South Minneapolis in July of 2006, still looking pretty damn scary after all these years. The mirrored shades were there, and he was still in shape. He seemed glad to see me. I had done some reading before I saw him, including a story I did about him after I sobered up. "I work to help people make a conscious decision and then begin to believe in that decision," he was quoted in the story, characteristically concise.

We'd had enough conversations in the intervening years for some of the mystique to drop away—it was a little easier when he was not the Lord God of my waking life. I asked him about the persona he brought to work every day.

"It was not your 'routine' delivery as far as treatment goes, but it seemed to work a lot better than taking the time to sit down and say, 'Happy day, good feeling,' and so on and so forth."

So part of it was tactical? Taking a sip of his coffee, he said it was a matter of tailoring the approach to the audience. I thought of a picture I had of our so-called primary group. That is me just off Marion's shoulder.

"There was rugged clients," he said. "They came from all over the streets, the penitentiaries, psychiatric wards. And they were set in their ways. And especially with me, I had this thing, 'Don't let them see me sweat and don't back down.' And I didn't try to present myself as a badass, but I was just, well, do whatever you're going to do, but I'm not gonna go and let up on this. And a lot of times, you know, I was walking around there for a while maintaining a particular aura that was free floating because there were some bad actors that came through there consistently."

Hearing Marion, who actually *was* a badass, admit that the place seemed rugged to his eye made me feel better. I had thought with some shame about how much Eden House, and some of the clients, freaked me out. The street vibe of the place made me feel like the white boy from the suburbs I actually was.

Sitting there many years later, he told me plain and simple that the reason he did not let me go was that weddings were slippery places; that in his clinical analysis, I wasn't ready, and he decided to just say no and see what I would do. It was far from a whimsical decision, but it was a patently unfair one. Then again, there was a sign in the main room of Eden House that promulgated three truths: "Nothing's Fair, Nothing's Fair, Nothing's Fair."

As I sat there at the coffee shop next to a rolling video camera, I told Marion that I remembered going down to his office to shove that therapeutic no up his ass. But I had left his office, stayed in the program, and had not gone to the wedding. What had he said? He remembered what I did not.

"You were on the verge, and I told you, 'Well, why don't you just get those two girls high too?' And you kind of flipped out, because those girls were the loves of your life, and just the thought scared you."

32

BOY ISLAND

On this evening the chief forces of the island were disposed as follows. The lost boys were out looking for Peter, the pirates were out looking for the lost boys, the redskins were out looking for the pirates, and the beasts were out looking for the redskins. They were going round and round the island, but they did not meet because all were going at the same rate.

—J. M. BARRIE, *PETER PAN*

Supply is the only issue of moment to an addict. Running low, riding high, all things in reach of an addict are subject to entropy—money, honor, the milk of human kindness—but the inventory of mood-altering chemicals serves as the maypole of every waking day.

It's helpful to think of junkies as like minds with a common interest, like folks who knit or clog dance. The activity is just part of it; there's also the endless rumination about every corner of the obsession. Even at Eden House, where many of us had been off the street for months, we loved our war stories. And they were usually stories of untold abundance. The night you got locked in the fully stocked bar, the weekend when the coke was measured by the fistful, that magical stretch when one was not too many and a thousand seemed like a very plausible number. Too much of a bad thing is always a good thing when you are a pharmaceutical autodidact.

The interest in what is on hand is writ even larger when the piles get smaller. Addicts often cluster, if for no other reason than to meet the humiliation of it all with numbers. And the dynamic of the group will help individuals elide over dry spells. It is a sort of numerical certainty that someone in the broader organism will be flush at one time or another, and if he is a good group member, he will share. Until the supply runs short. Then the little circle of sharing breaks down, and everybody starts leaning in over the now suddenly diminutive pile. Scientists could have saved time figuring out how to split an atom if they had convened a bunch of junkies. When things get short, a junkie's interest will not only dance on the head of a pin, it will tell you which half of the head of the pin looks bigger.

If you were going to come up with a hypothetical hell on earth for an addict, you might conjure an island, populate it with junkies, and then secrete some, but not enough, of a few treasured substances in their midst.

Fowl Lake in the Boundary Waters Canoe Area is actually a lot easier to access if you arrive from the Canadian side, but the annual fishing trip at Eden House consisted of far too many felons to mess with the border crossing. Once we got there, there would be a commute involving three lakes and two rivers so we could come in from the Minnesota side.

The twenty-three clients who got to go—I was in that lucky number—included two murderers, a rapist, a handful of strong-armed robbers and some run-of-the-mill losers like me. Dave, my buddy, was now chief elder. Most of us had not been off asphalt for years, and for some it was a first time in the woods. A very rough, remarkably urban crowd was loaded into vans for the long trip from Minneapolis, along with axes, filet knives, and handsaws. "What could go wrong?" said Tak, one of the clients who organized the trip, as he surveyed all the lethal hardware. People whose skills began and ended with three-card monte and selling carved cubes of Ivory soap as crack suddenly found themselves with a canoe paddle in their hands.

It was late May of 1989, and I was nearing the end of my tenure at Eden House. Apart from being so obese that I threatened to swamp a canoe merely by stepping into it, I had achieved a kind of stasis, a détente with the real world which suggested that I might not have to spend the rest of my waking hours making sure that I had enough drugs and alcohol to meet the day. My kids had prospered in foster care and were returned to Anna, who had successfully completed an inpatient treatment program. Hope floats, sometimes in a canoe.

I've never been all that handy in the woods, but after months of being trapped in the hermetic, noisy confines of Eden House, a sky full of stars and a horizon framed by lakes sounded glorious. But some of the guys on the trip were not people I would have chosen to split a six-pack with on the outside, let alone share space with on an island full of sharp utensils for more than a week. Scott was a whiner with a bad criminal history around women, Brett was a kid whose tenuous grasp on reality did not seem to need much of an assist from recreational drugs, and Vinny, God bless him, was a full-on nut ball who wore his devil-man beard with a great deal of pride. I was on antidepressants for the first time in my life, but many of the guys who came—there were two women on the trip—ate antipsychotics like they were Lucky Charms. Whatever it took, fine by me.

The counselors who ran the show—Jerry and Marion—were used to getting all the frogs in the wheelbarrow and headed in the same direction, and so what seemed like a script for a B horror movie actually had a kind of organized air. David and Tak worked hard as the clients "on top" of the trip to make sure that we had enough of everything to get by, even if we didn't catch fish. There was plenty of coffee, oodles of ciggies, and the counselors had everybody's meds apportioned into daily doses. We were good to go.

And then came the last river on the way in. It had been a very rainy spring, and the stream raced around its bends and through small drops. Right away, it was total mayhem, with at least four of a dozen canoes tipping and hapless nonswimming street bums floating everywhere. Nobody died, so we had a good laugh about it—until we realized that much of our preciously hoarded cargo had bit it along with the canoes. The cigarette supply was suddenly iffy, and the meds, well, some of the residents would be even more clean and sober than usual.

By the time we pitched camp, we were a bedraggled lot. When someone mentioned that we all needed a cup of coffee, we discovered that the big thirty-cup camp coffee pot had not made the trip. We had a teeny one tucked away that made a few cups at a time. "We have forty pounds of fucking powdered milk, but no way to make coffee?!" someone asked. There were feckless attempts to dry out the cigarettes and some misguided efforts at making cowboy coffee, but we knew that, basically, we were screwed.

Vinny, without his antipsychotics, took to making moonlight patrols, muttering as he thrashed around in the swampy parts of the island. He'd walk back into the light of the fire at night with his eyes ablaze. One night his grin was particularly epic, and someone asked him if the cat had swallowed his tongue. He opened his mouth very ceremonially to reveal a little painted turtle. It patched out on his tongue, trying to get away.

He had some trouble mastering the fishing, but at midweek he caught a big northern pike and began walking it around the campsite, introducing it as an old friend. If this were an episode of *Lost,* he would have been one of the "Others." "God answered my prayers on the spot; I cast out onto the water and said, 'Lord, gimme a northern,' and my pole started bending."

Much of the detail of the trip is easy to access because in order to keep some money coming in while I spent time at Eden House, I had pitched the story to the *Pioneer Press.* There was a fair amount of discussion by the leaders at Eden House about whether my notebook would put me at a remove from the therapeutic community, but in the end, they decided that I would need to graduate from the institution with some degree of professional momentum.

Reporting or not, I was completely seduced. For many of us, the idea that you could get into a canoe without beer and actually spend time catching fish was an epiphany that rivaled Archimedes's jolt in estimating the mass of objects. Jerry, one of the counselors, built a sweat lodge down by the lake out of a plastic tarp and some pine boughs. Apart from opening our pores and letting some of the grime out when we jumped into the cold water, it gave some of our time there a ceremonial air. Not to go all Robert Bly on the whole thing, but we did man stuff, no whiskey or narcotics involved.

Still, as the candle burned down on remaining cigs, and the coffee continued to arrive only in small dribbles, people began to get twitchy, especially the guys who were short on their meds. The *Pioneer Press* assigned a photographer to take pictures to go with the story, and when I paddled out to the Canadian side to get him, I asked three questions:

"Do you have a coffee pot?" ("No, I was pretty sure you guys would have one.")

"How are you fixed for cigarettes?" ("I don't smoke.")

"And I suppose a little Thorazine is out of the question?" (Long, quizzical stare.)

I explained that the island was a bit restless, more *Lord of the Flies* than therapeutic community, but Chris the photographer explained that he had worked in a number of war zones and that it would be no biggie. But he left a day early. His pictures were spectacular.

As was part of the plan, something about being out in the woods annealed some of the street right off us. The hardened dope fiends became guys who were suddenly afraid of the dark, the kind of deep-woods murk most had never seen in their lives.

In the context of the crew I was running with, I seemed like a direct descendant of Daniel Boone, more handy and adept than I realized. Now going on five months sober, I began to see that the hopelessness that had been draped over my every hour as an addict had been supplanted by a far more normalized reflex of finding fun wherever it showed up. Others were not so lucky. Brett tried to smoke his lithium on the trip back, not a pro move regardless of who was keeping the score. Scott freaked over some misdemeanor baloney and got kicked out. Vinny, well, he was a lost soul who was not destined to rest. Some of the guys from that trip, even the ones who had fun, went back out into the Life and did not make it back.

Midway into our trip, there was fearful talk of some guys on the lake with outboards and twelve-packs of Bud; drunken motorboaters from Canada. Someone said that they had yelled something untoward at the women in our group. It fell to Marion to recontextualize the situation:

"There are twenty-three of us. We are people who have been cut up, shot, beat with chains. Some of us shot dope into our eyeballs because that's where the best veins were. Nobody in their right mind is going to mess with us."

Tak was one of the client organizers on the trip. These many years later, I called him at Eden House, where he had become a counselor. I could hear the obnoxious pager in the background. It all came back to me, how we all came in and were dubbed Seekers, our names announced over the speaker for this and that. "David C. to the nurse's office." After serving as Seekers, we were brought up through a series of levels with privileges attached, all of us part of what was then called the "primary family." Really gooney stuff, but it worked for some, including me.

When Tak came in, on Valentine's Day in 1989, the house had been "on ban," or lockdown, for weeks. That meant no television, no radios, no board games, no passes, no nothing. He had a population sheet from the days when we were there. There were fifty-four men and eleven women. We quickly went through the names. Dead, in jail, back on the streets, nuthouse, and so on. About a dozen of us made it. After years of watching people come through and go back out, he had noticed some things.

Before we came in, he said, "You and I had had jobs, we had families, we had hobbies, things like that before we went off the deep end. A lot of the people we went through had none of those things. I had a guy in my office the other day who was forty years old and had never had a job. He wasn't proud of it, he just stated it as a fact. How's that guy going to make it when he leaves here?"

Still, each of us arrived with our big old tin cans clanking behind us. Tak had a massive heroin habit, and I had four treatments under my belt. We had done terrible things. I asked Tak if we were just gimped in some fundamental way, or if the drugs created a kind of temporary mania that was now behind us.

"We did what we did, and we each brought something to the table when we got involved with chemicals. Some of that stuff was not very nice," he said.

So then, those inner dope fiends were still standing at the ready, outriders on our current life?

"Sure," he said. "That's why you have to make sure that you don't turn into That Guy again."

Tak said that the time he spent after he first arrived with more senior clients demonstrated that we were not necessarily doomed to systematically screw up the rest of our lives. "You could see the guys who were about something, the ones who were picking up the cigarette butts and making sure that the place looked as good as it could. There was a kind of pride in being there, and a willingness to show others the way."

This time in treatment, either because of the stakes, the duration, or perhaps fatigue with living the Life, I was less interested in being some kind of junior counselor than in actually digging in and doing the hard work of recovery. I was, over time, a man about my business; the business of staying sober a day at a time, no matter what.

"By the time I got there, you gave me a sense of reality, a real no-bullshit attitude that went right to the core of what we were trying to do." Tak recalled. "I wasn't embarrassed to be who I was around you."

A lot of us brought in a huffy street pride, apropos of nothing. Part of breaking down that brittle facade was a mandate at Eden House that all clients went on public assistance. This meant that some of our food and lodging was paid for, and we got a check for $46 every month from what was left over. "For guys like you and me who had always managed to make our own way, who never had to rely on the state to get by, that brought some humility into the picture.

"You took me down to the line where we got general assistance," he said. At three months in, I was a so-called level 2 and allowed to take other clients out on errands. "I can remember standing in the line to fill out all those forms and talking to you about how weird it was to be going on public assistance. And you said, 'Wait until we go upstairs, and you get your picture taken, and they hand you a welfare card.'"

33

MOTHER HENNEPIN LOOKS AFTER ONE OF HER OWN

What if I had not been born in Minnesota, the land of abundant lakes, ample treatment centers, and endless forgiveness? What if I lived in a state or a country or a time—like now, for instance—where after the second or third treatment, they said, "Gosh, Mr. Carr, you seem to be having trouble getting the hang of this. Is this really a good use of the hard-earned tax money of the citizens of our state?" The state of Minnesota, along with the Feds, paid for at least three treatments, gave me general assistance while I was in the booby hatch, and, when I got custody of my children, issued me food stamps to feed them. A few years later, I got cancer, and it paid for all of that too. God bless the welfare state, God bless Minnesota, God bless the milk of human kindness.

Not a bad investment, in retrospect. Not only did the state not have to bear the burden of permanently placing the twins in foster care, but I had been a very good candidate to graduate from jail to prison, which is a very expensive proposition. As a citizen with the wheels glued back on, I have probably kicked back more than $300,000 in federal and state taxes. I'm hoping they drop a little of it on a loser like me. Insurance companies now treat rehab like a tune-up, funding a couple of weeks at most. But some are sicker than others. Redemption comes on a schedule known only to God, and as a civilized people, it's probably best to put good money after bad, hoping that the lightning eventually strikes. Am I right, or is that just me?

34

THREE-QUARTERS
OF THE WAY THERE

Call on God, but row away from the rocks.

—HUNTER S. THOMPSON

Recovery in a serious therapeutic community will harden one's resolve, freeze it like a big orange popsicle, with shiny, gleaming surfaces and nice, firm edges. But then it is time to take the popsicle for a walk out onto the hot, throbbing streets. And more times than not, the popsicle melts and leaves behind a sticky mess. I knew the syndrome and was now worried about what that sticky mess might do to my family—not the family of origins that I had tortured for decades, but this new one that I accidentally made.

So there I was in June of 1989, Chauncy Gardner just before he steps out into the world, six months of sobriety in my back pocket, on welfare, no job prospects, and pretty darned fat. Over the course of my treatment, I had watched my pal Dave. Dave was an old-school addict and drunk, and he was completely old-school in his recovery. Be accountable to self, make your own way, but do for others. He had a cartoonish, booming voice and a perpetually surprised affect. *"Really!!!!!???"* he'd exclaim in response to the tiniest thing, his massive, bushy eyebrows hula dancing as he said it. Dave made everything seem like some sort of grand caper, and his favorite metric in human affairs was whether something was "greasy." He had a finely tuned sensibility when it came to greasiness, and he saw plenty of it baked into my grand program of recovery. I decided to stick close to him.

Dave had wired up a three-quarter-way house on Oakland Avenue in South Minneapolis. Three-quarters (as opposed to halfway house) meant no hours to be kept, no minders, no ritual of morning prayer. Just a pack of addicts who found one another in weakness and formed a tribe. Use and you leave. Stiff on the rent, you're out. Simple stuff like that.

If you were going to pick a spot in which to immerse yourself in the economy of addiction, Oakland Avenue was a pretty good choice. A single step onto our crappy little patio and a shout of "Looking!" would have produced a score without getting out of your bathrobe. Crack whores walked a circuit, and there were bottle stores up and down nearby Lake Street. On some mornings when I was out early searching for work, I'd see some of my old running buddies making their way home, geeked out of their minds.

Which brings us to an odd, little-known corner of the junkie canon. When my name came up around the pipe, my former cohorts might have talked smack about me going in the booby hatch or probably suggested that I owed them money, but when the sober version of me saw them out in the world, they kept a gracious and respectful distance. No, they didn't want to join me in some circle of sober solidarity, but neither were they the crabs in the pot who sought to pull the potential escapee back into the boiling mire. They were happy that they were not me, but they were also happy that *I* was not me, at least the one they knew. Now, if I'd stepped toward them and told them that I was back in the game, that would have been fine and all—not much of a surprise, really—but a small, warm part of them would have been sad.

I had my moments when I would wobble, but then I would play it out in my mind. "Just this once" would become "just one more" and then "just a bit more," and then all would be lost, probably in the space of hours. I had no idea how Anna was really doing, but I had a notion that if I face-planted one more time, my temporarily displaced children would be lost to me forever.

Did I love them? Yeah, I loved them like someone loves puppies. They were cute, harmless, and tiny, exquisite examples of God's and nature's hand in forming perfect creatures. But were they mine? Really, really mine?

For most of my life, infants were pink little puddles that others assigned deep meaning to. I don't see myself when I see my children—I see the opposite, really. How could the likes of me have anything to do with the likes of them? But I learned to love them, even if they seemed more like remarkable beings on loan to me than my progeny.

That whole fruit-of-my-loin thing never did much for me. I've never loved my children because they were mine. I would make the perfect adoptive parent, give or take a set of character defects a mile wide. I love small people, think they are endlessly fascinating, and find questions of provenance and genealogy fundamentally uninteresting. My kids became mine through a series of overt acts, and when my patrimony was called into question later, I couldn't have cared less. It would not matter what the tests said. I knew they were mine because they became so in tiny steps across my soul.

While I was still in Eden House, the kids were returned to Anna from foster care. She had been through treatment and was working hard to stay out of trouble. Once I got out and began living in the sober house on Oakland, I'd bring them for overnights. Every sitcom cliché came alive when they visited. Here were these remarkable creatures in a house full of junkies, being passed around with hands that bore marks from injections, knife fights, and myriad bar brawls. These were hands that had hit people, mugged them, that had slid into their pockets and come away with filthy, stolen lucre.

And yet, there we all were, watching Erin and Meagan try to make their way around a blanket that had been laid out against the unknown history of the carpet. Dave was a father, and he taught me plenty about not just being a father but a man. One of the girls would produce an improbable amount of human waste, the kind of thing that merited goggles, and his huge, meaty hands—I often thought of him down the road when I watched *Shrek*—would scoop her up, and off we'd all go.

There was no plan. That whole one-day-at-a-time thing extended to all of my endeavors. When I first got out, I was busy just trying to do the next right thing. I never articulated to myself or anyone else that I would rebuild my life and eventually gain custody of the twins. Anybody who knew me, drunk or sober, would have found the notion preposterous. We kept it simple. Leave for the grocery store, actually buy some food, and then come back to cook and eat it. Go to recovery meetings and be of service. Empty ashtrays, stack chairs, make coffee.

Professionally, I was extremely small potatoes and kept it that way. Get a writing assignment from someone, work it, and turn it in on time. Everybody I worked with knew the score with me: I was fine until I wasn't. Editors broke off small pieces of work for me and then stood back to see what would happen. Good things, mostly.

Over time, life began to leak in. Dave's grand scheme about opening up a painting company actually became a viable enterprise. My stories began to take on heft and seriousness. We relaxed a little. Played poker. Went skiing. Took the girls on playdates.

Dave never let go of me. Even when I got my own place, and the girls began to grow, he came by every Sunday night so that I could go to a meeting—paying for babysitting was out of the question. He never made a big deal out of it, even after the girls caught the drift and began wailing at the top of their lungs because they realized that every time this giant lumbered into the house, I would be leaving. "Go to your meeting, we'll be fine," he'd say, peeling Meagan off my leg. When I moved into a nice house on Pillsbury Avenue in a crappy neighborhood, he bought the joint and moved in upstairs with his girlfriend Nancy. With his loud voice and massive footfalls, it was like having God as an upstairs neighbor.

While I went back into journalism, slowly, Dave stayed in the fray, working at a gigantic homeless shelter downtown, opening sober houses, and employing endless numbers of drunks and lunatics in his painting business. He married Nancy, a smart girl who knew what she was getting into and loved most all of it. His kids came floating back to him, the painting company that he formed with Tom, another Eden House graduate, prospered.

And after a long, good run, he started to get sick, his body reflecting years of hard living before he sobered up. There were other medical issues, and they began to pile up. Tom called me and said that it was probably time to come see Dave. He was in a hospice bed in a lake house he had bought with Nancy. No more booming voice, no more points of the crooked finger at greasy behavior, no more capers. He was swelled up and dying. Nancy let me be with him for some minutes. I held his hand, talked about the old days, about the pair of pants that we had shared at Eden House, about the house on Oakland. I gave his hand a squeeze and went downstairs in the house for a meeting a group of us were having in the basement. But I came back afterward and leaned down close to tell him this:

"I owe you every fucking thing in the world. You've done plenty. Now safe home."

35

HEAVY IN THE GAME

The past is at once perpetual and ephemeral.

—JONAH LEHRER, "PROUST WAS A NEUROSCIENTIST"

Scotty is or was a run-of-the-mill junkie who had star power; just something about him. He has always believed he was *this close* to joining friends who have gone on to big things: rockers, writers, comics. "Here's the thing about that. Just through sheer repetition, perseverance, doing something over and over, after awhile, everybody's got a good movie in them, everybody's got a good book in them, everybody's got a good song. Seriously. My dad used to tell me that," Scotty said. "We all got that in us."

I'd agree. Fate and circumstance, along with a willingness to punch in, is often all that separates the lucky from the luckless. Scotty was ready to talk when I saw him. While others thought that the idea of reporting one's past was odious and nonsensical, he thought it made perfect sense. Everybody should have a book about himself, right? We met at a coffee shop in South Minneapolis, his joint. He had on one of those muffin hats that is, depending on whose head it's sitting on, either very rock or totally dorky. Other than some dental work ahead of him, he looked fine.

As we sat outside, Scotty seemed to know everyone who happened by, and the camera I set up to film the interview added to the theatricality of the moment. I felt a bit like I was interviewing a veteran rock star like Iggy Pop. At every turn in the conversation, he made it clear that back in the day there was a game going on at a whole other level, one that I knew little about.

As he recalls it, we met at the CC Club, a South Minneapolis nexus of rockers, dopers, and scenesters. We had some drinks and then went across the street to where Tom the comedian was living with a bunch of other maniacs. For reasons I can't recall precisely, both underwear and pizza boxes had been affixed to the wall with very large nails. There was a card table framed by guys without shirts who probably should have kept them on. There was a lot of sweating going on, Scotty said.

"There's like two ounces of crack on the table, and you and I were kind of hitting the booze, and we thought this was pretty funny, I think, at the time."

By my version of events, he was a chipper like me who occasionally got in on some larger action, but he made it clear that he was a player. I thought I had middled the space between him and Anna, working that gap for cash and a taste.

"Between you and I? Nah, between Anna and I more so than you and I. You tried to run middle ground, but I already knew her from Kenny, you know?" he said.

The dope business, like all commercial endeavors, is built on relationships, and those alliances are brokered, commodified, and one-upped. Having someone between you and a source was not just a hassle, it was expensive. The straightest lines are the cheapest ones. The term of art for one's source is "my connection." There are many aspects to that, by the way. Wiseguys always describe each other as "connected," so there's that, but if you run with the metaphor a bit, a junkie's connection was a route to life itself. That primary relationship was nurtured; tribute, along with yesterday's dope bill, was paid.

I have since covered both politics and Hollywood, cultures where abject fealty is refined to an intricate art, but you haven't seen ass kissing until you have seen a roomful of junkies surrounding someone who has a bagful of coke. A wan little joke from someone who is holding

221

becomes an occasion for everyone to jackknife with guffaws, holding their stomachs as if they had just heard the funniest thing ever. I've been both those people before, the one with the coke slut in front of me who was doing every fan dance in her repertoire, and the one who is all damp and sparkly at the every utterance of the one with the dope. It's sickening to think of, even now.

Like a lot of veteran dopers, Scotty knew how to float and ingratiate in opportunistic ways.

"You introduced me to a whole set of crew that I would never have come in contact with had I not met you, and probably I had some ins that you would not have met had it not been for me," he said. "It wasn't like we all became friends or anything like that. You know, when you're a junkie, you're out for yourself. It's that sad, and that's the truth. It's like looking back on relationships with all of those people, you know, the drugs took priority."

Scotty understood and articulated the fundamental transaction between people with a common affliction. He mentioned how we both used Dave, the bouncer at the Uptown, as a bit of muscle to be called on when required. Big scary guy, fiercely loyal and lionhearted, someone you could unchain from the hood of the car when the need arose.

We had an alliance of convenience, but as Scotty recalled, there were some bumps along the way.

"We were at the CC Club. It was the third booth back, in the red booths. We were in the bar. It was one of those moments where I don't know where it came from. I didn't do anything to you; you were like a brother to me. I didn't understand it. You were like, 'If you ever fuck me over, I will kill you.' And you had this crazy look in your eyes. You weren't attacking me; you just put your hands around my neck, and you looked me in the eye, and it was like, 'If you ever fuck me over, I will kill you.' And I was like, 'Dude, what did I do?' I was dumbfounded. And I figured out that it was psychosis. You were psychotic at the end, and you scared me. Your addiction was frightening to me."

Scotty, who said he started doing drugs when he was eight years old, said that most of the abuse I handed out landed pretty close to home. He hinted that I was a couple fries short of a Happy Meal, a person who made a habit of punishing himself.

"Beatin' yourself up; you were all about self-abuse."

"Whatever," I said.

"Well, not 'whatever,'" he said, pulling me up short. "You were abusive to yourself. You liked that part; that's kind of sadistic. It is what it is. Right?"

Probably more masochistic, but I get the drift. His concern for me, then and now, is genuine, but then he says this: "The drug thing really fucked my life, fucked up a lot of relationships, like with Anna. We have not talked since '86 or '87. I mean, to be frank with you, Anna and I were planning on killing you at one point."

Well.

"There was a hit on you for taking the twins. She wanted me to do it, and I was like, I hate the motherfucker enough right now that it would be no sweat if I could come up and pull a Tupac on him, but I'm no killer either, right? She was pissed off to beat the band, man. It happened to me too. My daughter was taken away from me when she was eleven months old," he said.

Was she really pissed off enough to talk about killing me?

"She was venting. You'd have to ask her."

36

A LARGE UNGUIDED MISSILE

By my recollection, when the twins went into temporary foster care, I handed them to some faceless, kindly county bureaucrat. I could not recall that moment with any specificity, but it had to be freighted with tremendous sadness: besieged by unseen forces within, the father, with the gentle encouragement of his parents, admits that he is worthless and that strangers must step into the breach, pry the children from his hands, and take them to a safe, happy place.

Never happened, at least that way.

A while ago, I stopped in Edina, a suburb of Minneapolis, to see Zelda, who with her husband, Pat, had been temporary foster parents to the twins. With their own children mostly grown, Zelda was in search of something else. She saw a *Phil Donahue Show* about the need for foster parents in New York, figured there was a need in the Twin Cities, and called Catholic Charities. Erin and Meagan were two of six children they ultimately cared for. When I stopped by to see Zelda, we got so busy talking about the twins as they are now that we never talked about those months.

In retrospect, the twins and I were incredibly lucky. The girls were randomly but fortuitously assigned to two incredibly talented and committed foster parents.

I called them back in the middle of book writing because I was confused about how the handoff had occurred; the specifics of who had brought them my children. Because the twins were eventually returned to Anna and I, Catholic Charities had none of the relevant records. Zelda picked up and had Pat get on the other phone so we could all remember together. As they spoke, a memory I had lost returned to me.

They reminded me that two days before Thanksgiving in 1988, I arrived at their home with seven-month-old Erin and Meagan, my mom, and all of the clothes and stuff we could carry. I was between detox and Eden House, still using, but about to shut the door. They loved those babies from the minute they saw them. Their father? Not so much.

> ZELDA: You were very serious, very somber, and it felt kind of belligerent, like you really weren't interested, like you really didn't want to talk to us much but we were a necessary evil. This was a good place to put the girls. You were that way and—

Pat interrupted. And you were high.

> ZELDA: You were a bit disheveled.

> DAVID: So, disheveled and high.

> ZELDA: Yes.

> PAT: And you fell on the floor.

> DAVID: What?

> PAT: You just kind of lost your balance and fell on the floor, and I remember thinking that if one of the babies was there, the baby would have suffered some pretty severe injury.

> ZELDA: You wanted them perfectly taken care of. You were

very blunt. Adamant, blunt, and direct. I don't remember what you said, but you were aware enough and alert enough to want only the best for these kids, and did we meet the test, and so you did ask us direct questions.

PAT: I remember thinking, this will never work.

ZELDA: Why?

PAT: I guess maybe your mother had told us that you had been in treatment before or something, and looking at you, you were so far out of it. I just thought that this was a way of exiting the scene, the responsibility with your children. I read it all wrong.

When I got out of Eden House, we all went out to dinner at a barbecue joint. Erin and Meagan showed some of their dad's skill at putting away food and some gestural elegance with the rib bones as well.

ZELDA: The next time I saw you, you were a different man. You were so good with the girls, and you're not the kind of father that [baby-talked] to your girls. You talked to those two little girls just like they were two little people, like they were right on your level, and the three of you were doing a great job.

PAT: I was really impressed with you as a parent. Like Zelda said, you treated these little babies as adults. You conversed with them as being on the same level as you were.

They picked me up at our place on Dupont, which, truth be told, was kind of not so great.

ZELDA: Your car looked like it would hardly go. You didn't have a cleaning lady—you could tell that, the place was a bit disheveled—but you had all the stuff they needed, like their snowsuits, and you put those kids in those snowsuits like lickety-split and zipped them up, no fooling around, and it was so great to see you so capable and so competent and so efficient. Efficient, capable, 'Let's go, guys,' and they were in their suits and out the door and down the steps. You just took charge.

Probably the same snowsuits, or some other hand-me-downs. But a different guy was zipping them up.

37

MATERIAL WITNESS

For years, I beheld my children framed by guilt. Not just for what I did when they were in utero and when they were very young—my amends are in the choices I have made since then—but I felt a share of remorse about how I ended up with sole dominion over their lives. Anna has always maintained that I stole them at a weak moment in her life. And without ever saying it aloud, especially to her, I thought a case could be made. Was I a steadfast single parent or a kidnapper with a good attorney?

While I was in Eden House, Anna went to inpatient treatment and came out determined to parent not only our children but her other two as well. The twins spent three and a half months in foster care and then, with approvals from the county, were returned to the care of their mother. She was making an earnest attempt at sobriety and creating a safe, happy environment for her children.

It was clear that absent the handcuffs of addiction, Anna and I were not going to be together. While I was in Eden House, she began seeing other people, and I had started to sneak out to see Doolie, my old girlfriend. When Anna came to visit me, we got in a fight, and I gave what I remember as a playful bite on the lip on the way out. She remembers it more vividly and probably correctly as one more time—the last—that I assaulted her, and this time I was not high.

As a sober person, Anna could be incredibly competent. But she'd never had a real job, at least not for long, and so the money that went with the drug lifestyle was very important to her. Even in those first few months after she got the kids, she felt a need to keep a hand in the Life, to keep the money and the connections rolling.

I also wanted to get back to business, but my business was writing. I cut ties with all of my drug buddies, except the ones I owed money to. (At Eden House we were told to get straight with everybody on the outside—even dealers we owed money to—unless, of course, getting in touch put our sobriety or lives at risk. When I met with one guy that I owed, I told him that I was done but needed to make good with him. I can remember the dumbfounded look he gave me as I handed him a couple hundred bucks in twenties.)

But Anna really had no choice other than welfare. True, she had real friends, but in professional terms, she was a commodities trader whose product and skill was a trigger back to the old ways. I would come by on weekends in the early summer of 1989 to pick up the kids, and even though I tried to keep my eyes slightly crossed, I knew in my heart that she was dealing and probably using, if for no other reason than she had no visible means of support.

But who, really, was I to judge? I was staying sober in increments sometimes measured in hours, crawling along on bloody stumps and hoping to make it through the day. If she was using, my response was simple: "better her than me." The kids seemed OK, her ex-husband, Steve, was around to help, there was food in the house, and I was living in a three-quarter house where there was no room for anybody else on a permanent basis. Weekend visits were fine, fun even, as they cuddled up in their baby buckets for the night, but I mostly took them out to my parents and stayed there because they had cribs in the basement. It was a cobbled-together existence, but it was working.

But then, as the summer progressed, things started to look grim at Anna's house. I would arrive, Anna would be nowhere in sight, and

Steve would say nothing but roll his eyes and nod his head upstairs. I knew from experience what was going on up there, and I knew that it was my job to stay downstairs.

Other times, when I came by, Steve would be gone and Anna would be tottering around the house. She had a way of moving and talking when she was geeked, almost delicately, with a great deal of deliberation. Clothes started to pile up, and sometimes Erin and Meagan would be thirsty and wet. Anna's two other kids were at loose ends, running around, and I would open up the refrigerator and find very little. Diapers, the coin of the realm with two toddlers, became my responsibility. I brought them and small money whenever I picked up the girls. But it seemed to be turning back into the kind of mess that a pack of Pampers was not going to fix.

A normal person would have called somebody, anybody, but I felt a loyalty and a lack of judgment toward her that is difficult to explain now. The idea that anyone like me, with my history, would point a crooked finger at someone else seemed preposterous. I worked my little stories, hit my deadlines, went to recovery meetings, and came and went quickly at the house on Oliver Avenue.

Going back over journals from those days—the newly recovered tend to memorialize *everything*—I was clearly feeling my way in a new world I did not fully understand. I knew how to be The Problem, the one who had to be managed, but being cast as a grown-up—a parent, no less—was a leap I couldn't quite conjure. When I talked to Anna all these years later, she clearly believed that I had a plot to snatch those kids, but in those early months, I never actually thought those twins would be mine to look after for the long haul.

Reporting it out, I realized that you cannot steal what someone gives you hand over fist. Not because she didn't love them—she did and still does—but because she was so buried in a vortex of dysfunction that left her no choice. Journals, legal records, and interviews with people who were there demonstrate a pattern of attempts at accommodation and reconciliation on my part that were followed by disappointment and busted deals.

The twins were certainly not the problem. All of those nightmarish stories about crack babies may have tugged at the heartstrings, but I don't know how much truth they actually contained. I can say with certainty that these little babies born to addicted parents seventy-five days before their due date were prospering. Their medical records indicate that they had breathing and heart issues that resolved once they were in a postnatal environment that was somewhat healthier than the prenatal one. Meagan was fussy and needy, while Erin was reflexively happy. I called Meagan "Noodles." I'm not sure why, but it may have been a nod to her preference for pasta and a bit of an ode to a cartoon gangster on TV who went by that nickname. Erin was nicknamed "Beefaroni" because she loved her vittles, and that passion was reflected in her cheeks.

If I took those children, I took them in very small increments. I had no idea what I was doing, but children teach you how to parent them. Leave the house without an extra diaper, and they will have some brutal, smelly event at a McDonald's. Let them wheedle their way into your bed so you can get some rest, and you will be fighting them off every single night of their young lives. Gradually, slowly, the three of us developed a routine at bedtime when they stayed over, with baths, prayers, and stories—stuff I had been raised on or had seen on TV.

As we spent more time together, they began to know me, and I came to adore them—madly, deeply, truly. We developed other rituals. When it came time to actually turn off the light, I would sing a song of my own making:

> *[To the tune of nothing in particular, but very uptempo]:*
> *Oh, I've got the nicest girls in town,*
> *I've got the nicest girls in town.*
> *They are so nice, they are so sweet,*
> *I love them twice, they can't be beat.*

> *[And then a real strong Broadway finish, with every note*
> *held and punished (with apologies to Ethel Merman)]:*

231

Oh. I've. Got. The. Nicest. Girrrrrrrrrrrrrrrls.
Innnnnnnnnn.
Townnnnnnnnnnnnnnnn!!!!!!

If that sounds like some after-school special, with the fat ex-junkie dad singing to his misbegotten daughters, well, it is what it is.

————

As the summer of 1989 progressed, what had been weekends of responsibility deepened. Anna began missing the twins' medical appointments, so I took over those. And at least three times, she did not show up when it was time to pick up the kids, setting off a mad scramble to find her or find a place to put the kids while I worked at a legal paper. For two feature stories a month, I was able to rent the apartment owned by the publisher of the *Minnesota Lawyer,* and I did all the freelance writing I could get my hands on.

The unmanageability of addiction does not begin and end with the addict. All those around them begin to pivot and react to the pathology in their midst. After awhile, I came to understand just a small bit of the mayhem I had inflicted on bystanders. In October of 1989 I found a sheriff's note on Anna's door, saying that the house was being foreclosed on. She was inside, surrounded by a collage of junk, puttering around and saying that it would all work out, that she had some money coming in soon. On October 20, I stopped by to get the girls. They looked remarkably out of sorts. Anna talked absently about being short on diapers again and that Steve had said he was bringing some food over, but he had not come. In truth, he had mostly pulled out a couple of weeks before, no longer able to abide what was going on.

I mumbled something about bringing them back soon, and we went to the nearby 7-Eleven on Penn and Dowling avenues in North Minneapolis. The twins were frantic, wailing their heads off, so I could not bring them in the store. More so than most parents, I was freakish about leaving them in the car, a body memory gripping me when I stepped away even for a second. I waited until the spot right in front of the door opened up, and I went and quickly bought diapers, milk, new bottles, and some bananas.

While I changed them, they each drained a bottle of milk. And then another. They ate the bananas with an animal intensity while I stood outside the window of the car and stared at them. I decided not to bring them back, not really knowing what that meant other than the fact that I would need more clothes and more money.

On a trip back to Minneapolis in 2007, I sat outside the convenience store, which had changed names and owners many times. I stood in the snowy parking lot with the nineteen-year-old version of the twins and tried to remember if I had really thought about what I was doing. Did I sense that what seemed like a rolling tragedy was actually the beginning of a spectacular adventure? Not quite, but something about standing on that forlorn patch of tar gave me goose bumps.

38

A VERSION OF NORMAL

In my replies, I tried to console him by pointing out how hard it is for human beings to think beyond their immediate situation. It is a matter of feeling and not of reason: prone to consider the present their abiding lot, they are incapable, so to speak, of seeing round the corner—and that probably applies more to bad situations than to good ones.

—THOMAS MANN, *DOCTOR FAUSTUS*

Where do victims come from? Are they conjured by fate, manufactured by punishing circumstance, or is the hand that strikes them seemingly from out of nowhere actually their own in disguise? Anna's life has been a litany of woe. She pushed through a tough upbringing by being smart enough to see an opportunity and take it. Still, much of the rest of her life has been like a bad indie movie: a tableau of trailers, health fiascos, bad men, and busted dreams, along with the occasional pair of handcuffs. The Irish in me wanted my children to be loyal to her—she was family—but I was at a loss to explain why things always went so badly for her. I have heard enough of her version, often at very high volume on the phone, to know that I am cast as a cunning narcissist who tipped her over, took what he wanted, and kept moving. But I have been out of her life for years, and even stipulating the damage I inflicted, things still refuse to go her way.

When her house was foreclosed in November of 1989, Anna was very much at loose ends. The twins were with me, her other two children remained, but something was about to give. They too wanted to come with me when I left, not because I had been good to them—I had been in an accident with her son in the car while I was no doubt intoxicated and I was a monster for much of the time they knew me—but because even at the tender ages of five and two, they could see the trend. In the second week of November, I called her family, and they intervened, sending Anna to detox. She came out and began using. Her children were now scattered to her family and me, and she was in a house full of the detritus of her past, with a cord from a neighbor providing a little bit of electricity. The appliances had been sold. It was, as I recall, the saddest place on earth. My father, who always liked Anna and understood the mania of addiction, went with me to try to help her with her next move. She refused to go back to treatment and said that she would travel to her parents' house in Texas to regroup. It took her a week to pack up what she could carry. It was hard to watch, even for somebody like me who knew every inch of the bottom. When she left, I told her that I would send the kids along in six months after she got settled. Did I mean it? I have no idea. I didn't know what she was going to do from one day to the next, and I did not have much in the way of plans myself.

In the third week of November 1989, she and her other two kids took a long, brutal bus trip to Texas. Many years later, sitting with me outside a hotel in Arizona, she doesn't remember things any better than I do.

"I started using again; I knew I needed help," she said. "I felt like I had taken care of the kids all this time, I felt like you could help me. I never in my wildest dreams thought you would take them from me and never return them."

Me either, really. Sitting with a camera trained on the mother of my children, I feel like a voyeur, less O. J. Simpson than Kato Kaelin, a bystander at terrible events. Anna is a talker, direct in her speech, but she has correctly surmised that talking about my life will mean talking about hers. Today is ugly, not on purpose, but it is a moment defined by savage, intimate things between us, long buried. In the ten years since we had seen each other, the past came up only in bursts, a sudden screaming match when the patina of civility between us crumbled. We were two people terribly disappointed in our former selves and terribly disappointed in each other. She talked about leaving Minneapolis back then.

"I knew I needed a change, I knew I needed something. Going to my parents' house, that was not what I needed. It takes about six months for your brain to start working again. It's a six-month deal. You don't get it in two weeks, you don't get it in a month, you don't even get it in three months, you get it in six months, minimum. So I gave it my little shot, and, of course, I couldn't do it. I think I was at my mom's a month or two, and I was served with child abandonment papers, and I felt like a wounded animal."

It was actually six months later. In that time, she came back to Minneapolis in early December for a few days and saw the kids twice, for about two hours. She was in the bars drinking, which was a new and unwelcome trend. We dropped her off at the bus station, and she called a week later from Texas, saying she had been assaulted on a date. In February of 1990 she called and said she needed money to come back to Minneapolis to be with the kids. I sent some small money, but she called a week later and said her plans had changed. According to a journal I kept at the time, she called on March 2, on March 16, on April 7, on April 15—the girls' second birthday—and April 23, each time saying she was on her way back to Minnesota. It became clear that she wasn't coming back any time soon.

We made do, and the new normal set in. My family began to believe that I was actually about something, that I had finally made a commitment that I could live up to. My mother went to garage sales in the tonier suburbs, coming back with barely worn matching outfits that were very much in style. And she didn't just drop off those clothes—she came back every week to pick up laundry and leave clean clothing, organized by color and folded into daily piles for fear that, left to my own devices, I would make poor choices. My sister Lisa began providing day care for the twins at some insanely low rate as I worked more and more. Each day when I came back to pick up the girls, they were a bit more schooled in becoming young ladies. My sister Coo was the source of fun and regular dinners out. Friends would drop by without announcement, knowing we were mostly around and that the twins would always have some new trick up their sleeves.

I began consulting with a lawyer on a regular basis because at some point it became clear that what had started out as a temporary patch was settling into something more permanent. On May 11, 1990, I filed a petition with the court for temporary sole physical custody.

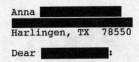

FILE COPY

St. Paul

May 22, 1990

Anna ██████████
██████████
Harlingen, TX 78550

Dear ██████████:

I am enclosing and serving upon you the Ex Parte Order signed by Judge Larson on May 11, 1990 granting temporary care, custody and control of Erin Lee Carr and Meagan Marie Carr to Petitioner, David M. Carr. The order further restrains and enjoins you from removing or causing the removal of the minor children from the jurisdiction of the Minnesota court. I am also enclosing the motion and affidavit filed with the court in support of Mr. Carr's ex parte motion.

Mr. Carr tells me that you have retained an attorney in Minnesota, however, neither Mr. Carr nor I have heard from your attorney yet. Please identify your attorney so that our future correspondence can be with your attorney.

Very truly yours,

O'NEILL, BURKE, O'NEILL, LEONARD AND O'BRIEN, LTD.

By
Barbara Saunders Lutter

BSL/bml
Encs.

237

In Anna's eyes, I was a thief, something I had never believed about myself. Through the years, she had come to believe that I stole her drugs, her money, her heart, and finally her children. If not for me and the misery I brought, she believed, everything would have turned out OK. She is not great on the details that went off in the maelstrom we created, beyond pointing out that any narrative that suggests that I was a fair and good man is a false memory.

39

LESSER EVIL

Personal myths are described by William James as a badge of fallen nature, a way of helping the self elude unspeakable truths. I have mine, and Anna had hers, and much of it would not be reconciled.

I remember being supremely confident that not only would I prevail in the matter of the ultimate custody of the twins, but that I would be an adequate and perhaps gifted father. But as a matter of history, I had not demonstrated that I had the capacity to take care of a friend's ficus plant for a week, let alone play a singular role in nurturing and raising twin baby girls. Perhaps because history has acquitted the outcome, I always believed that the legal case was open and shut.

In this formulation, when I started pursuing custody, I was just a beefier version of Mother Teresa, all selflessness and calm, and Anna was a nasty basket case. Eighteen years after the case was decided, I went to see Barbara, the attorney who helped me obtain custody of my daughters. Back then she was a junior associate at my uncle Joe's law firm in St. Paul. At the time, he was still trying to find a place to put the death of his son, Tommy, and I think it gave him comfort to know that he was helping me and mine find our way. Barbara had never been involved in a family-law case, and I was manifestly unable to pay, so we were something of a match.

Barbara is now, as irony would have it, a remarkably successful family law attorney in the suburban Twin Cities. In truth, I was there mostly to say thank you. I had spent enough time looking into the history of our little family to know that Barbara had done an amazing amount of legal work to bring our future forward and had received exactly nothing in return, save the knowledge that she had represented my interests avidly. Because I was confident in how I came to be chosen to parent Erin and Meagan, driving out to her office was a courtesy call, with not much thought to any reporting to be done.

She did not look much different from when I showed up at her office back in 1989. I quickly ran the CliffsNotes version of the case, with special emphasis on how recovery, nascent as it was, had left me qualified to take control of these girls' destiny. These many years later, Barbara hesitated when I ran that bit, and then told a different story. She began with the moment I first walked into her office.

"You were rough . . . you looked, you looked unwell," she said. "In the first place, you weighed, I bet you weighed close to three hundred pounds. It was in the winter, and you had on a very heavy coat, but it obviously didn't fit you, it was raggedy. If I had seen you on the street, I would have thought you were homeless, because you were very rough. Your hygiene was bad, your eyes were rheumy."

But even so, I was a man about my business, right?

"I wanted to help you, but I'd never seen anybody look rough; I'd never seen a client look like that," she said, looking at me to see how all of this new information was landing. "I wasn't used to having clients look like you. I didn't do criminal, I represented banks and mortgage companies, and so to have you come in and want custody of two little babies, um, I struggled with whether or not that was even a realistic goal that we should consider, because I didn't know if you were in a place physically, emotionally, or financially to provide for babies. I didn't know if you had any idea what it meant to be a parent and raise children, and it wasn't my job to have that discussion with you. I couldn't tell if you were following along well enough to understand the impact of what this would mean to your life."

Her recollection created some significant dissonance with what I had thought were indelible memories of the time, but then, she had been the one taking notes. Our every transaction and conversation had been memorialized in comprehensive form in a file she gave to me.

"I had no idea what you were using," she said, admitting that she preferred not to. "Even to this day, I don't think I ever knew." I told her that my last stop before I sobered up was shooting coke. "Oh, my good God, David."

So other than being addled from an unspeakable habit, a little smelly, and a touch on the amazingly obese side, I was good to go. Ready to star in one of those car commercials where the kids crack wise in the backseat while the dad says something sage and knowing into the rearview. Except I didn't have a car. And the kids did not belong to me. I had never married their mother or established my paternity. I had no insurance, and I had not paid taxes in several years.

Instinctively—Barbara was and is a brilliant attorney—she became my player-coach, working to help me build a life as much as build our case, even though she barely knew where to begin. She started with the health of the babies and then got into the basic blocking and tackling of raising them.

"The girls were crack babies, and I remember we were concerned that you understand fully the impact, if there was any impact on their development, and so we tried to get that checked out," she said. "And we talked about how you take care of babies. Then when the babies were finally with you, you kept extensive notes about what you did, because I was really concerned that if a judge saw you in that shape, his first impression would be similar to mine, and we wouldn't have a chance. It didn't matter what Anna looked like."

She was a lawyer in possession of a bad set of facts who made do with what she had.

"I remember asking you, 'Keep track of when you feed them and how you make the bottles and how many times you change their diapers, and when you do the laundry, and how you put them to bed, and get a routine established for your day so that there's something predictable that you can count on and get yourself into a routine with the kids.' I asked you to keep journals, do you remember that?"

Revisiting the issue with Barbara, I talked about how we managed to convince Anna to take a drug test when she finally did come back from Texas. We made visitation conditional on a clean result, and she agreed to be tested. She came up positive for cocaine and pot, a slip that we exploited. I remembered this as a clever linchpin in our legal strategy, but Barbara reminded me that Anna had failed that test over and over, that she moved in with one dope dealer when she got to town and then moved in with another. How she missed appointments to see the kids, missed court dates, switched lawyers, and eventually just gave up.

I didn't steal these children. One day I didn't bring them back, we moved in for a bit with my parents, and then I found a place. But I did not take them; they were given to me. A four-inch-thick file that Barbara gave me was full of Anna's nice tries, broken promises, and full-on face-plants.

I would drop them off for a visit with Anna, and Meagan would cut her own hair, or end up in the ER because she had stuck eyeliner in her eye, or had cuts all over her legs from using a razor in the bathroom. Anna would be sober and reasonable for a while, and then something would happen, and she would fall down.

In her affidavit at the time, Anna describes it differently. Because I had served time as a wrecking ball in her life, she felt that I was hardly entitled to pull this holier-than-thou crap in court and that she deserved custody regardless of her fitness at the time. In her filing to the court, she said I had:

1. Ruined her life. True, but it was sort of tit for tat.

2. Physically and psychologically abused her when we lived together. Dead bang true.

3. Left her when she became pregnant. False.

4. Forced her to leave for Texas by my abusive behavior. False. I was long past terrorizing her; she was doing a pretty good job of it herself.

5. Ignored the fact that she had been sober and fully employed since she moved to Texas. True to an extent, at least in terms of the ignoring part, because it was all lies.

6. Reneged on an agreement to send the children there along with child support after six months. True, but I had my reasons.

7. Ignored the fact that she called constantly when she was in Texas. Almost never, and if she did, she was geeked or drunk.

8. Used her absence to make a move on custody. True, to a point. I had the children, but no portfolio to go with that fact. And she continued to say she was coming back and never seemed to pull it off.

There is an embedded bias in the legal system toward the mother in custody matters. And once push came to shove, she decided that maybe I wasn't their actual father. Those were confusing times, after all, she said. Frankly, I couldn't have cared less—I had already decided I was their father—although there would have been profound legal consequences had it been discovered that the kids I had been taking care of did not share my genes. On June 6, 1991, a letter arrived saying the following: "Based on testing the genetic systems shown on the attached protocol, falsely accused males can be excluded in 96 percent to 99 percent of cases. The results obtained in this case do *not* exclude David Carr." The dry scientific rhetoric did not disguise the fact that most people who ended up being tested were hoping to be excluded, while I was looking for precisely the opposite result.

While I was going back through the journal entries Barbara gave me, I saw that I had been nominated for something called the National Victory Award. Each state has a nominee, someone who has overcome some difficulty, and there is a ceremony at the Kennedy Center in Washington, DC, and coffee at the White House. Although I generally loved attention, this version of it was keenly embarrassing, which may be why I never mentioned it to anyone after it happened. One of the nominees for the Victory Award had been shot, lost his sight, and sailed across the Atlantic Ocean by himself, or something really extraordinary like that. And then there was me. People at the various events for the award would politely ask me why I had been selected to represent Minnesota, and I never could think of the right thing to say. "Um, I used to stick things up my nose, and now I don't anymore, and, um, I'm raising the children that I brought into this world." We stayed at the Watergate and I journaled the trip:

fields. Housekeeping eventually brought beds, but it took forever for the girls to quiet down from their trip.

went out to cheverly in the morning after a walk on the potomac and breakfast. great to see linda and the kids. we hung out while mom and john went to some reception. Linda ansd i took the kids on a trip on the metro in the middle of the day and had a blast. got to the hotel late and kids dropped like rocks.

sunday morning we all went out to brunch in maryland and ther to a soccer game of timmy's in bowie, md. we went back to the hotel and mom watch3ed thwe kids wh8ile I covered the wellstone-boschwitz debate. John came with and we had a lovely time. I sat up most of the night and wrote the story, got up 2 and a half hours later to modem the story back to the twin cities. mom and i took the kids out for one of the most greasy deli's i have ever seen in my life. Korean guy's going "wha you want?"

went home and tried to nap. grandma took both of the kids because I hadn't slept, but after an hour she brought a wiggling meagan into me and said that I was going to have to punch in. Tired as we both were, we eventyually gave up on trying to go to sleep and punched the little mermaid into the video player. I will always rember how lovely little meagan looked framed by that huge bed, a self-satisfied smile on her face. one hour later, the same little bugger was tearing around the white house and making something just short of a scene ... she went tearing across the room laughing her head

off when it was time to get a picture taken with Mrs. Bush.

To David Carr
with best wishes, Barbara Bush

```
we left early, dropped the kids in cheverly and then john
took us out to dinner at dominiques in d.c.
then it was off to the victory awards and a lvoely party
following.

we went out and picked up the kids in cheverly the morning
following and then spent the afternoon heading back thru
cleveland to our home. meagan was wound up out of her mind.

the above few paragraphs don't even begin to describe how
wonderful the trip was, but I am still too tired to be more
descriptive
```

It was still a sweet, sweet time. My mother and I flew with the twins, and we both had suites at the Watergate Hotel. I was very excited about the trip—I went to Brooks Brothers and bought an unfortunate pink dress shirt, which I still have. The file from Barbara noted that the day before we were going to leave, Anna tried to get a judge to stop me from taking the kids out of the state. Nice.

As my attorney, Barbara had an iffy, nonpaying client and a lot of other question marks. "I guess I'm competitive enough, I wanted to win," she said, "especially since Anna didn't have a lawyer for part of the time, and I thought, 'If I can't even win a case without a lawyer on the other side, what kind of a lawyer am I?'"

It was not, however, a popular case back at headquarters. "Inside the firm, they started questioning," she recalled. "'Why are you spending all this time on David Carr? He's not paying us, this is a free case. Just put in your appearance. He's a drug addict, Barbara, this is a lost cause.'

"Your journal started out being kind of random ideas that weren't connected. There'd be no organization, no rationale from point A to point B," she said. "And over time you became a writer again. Your journal started making sense, and it would tell a story—had a beginning, a middle, and an end. The random ideas were minimal at the end. And I would say that's kind of a metaphor for what was going on in your life at that time, because you were putting your life back together too."

nov. 24

both of the girls have ear aches and it is the day after thanksgiving so we had to go to the emergency room at the University to get a bottle of pink stuff. they are really sick and we hav3e huge plans for tomorrrow, so I hope lightening strikes and they get better in a hurry,...

Meagn was sitting just off of my elbow while I worked late tonite... she ate popsicles, read books, and agreed immediately with everything I said. probably had something to do with the fact that she felt like she could be put back to bed at any moment. it was quality time. I typed and she chattered, sich as she was.

thansgiving was very spiritual. two years ago at this time, I was sitting in detox up to my armpits in a tub of Dreft to soak all the marks I had made with needles. two years ago, my kids were on their way to foster care and I was on my way to treatment. thank god and every one that the war is over .... right now, there is little money in the bank, the wolves are away from the door and life is good. This is a miraculous planet we live on and I feel like exhibit A ... not to mention the father of exhibits B and C.

bye for now.

Speaking of exhibits, after much adjudication and negotiation, the Hennepin County Court eventually decided that I was "a fit and proper person to have the permanent care, custody, and control of said minor children."

History suggests that things turned out as they should have, but Anna's suggestion that I was not the obvious choice for the twins' custodial parent found significant traction when I went back and looked at the record. I had won a tallest-midget contest with Anna, nothing more. Each of us had a history of relapse, and mine was far more extensive than hers. The lie that I told myself—that I was made entirely new by my decision to lay off drugs—kept doubt at a safe remove. If I really examined my fitness in all of its dimensions, I would have been paralyzed. I was sober, Anna was not, and therefore I was not only eligible to take custody of human souls, but qualified. It became a fairy tale that kept me alive and allowed me to make it come true. Everything good and true about my life started on the day the twins became mine.

40

CALL WAITING

MARCH 1990

ANNA: Why can't you just spend a little money to send them to me? I'm asking you, begging you, to send money so they can come see me.

DAVID: No.

ANNA: I can't fucking believe that you took those babies from me, stole my money, stole my drugs, and you don't even have the decency to send them to their mother!

JULY 2007

ANNA: I have not seen those kids in ten years. Ten years! I'm asking you, begging you, to spend a little money so that they can come see me.

DAVID: No.

ANNA: After you stole my money, ruined my business, ruined my life, really, you can't fucking find it in your heart to spend a little money to send them to me!

41

NO, THANK *YOU,* BABY JESUS

Like a lot of people fairly new to recovery, I was not one to keep my light under a bushel even though I didn't really know what I was talking about. I brayed about my new purchase on life to almost anyone who would listen. As time wore on, I began to speak in service to others. I spoke to youth detention centers, prison inmates and guards, detoxes, and in one memorable instance in 1990, to a committee of Catholic bishops. My brother John worked with them and arranged to have the bishops hear from his little brother, one of God's wayward children.

When we got together to talk at a coffee shop in Minneapolis in 2006—he was visiting from Washington, DC—he recalled that when I was using, I drove my mother crazy. "She'd say, 'I don't want him dead, but I want him hurt bad enough so he stops.'"

After I finally managed to stop, John had me speak to the bishops. He felt I carried the message very well, had an impact on the assembled, but pointed out that I was a handful afterward. "We were having lunch or whatever, and you leaned over to Cardinal Hickey and you said, 'What's it feel like to be called Your Eminence?'"

When John got home, he sent me a copy of my remarks from that day.

> *Those folks who manage to stay clean for a month are really still very sick, vulnerable people. In that sense, the unconditionally loving arms of the Church could possibly mean the difference between somebody living or dying. It was hard to avoid a spiritual dimension in my own recovery. I woke up to a miracle every day that I was clean and crawled into bed each night grateful.*
>
> *Part of the program that I am living every day requires that I take a fearless moral inventory of myself and share it with another person. The priest listened impassively as I described leaving my children parked outside the crack house on a cold winter's night. He didn't react when I talked about leaving them hungry while I took another hit. When I was finished, I was crying. I asked how I could ever be forgiven. Each sober breath you draw is an act of grace, my friend said. You are making amends every day you do not use. I found enough comfort in what he said to forgive myself . . .*
>
> *I am not a big believer in the "war on drugs." There is no war, and there are no sides. There is only addiction and the human and social consequences that go with it. The Church can do more than mitigate the gravest of those problems. In my opinion, by demonstrating a willingness to minister to those afflicted with this disease, the Church becomes better . . . The Church has the proximity and the people to make a difference in what seems like an insoluble problem.*
>
> *In today's environment, drug addicts have become almost like lepers. It seems like it is an entirely appropriate place for the Church to serve. Helping people rebuild their lives sounds like noble work to me.*

42

POWER TRIO

When a woman, any woman, has issues with substances or has kids out of wedlock, and ends up struggling as a single parent, she is identified by many names: slut, loser, welfare mom, a burden on society. Take those same circumstances and array them over a male, and he becomes a crown prince. See the lone white male doing that dad thing and, with a flick of the wrist, the mom thing too! (I found out later that regardless of that conceit, I was not Erin's and Meagan's mom. Their mom was their mom.) Why is it that the same series of overt acts becomes somehow ennobled by gender?

I'm not saying that raising children, especially by yourself, is a trip to the Caribbean, but single parenting is as old as reproduction. Families declare themselves in all sorts of versions, and ours happened to be two adorable toddlers stapled to more than two hundred pounds of large, white male. Still, people who knew our circumstance marveled at its idiosyncrasy. And people who had known me before the twins wondered all the more. My mom, who knew me best, did not doubt my intent, only my constancy.

I knew how to change a diaper. Having worked in nursing homes, I had cleaned up ancient crones, young mentally retarded kids, and surprisingly strong old men who did not like some stranger pulling down their pants. And I had good, fast hands from my days as a waiter. But what of my heart? Had years of self-seeking left it atrophied, incapable of responding to the pitter-patter of little feet? Not so, as it turns out.

Having children has an enormously simplifying effect on life. Far-ranging, drug-induced ramblings about the meaninglessness of life defined by Sisyphus on one pole and Kierkegaard on the other were replaced by a more prosaic—and ultimately more engaging—issue: Now that I have produced these children, how will I hunt and kill enough food to keep them thriving? (Other questions came along for the ride: *Is frozen corn a vegetable?* It is when I am doing the cooking. *Do those awful pink-meat hot dogs count as a serving of protein?* Here, have two. *How many times a week can you legitimately serve generic macaroni and cheese?* I say five.)

Like most single parents, I was constantly impaled on a fence between making money to meet my kids' physical needs and being present to meet their emotional ones. There was almost no work I would not do. I wrote for a state-sponsored drug policy newsletter, I did rock band profiles. I wrote a politics column for the *Reader*, I did features for the Minnesota Twins baseball program. I did a collective profile of the meanest divorce lawyers in town for the city magazine. The magazine editor, Claude, thought the first write-through was flat—he was right, I was incredibly busy and mailed it in—and called to say I could take the kill fee or try a rewrite; it made no difference to him. The stakes were high, with $700 hanging in the balance. It might as well have been $10,000. I drilled in and wrote it with all my might. Claude called back and said, "I like it. It's got people, it's got mood, it's fun and well written." I hung up the phone and dropped to my knees and wept, muttering a prayer of thanks and relief.

The God thing was weird. All the theological debate seemed at one remove, and a higher power was in our midst simply because we needed one to be there. It solves some practical issues—I had no time to come up with my own version of a creation myth, so that all-powerful God of the Catholic realms that I had been raised on came in very handy. In July of 1989, we went to St. Stephen's, a church in inner-city Minneapolis, to baptize the white-cosseted twins into a community of faith. My family, Erin's and Meagan's new godparents—my brother Jim, my sisters Missy and Coo, and my friend Chris—and the folks from the rest of my life were present for the big occasion.

We had a picnic in Powderhorn Park afterward, and I can remember standing on the hill overlooking the party, watching as Erin and Meagan were passed around like treasure. It felt glorious, like I wasn't really faking it, that I was in fact a parent and my kids belonged somewhere. The guest book from that day is full of raves about the demeanor and coiffure of the twins, including the little ribbons my mom taped to their mostly bald heads.

"A picture of loveliness," wrote my friend Nick. "And then there's the father."

If Anna was in and out of the lives of the children, Doolie came in and out of mine. The things that brought us together were still there—

intimacy and mutual attraction, a shared sense of humor—but now they had to travel across far too much rubble from the past. Doolie was happy that I was flexing my muscles as a parent, but she knew where the babies came from and what a duplicitous, violent bastard I had been. She forgave by turns but could not forget, given that Erin and Meagan were constantly entwined in our legs when we were together. There was some drama, nothing like the past, and we gradually began to go different ways.

I joined a single parenting group where I was the lone male in the room and began to develop connections in various programs of recovery. The twins were not a burden in dating matters. Precisely the opposite. Among the pieces of business I put together was a column called "Because I Said So" for my friend Marci's family newspaper. The picture that ran with it communicated innocence and decency, not generally what I featured.

BECAUSE I SAID SO . . .
Musings of a Single Father

BY DAVID CARR

Readers would look at that picture and the cloying copy that went with it and come away with a nice first impression. *Oh, he seems sweet, sitting there with those nice babies and all. Doesn't it look as if he could use some help?* I wasn't exactly working the Mr. Mom thing, but I didn't bury it, either. For one thing, anybody who dated me had to know that if there was any finishing game involved, it would be at my place. It was important to get the babysitter off the clock as fast as possible. The columns made our little upper duplex, generally a nexus of mayhem, sound like a kind of wonderland.

Take sleep—if you can get it. I still can't figure out how anybody who is home as many nights as I am gets so little shut-eye. Recently, our little trio did the hand-off for two solid weeks with that alien cold bug that has been going around. I think I slept more than four hours once. By the time I finally got sick, the girls were feeling good enough to launch a 4:30 a.m. raid. I woke up one night to the pitter-patter of little feet and then opened my eyes a crack to see one of their stuffed animals staring me right in the face. I looked down the length of my bed and there were eight more stuffed animals lined up. The twins entered the room, chattering as if it were mid-day.

"Mind telling me what's going on here," I murmured into the pillow.

"We're doing a show for you," they said cheerfully.

Men who fancy themselves players will often get a really cute, frisky dog, a warm-blooded accessory that precedes them down the sidewalk, wagging its tail and making nice. Now, I never was much of a player, but I can tell you that twin girls—friendly, sweet, adorable—make every dog seem like a pit bull by comparison. When I was out and about, the twins signaled many things about me: That I was already involved and hence not a threat. That I was in touch with my androgynous-man-woman spirit. That I was responsible enough to be let out of the house entrusted with two gorgeous little girls. Only the last part was true, and only because there was no one to ask for permission.

Our first place together was at 2612 Dupont Avenue, an upper duplex that was sort of creepy and mouse-ridden, but it was ours, giving us defendable space that was not in my parents' basement. We did not have a car that worked, and we ended up schlepping to buses on many brutally cold winter days. (To this day, living in suburban New Jersey, where a bus to New York is a way of life, I detest riding it, in part because it arcs back to a time when I had no choice.) We went through a couple of junker cars and eventually bought a rolled-over white Volvo wagon that the twins called "Beauty," not because it looked good, but because it ran. My pal Billy pounded out the dents, sold it to us on the cheap, and then made sure it kept running, one of the many not-so-random acts of kindness that helped us achieve normalcy.

I was a single parent from the time my girls were one until they were six. Whenever the subject comes up, people always wonder "how I did it." I didn't. People rooted for us, in part because of the novelty, and in part because of the stakes.

Nancy, a pal I had a long-running crush on from the days when I worked with her at the Little Prince, conjured a home for us using a black belt in thrift shopping and glue guns. When we moved into a place on Pillsbury, she found giant rugs, cool lamps, toy boxes, couches, and on and on.

My mother dressed those children and gave me constant lectures on the importance of good grooming, if not for me, then for them. She knew that if it were left to me, they would walk around in gunnysacks, and dirty ones at that.

Every Sunday I went to a meeting that I needed to go to because my friend Dave showed up, rain or shine. Even though I had stepped out on Doolie and had these girls with another woman, she was more than happy to stop by and take them off my hands for a few hours. My pal Rick from Eden House, now back in the middle of his old quasi-gangster life, always seemed to have time to drive us wherever we needed to be. Chris, their godfather, was the same way.

Fast Eddie was my ace in the hole. On a bitterly cold morning in November of 1991, my unfortunate Grand Prix threw a rod on Excelsior Boulevard near Lake Calhoun. He was there in ten minutes, bundling the twins into his warm car.

Some of the interest in us was not so sweet: A checkout lady at Rainbow Foods watched Meagan melt down over a pack of gum and prattled on about how "Daddy is having a little trouble with the babysitting." Having heard this more than once, I turned to her and said, "It's called parenting, you twit." Without fail, when one of the kids got hurt in a public place, skinning a knee, some woman would swoop in out of nowhere. More than once I had to elbow aside someone with a hiss. As far as I could tell, taking care of my children did not require ovaries.

To feel the trust and dependence of small beings is a terrible and beautiful thing. Not ennobling, precisely, but it allows anyone, even me, to access his better nature. One night I was crashing on a brutal deadline. I decided at about three in the morning that I needed to just lie still for a moment. I went to my bed in the next room and laid down, but left my feet on the floor so I would not fall asleep for the night. Dozing in that state, I heard a noise from the office: the sound of my air-conditioner being set on the floor. I sat up, and when I walked in, there was a geeked-looking crackhead halfway in the window. With the girls sleeping behind me a few rooms away, it was fight or flight. Slam the door and call the cops? Naw. Fight.

I would love to say that I advanced and kicked his face so hard that it gave him a mouthful of bloody Chiclets, but it was really more of a shove with my foot than a kick. He left.

But at some point, everyone would go away, and it would be just us. "Just us," I would say. "Just us," the twins would say.

It could be glorious, but it was also capable of being its own fresh hell. On some nights I would find myself outside the door of our apartment, saying a prayer that was really a mix of swearing and muttering. *Dear God, please know that these little girls have me on the run.*

Meagan was not a good sleeper, which meant that she would wake up Erin, which would mean that I would be up, sometimes night after night with one or the other. Absent alcohol or coke for artificial stamina, I began to wear out. Wendy, a playwright who lived downstairs from us on Dupont and loved the girls, called the cops one night because she was absolutely sure that no one with a pulse could sleep through Meagan's wailing. But there I was, in a coma born of exhaustion.

My journals from the time are filled with desperate entries that sound like they were written from a foxhole. Like a lot of newish parents, I wrote longing sonnets about sleep and often wished there was someone, anyone, to take the weight. Women often marry men in the belief that they will grow into something else. That never worked on me, drunk or sober, but these little women landed on me with profound effect.

My pal Dave the businessman, a very successful guy who adopted me in recovery, seemed to know when the cavalry was required. Our first Christmas on our own was looking a little lean. He came over, peeking around to make sure the girls were in bed, and then carried in bag after bag of presents. He and I crept around my house, stashing goodies.

Many years later I told Dave that given the amount of help we had, it was not as difficult as some of my friends and family thought. He disagreed. "You were living in a shithole," he said, taking a bite of a burger at a joint in Edina. He said I had "no money," that I was "fat, smoking, eating all the shit you shouldn't eat; you were like a time bomb. I thought to myself, This guy is just hanging on, just barely hanging on. Rarely did you smile, did you laugh—that's one of the things I remember the most. Unless you were with your girls.

"But what you didn't talk about was how hard it was for you to stay straight. You always knew that you were just one second from going right back over, but you knew your girls depended on you, and you were bound and determined to do it."

43

TYPING TOWARD BETHLEHEM

In the years since I reentered the journalism business, I have always been convinced that I got back on the horse through the kindness of others. True to a point, but only to a point. After talking with editors I worked for and with, it was clear that I mostly hacked my way back in.

"You made an assault on the profession," Erik said, sitting outside the Les Halles restaurant in Washington, where we both had turns editing the *Washington City Paper*. "It was a full-on assault. There's no other way to describe it. Your ambition and your energy and your every move were calibrated very closely. You don't look like one, but you are a climber."

At bottom, most of my success has derived from a fairly common characteristic in reporters: The most interesting thing to me is what I'm told can't be found out. When I hear that, an autodidactic impulse kicks in, and I will turn over every single rock. And because I had been in some tight corners before and had known real fear, if I found something that was true, I was happy to just write it up and deal with the fallout. No big.

In those early years back as a working reporter, I wrote media coverage that deconstructed the shortcomings of the daily paper. My political coverage was savage and ill tempered—I once said that a U.S. senator from Minnesota let "his moral compass spin like a prop on a C-130." When one of the biggest lawyers in town bilked his firm, I did forensics on his motives. I wrote stories that suggested developers were getting one over on the city, that local officials had manifest conflicts, and that the liquor industry had outsize influence.

Looking at the clips from those days, the reader does not hear my twin girls racing around in the background, or the dormant addict keening for just one more romp. The clips are all of a piece—a reporter in command of his information and revelation of same.

There was plenty of professional awkwardness to begin with when I was attempting to rehabilitate my reputation after a very public pratfall. Part of the problem with authentic recovery is that you are stuck with the same rhetorical set that you had when you were chronically relapsing. *This time, I'm really about something. No, this time. No, now, I really, really mean it. That was then, today I'm completely done with that shit. OK, I know I said it before, but once and for all, it is over.* Unless it isn't.

The addict shares the skepticism of those who behold him. Part of it is practical—you have to do the hard work of staying sober—but part of it is mystical. Guys I thought were perfectly fine, running a better show than I ever dreamed of, were the ones who jumped off a bridge, ate a shotgun, OD'd. Yeah, sure, better them than me, but shit, what if it *were* me? The defining characteristic of recovery from addiction, or any other chronic health issue, is that you are fine until you are not.

To the normal person, it can seem completely baffling. In my case, why would someone who was quick out of the gate as a writer with nothing but future piss it all away through self-seeking self-destruction? But civilians are equally bewildering to the addict. I've watched people drink a glass and a half of wine and push away the rest. What exactly is the point of that?

Regular people, people who are not drunks or addicts, will drink too much, get a horrible hangover, and decide not to do it again. And then they don't. An addict decides that there was something wrong with his technique or the ratios. *Too much coke or not enough. It was the gin; from now on, brown liquor only. And water, I forgot to drink water. Or maybe it was the lack of food. Next time I think about doing shots on an empty stomach at three in the afternoon, I'm going to order a grilled cheese. That should make a huge difference.*

Addicts are not types. They walk among us. The quiet, prim girl maintaining the computer servers who is sick a lot. The manically controlling überbitch sales manager. The meek, undermining quisling who runs the office and is up in everybody's business. The back-slapping boss who seems so happy about everything every day that it calls for just a couple of pops. Drunks all. Pill heads. Coke fiends. All flavors, all living nights full of desperation and longing, followed by fitful, mortifying mornings filled with desperate oaths to never let it happen again. But it will.

Jay, the editor of the business magazine who gave me a choice of treatment or unemployment, said the fact that I was able to work again had to do with a reputation for industriousness that may not have matched my penchant for spreading mayhem, but it was measurable.

"It's a small town, and you had a big reputation," he said. "Everyone knew what to expect, everyone knew that there were some high positives and high negatives, that there was going to be some irregularity, pushing on the deadlines, you might not get precisely what you were expecting. There would be too many words, and also it would be highly readable and that it would be engaging to anyone who is going to read it. The risk was always worth it, and people would want to read your story and see how that turned out. Beginning, middle, and end, you thought through them. You had the ability to write prodigiously, write four thousand words in a six- or seven-hour stretch."

A lot of people take the geographic cure after they sober up by engineering a move so that they don't have to hang around the same corners. If you evacuate the scene of your crimes, you don't have to beg your way back to solvency by asking for work from the same people you screwed over a scant few years before. Some different editors were in place, but much of my reentry into journalism was at the *Twin Cities Reader* and *Corporate Report*, both places where I had fallen through the ice. Leaving town was not really an option—I had an entire support group that I would have been a fool to walk away from.

At the *Reader*, I did a variety of things as a freelancer, including a cheesily dubbed column, "Politics as Usual." Given the benefit of hindsight, I was wildly wrong in some of my predictions—I said that guy named Wellstone never had a shot until it seemed like he did—but the discourse was very modern, almost bloglike, with a directness and pithiness I sort of wish I could access now. I still covered crime—one of the more important stories was about a serial rapist who had a bead on the women in Minneapolis, but the police remained clueless. I often got ahead of the dailies by simply stating what was in plain sight instead of submitting to the straitjacket of spokespeople and prepared statements and pat answers.

I called Tony, the former chief of police I bumped heads with on occasion—when I wasn't pinballing through arrest and booking a floor below him. Chief Tony had a collection of misfit cops that he took a special interest in—sometimes the more wounded the better—and I found the same soft spot back when I was using.

"You were a serious working fuckup, no question about it." He may have heard a few things about what I did when I wasn't working stories, but nothing that rose to a level requiring investigation. We had in common a high regard for cops and a low regard for the politics of butt covering. "You were tough, but you were not cynical and did not want favors. You were a tortured soul trying to get it right, and I was impressed," he said. "There was something real about you, not facile or smooth. You were always kind of a struggler, and I loved working with you."

Sometimes a professional history that had its share of tin cans clanking along behind it had its upsides. Other people who'd had a public stumble figured that someone with his own empirical knowledge concerning human frailty might be less apt to make snap judgments about others. People with complicated stories didn't mind, and in some cases sought out, someone like me who had a complicated past.

Lyle Prouse, a captain with Northwest Airlines, was a ramrod former marine who began the morning of March 8, 1990, with his usual thirty push-ups, even though he and his crew had been out drinking hard at the Speak Easy bar in Moorhead, a Minnesota town just across the border from Fargo, North Dakota. He went out to Hector International Airport in Fargo to captain a 6:00 a.m. flight to Minneapolis, and an official from the FAA was there to meet him, having received a call about some hard-drinking pilots. There were some concerns about the so-called "bottle to throttle" rules, which called for a full eight hours before anybody who had been drinking got into the cockpit. There was a series of conversations, some confusion, and while the FAA guy was on the phone, Lyle and his crew took off with fifty people on a 727 to Minneapolis. After they arrived at nine-fifteen, a blood alcohol test was administered, and Lyle's result was .128, over the legal limit for driving a car. Hello, Jay Leno punch line; good-bye, career. Lyle was sentenced to sixteen months in a federal prison.

There was a mad scramble for "the get," the big interview before he went to jail, including *Oprah* and *Geraldo*. Peter, a Minneapolis criminal defense attorney, caught the mother of all DWI cases. I knew Peter three ways: He did a lot of federal criminal work, which put him on my beat, we both drank at McCready's back in the day, and a couple of times when I got in jams, I called for free legal advice. He called me and offered me the exclusive, which I wrote up for *Corporate Report*. Instead of being a tabloidlike story about the lunatic who flew a plane drunk, it detailed a far more nuanced version of events, including the shades of gray that live in all good narratives:

> Since his arrest, Prouse has been dealing with his
> alcoholism, spending 60 days as an inpatient and

uncounted hours subsequently in various support groups. The former captain explains that, by giving an interview, he hopes to help get out the message that people can and do recover from the disease of alcoholism. He is noticeably eager to share the message of recovery, but chuckles bitterly at the suggestion that he might be on the type of "treatment high" experienced by newly recovered people who seek to let the rest of the world in on their secret.

"I certainly don't have anything to be high about," Prouse says. "For 52 years, I set very high standards for myself and the people around me, and I was lucky enough to hit most of them. Then this happened."

I went back and asked Peter why he gifted me with a huge exclusive. "You were in recovery, you knew the score, and Lyle trusted you," he explained. "It wasn't more complicated than that."

Lyle did his time without complaint or excuse, made amends, and ended up not only back in the cockpit but training other pilots.

Given my habit of going on and off the wagon as much as a stagecoach driver, people in the racket were leery of me even when I had a couple years of sobriety under my belt. I didn't blame them. When I set about climbing out of the ditch I had sailed into, I viewed any assignment as a terrible kindness, a selfless act on the part of some editor who did it instead of giving to the March of Dimes.

No editor gave me more time or more significant assignments early in recovery than Terry, the editor of *Corporate Report*. I was surprised that he gave me the time of day, let alone a two-part series on a pension fund chief who had been found shot dead down by the river with his pants around his ankles. And there was the story of Lyle, the airline pilot. I had always assumed that Terry, a skeptical man with a huge laugh, had a soft spot for me.

In August of 2006, I stopped by his St. Paul office, where he worked as a reporter for the *Star Tribune*. We walked over to the Saint Paul Hotel for lunch, and I could tell he thought the book was a stupid idea, built on the kind of self-involvement he would never truck as an editor. His soft spot was nowhere in evidence, in part, I think, because deep down, he was always amazed that I had gone a very long way with a fairly modest skill set. It was less professional jealousy than curiosity. He knew, as I did, that he was every inch the journalist I was, if not more. I can remember time and time again back in the early nineties walking into his office with flow charts of pension funds or a thick book of FAA regulations and having him stare silently at the stack for a while, chewing on a pen, and then play it back to me in a precise but casual explanation that would have taken me days or weeks to figure out.

After many years, we sat down in a booth and ordered lunch. When I got out the digital video camera, he said nothing, but you could tell from his expression that he thought it was the dumbest thing he had ever seen. As soon as I put the camera on his mug, it captured the mix of sourness and skepticism. We got started when I made some awkward reference to his kindness in working with me at a time when others were not exactly lining up. He said it was not like that at all.

"Um, no, in fact, there was probably a lack of charity in it. I didn't know you, and I had a pretty negative view. I think some people got really caught up in the romanticism of it. There was just a kind of a Hunter S. Thompson view of you, kind of romantic, and I had sort of the opposite view. You bowl a lot of people over with your charisma, I think, and me being the sunny, dramatic person that I am, I never listened."

He reminded me that he first started working with me because I happened to be attached to a big, fat exclusive about Lyle the pilot.

"It was exciting to think about. I can remember pitching it to our publisher, and I was fairly new at the job. I didn't just want us to be a business magazine. I wanted us to be a great magazine, and of course I was just thinking the biggest possible things, and then the biggest possible thing sort of landed in front of me.

"It's a national exclusive, so first of all, it's attractive right there," he said. And the guy who brought it in? "Maybe I was too egotistical to think about the possible repercussions or the difficulties of a big story, that you went out and got it, but maybe you're not in game shape yet."

Then again, he said, it wasn't like I had been "lying around in a bunk bed eating Cheetos or anything like that. You were back working, and you had a reputation for doing and getting big stories. It wasn't as if you were a fabricator or some ridiculous thing like that. It would be a great story if I said I was somehow helping you to get back in the game, but that would be ridiculously egotistical and untrue. It was much more pragmatic than that, I think."

He said that I prospered because people liked to tell me things. As he talked about those days, which were heady ones for both of us, I think that some of the excitement came back to him about the fact that the little business magazine in the Midwest was going to break a huge story. Like a lot of good editors, Terry has a way of talking about the business that makes clichés ring true.

"There's a passion, there's a knowing," he said, eyeing his food as it got cold. "In a way, you almost have to know how to be a journalist before you commit to being one." He paused, putting two large hands flat on the table. "If you find out something you can do well, I don't care if it's whittling wood, or fixing a car, or writing a lead, if you find out you're good at being a reporter, you just want that over and over again. You want that reinforcement, you want that feeling. *I know what I'm doing*. It feels good to know what you're doing. A lot of people walking around don't know what they're doing, in anything. In any way. And this is something that is pretty easily measured. Did I win today?"

Terry won a lot and helped a bunch of others, including me, take a few victory laps. It was a privilege to listen to him ruminate about this thing of ours, all the more so because he dropped dead unexpectedly a month to the day after we talked. He was forty-seven, and not only one of the good ones but one of the best.

Journalism may involve typing, but excellence is dependent on the respect and trust of others. People have to be inclined to tell you things, but those relationships aren't made over a drink after work or a quick lunch. Sources are built one story at a time. They tell you stuff, you report it out, you write it up, you get it right. On to the next—and sometimes bigger—story.

One of my best long-term political sources was Brian, a gay former activist who became a highly effective Minneapolis City Council member. Some saw him as preening and self-regarding, but he was a consistent voice for downtrodden folk who did not get a lot of play downtown. He was a master of playing the press to his own ends, and I was one of the violins that he picked up when it served his or his constituents' purposes.

In January of 1991, I was pretty much back in the swing, and I got a call from Brian, summoning me to his office. Most of the time, talking with Brian was like spending time with a particularly large, handsome Siamese cat. He would narrow his eyes and think of something delicious he was about to share, all but licking his paws at the thought. I have no record of the following conversation, but Brian asked me if I was comfortable with keeping a secret. I was. He said this was a very big secret. I told him not to make me say it twice.

"I have AIDS," he said. Ever the conductor, Brian wanted to roll out the story in his own way and on his own schedule. We/he decided that *Minnesota Monthly*, a literate local monthly that was owned by public radio, would be the right place to drop the bomb. We diagrammed the sourcing, the reporting, and a black-box agreement with the editor there.

The day the story dropped, at the end of April, we had copies delivered to all of the local television stations just before the six o'clock news, all but forcing the anchors to read right out of the magazine.

"Our story," as Brian would call it at the time, was all about living with AIDS, but that's not how it turned out for him and many other people who were diagnosed back then. Sometime at the beginning of the summer, I put down the notebook and became part of Brian's care team. The whole journalism thing lost salience, and I accessed skills I had learned from working as an orderly.

Brian headed toward that last door regally, a pasha surrounded by his beloved Oriental collectibles and a care group peopled by family and friends. There was something appalling about what was under way, but he brought his own catty humor to the matter at hand. I drew night duty one week, which meant sleeping near the hospital bed he had installed in his living room. I woke up in the middle of the night and heard nothing. No coughing, no stirring, no nothing.

I crept up to his bed in the darkness, terrified by the silence, and leaned in very close. Very. Close. A bored voice broke the silence:

"I'm still breathing, David. Go back to sleep."

Brian died that August.

44

CALL US BACK WHEN PIGS FLY

Fresh off some fairly well-received exclusives, I thought I could buy me and mine a bit of security by getting a real job, perhaps at the *Minneapolis Star Tribune*.

425 Portland Avenue
Minneapolis, Minnesota 55488

Star Tribune
MINNEAPOLIS / ST. PAUL

March 27, 1991

David Carr, Minnesota Lawyer
123 N. 3rd St.
Minneapolis, MN 55401

Dear David Carr,

Thank you for sending your clips. We don't have any appropriate openings right now and don't anticipate any in the near future.

You do appear to be a good, solid journalist and I would like you to keep in touch.

Yours,

Linda Picone
Deputy Managing Editor

LP/aks

45

WARD CLEAVER'S LITTLE PROBLEM

Heart and head are the constituent parts of character; temperament has almost nothing to do with it, and, therefore, character is dependent upon education, and is susceptible of being corrected and improved.

—GIACOMO CASANOVA

Erin and Meagan grew up with a broad understanding of what "normal" was supposed to be. They knew from spending time around both their mom and me that there were all sorts of approaches to making your way in this world. They didn't judge our lack of money, in part because they never wanted for much. My friends were gay and straight, black and white, lawyers and junkies, filthy rich and dirt poor. We might spend an afternoon swimming at a pal's mansion and then on the way home stop off to see a buddy who worked in a homeless shelter. It was less about some crunchy, encompassing notion of all God's children than a measure of my fairly textured life.

One of my favorite pictures was taken when the girls were about four. We were at Loring Park in Minneapolis on a Monday night for movies and music. I don't remember what the movie was, but the band The Wallets played, and my kids cruised the crowd and profiled like the scenesters they were. They were confident young ladies, pretty and very much together.

Much is visible in that picture. Erin's bear hug on her sister and the world continues to this day, and Meagan's attempt to please both me and the camera with an outsize smile in spite of the fact that she is being choked a bit reflects her principal engagement with life. There was nothing pitiful or weird about us. And they heard from their mom often enough to know that she loved them as well.

Around that same time, I bumped into Barb, my first treatment counselor at Parkview. I went through Parkview twice in the mid-eighties, first as an inpatient and then as an outpatient. She had my number the whole time I was her client, and knew who I was—probably better than I did at the time. Barb was very touchy-feely with a lot of her clients, but she always hopped around on one foot near me because the other was up my ass. She frequently suggested that I was (a) full of shit, (b) often unwilling to do the hard work of recovery, (c) a manipulative, deceitful person around women, and (d) a decent man under all of the arrogance and defensiveness.

We had a nice lunch in 1991 at Lawry's, a restaurant in South Minneapolis, and I bragged about how splendidly things had turned out, how my life of duplicity and corruption was finally behind me. She listened acutely, smiled, and congratulated me on my good fortune. Then she gave me a business card from her private practice, saying I could call if things ever got bumpy.

As I recall, I phoned her the next week.

I called because underneath the whole Ward Cleaver/punk-rock dad thing, I was still hanging on to a part of my former self. I had maintained ongoing relationships with some of the darker women I knew out on the street, none of whom had anything to do with the kind of loving, sober bonds I was supposed to be developing. Sexually, I was still a perpetrator, with late-night visits from women I only had sex with and sometimes gave money to, in part because I no longer had pockets full of drugs. Some of them were party girls just trying to get from one high to the next, and others were working girls I had known.

The low point came when I was driving down Lake Street near my house on Pillsbury one night when the twins were away at my mother's, and I saw Rita, a girl I knew from the old days. She waved, and I stopped. When she got in the car, it quickly became clear that her jaw had been wired shut after it had been shattered by a beat-down from her pimp. I asked what in the world she could be doing for johns on the street in that condition. Rita offered to show me, and my stomach lurched. I gave her some money instead and dropped her off a ways down Lake Street.

For all appearances, I was dating normal women—women I knew in meetings, women I met doing this and that—but I still was leading a double life, using women who had already been knocked around plenty. I was allegedly raising my daughters to be nobody's object, yet I was willing to objectify and use someone else's daughter. For all the real things I was accomplishing in terms of family and business life, the perpetrator within me, the addict trying to get over, was still drawing quiet breath. And that feeling of being a fraud is a toxic, slippery way to go, one that endangered everything else. I showed up at Barb's office and told her that I wanted to be the man I pretended to be.

"Then quit pretending," she said. Week by week, appointment by appointment, she helped me integrate being a man, a father, and a human, which was all very complicated business for somebody who'd lived as I had.

Fifteen years later, I was again sitting across from Barb, this time on a patio in South Minneapolis. She'd had her own share of travail, but looked great and was still the same alloy of steel and empathy that I had so admired.

In order to get through a lot of the reporting, I had adopted a sort of clinical tone when I interviewed people, even those whom I'd hurt or maimed or loved. But this was different. The custody of the conversation reversed almost immediately. Not only was I revisiting behavior that anyone, even me, would find revolting, but I was doing it with someone who knew every inch of me, the history, the good and the odious. Barb was glad to see me, but none of the apparatus of reporting—the video camera, the tape recorder, the notepad—put me at a safe remove. Part of it was her clinical expertise. She was a licensed social worker, not some multidegreed nutcracker MD, and had ferocious instincts where I was concerned.

More to the point, I was twitchy because I was talking with Barb about stuff that happened when I was stone-cold sober, when everyone around me was marveling at the turnaround in my life. The question of whether chemicals induced behavior or revealed character seemed to hang a little too close for comfort when I was sitting on that patio with Barb.

Back when I was her client at both Parkview and in her private practice, she had watched me work the recovery stations of the cross: the defiant first-time treatment dude, the repentant relapser, and then the fully sober guy who was still capable of virulent pathology that had nothing to do with chemicals.

"You were kind of hard nosed," she recalled from treating me as an inpatient at Parkview. "I don't remember you needing the Kleenex that much." Years later, when I saw her in her private practice, the Kleenex, big fistfuls of it, came in handy. "You would never have stood for some-one else treating your daughters the way you treated women." She fixed me with a gaze that was freaky in its knowingness. "Never."

She made it very clear that she thought I was sexualizing the atmo-sphere of the home—that even if the twins didn't know precisely what was going on, they knew something was wrong. "You had to make the changes at home with your girls if you wanted them to be little girls and have a respectable dad," she said, suggesting that a jerk who would hook up with women in meretricious ways could not be the same guy who tucked in his babies with a story and a prayer.

"That was part of who you were and what you brought into that home to your girls," she said, still holding my gaze. "Sometimes you even brought the women themselves home, and because the girls were asleep, or they were off for the weekend with their mom or whatever, you told yourself that it didn't hurt them. What I wanted to help you see was, they're going to be affected by this because this is part of you."

She said that I presented some therapeutic challenges.

"We all need boundaries, but yours, um, were tough. For some people, I think you would have been hard to crack because you had that street sense about you. But there was also that other side of you that could be a parent of two little girls who otherwise wouldn't have had a parent. You're very duplicitous in that sense; it was kind of in and out, in and out. There was this hard-core addict part of you, but there was also this really genuine, nice guy, fun guy, intelligent guy— what the hell is he doing here? It was just back and forth, and I would kind of go, 'What happened to you that you're wrecking your life with this?' Because I just thought, Man, this is just nuts. You could have it all."

Eventually the street and the women who were part of that life became part of a past that I could no longer visit, even as a tourist. Like my friend Tak, the former client and now counselor at Eden House, told me, when you come in from the street, from the game, some of those slimy, loathsome reflexes come with you.

"You played games with everybody," Barb said. "There's that side of

275

you that—I don't know . . . you lie or you put on kind of that, oh, arrogance is the only word I can think of that fits."

Beyond her expertise, part of her effectiveness had to do with gender. It took a woman to explain to me that you couldn't compartmentalize life—be Ward Cleaver one day and some street version of Casanova the next. I had to learn to be a man, no pretending involved.

46

STILL LIFE WITH ALIEN

And here might be the moment to squirt one perfect tear, all bit-
tersweet and shimmering with dreamy resignation. Except that
as the serpent once sunned its coils in Eden, patiently awaiting
the opportunity to let the biggest cat in eternity out of the sturdi-
est bag, so a pack of Camel cigarettes stands in these wings,
waiting to come on and do its most unexpected stuff.

—TOM ROBBINS, *STILL LIFE WITH WOODPECKER*

Cancer is the alien among us. One day you are just ambling along
when a little spaceship lands somewhere in your body, and you
are abducted from within.

I had the odd experience of self-diagnosing the invasion. Late in
November of 1991, I was rushing out the front door of our house on
Pillsbury. There had been some melting and refreezing, and a gutter
over the front steps was broken. When I hit the bottom step, my right
leg folded back underneath me. It hurt so much that I threw up. I slid
back up the steps on my butt and rang the bell, and the sitter who was
watching the girls called an ambulance. I had pretty much shredded the
meniscus in my right knee. It was surgically removed on November 21,
leaving me on crutches with twin two-and-a-half-year-olds. It was pathetic, and about to get more so.

On the night of December 8, 1991, I noticed that a couple of
weeks on crutches had built up my neck muscles on the left side.
Like, remarkably. The next morning, I got up to make sure I wasn't

crazy, and when I looked in the mirror, it was noticeably bigger. Overnight.

Lemme see, uncontrolled growth right over my lymph nodes. Gosh, I think I got a little touch of cancer here.

I wheeled the twins out the door, and we went to CUCH clinic, a low-cost public health clinic affiliated with the University of Minnesota. Soon after I was examined, a bunch of other doctors and medical students came streaming in for a look at the giant tumor on the left side of my neck. *Son of a bitch.*

The twins were sitting together on a single chair, happy they weren't the ones being poked and prodded, but looking up in wonder at the number of doctors filling the room. I was referred to the University of Minnesota for a biopsy, but I already knew that things were not going my way.

I had Hodgkin's lymphoma, a cancer of the immune system, and a "good" cancer if it is your turn. Curable if found in its early stages—and we were in pretty early days in spite of the tumor's impressive growth. Now all the doctors had to do was go most of the way toward killing me in order to save my life.

I tend to keep my mouth shut when the subject of my cancer comes up. It came and went, nothing to see here, keep moving. But after spending time with my massive medical file and reading a story I wrote later for the *Twin Cities Reader*, it is clear that my time with the alien left me marked. My own private Area 51.

From the time I was little, I loved watching movies about aliens. Years after I saw the 1951 classic *The Day the Earth Stood Still*, my dreams were filled with steel-noggined guys who spoke in detached, tinny voices as they ordered the world to submit. The aliens at hand were different. They were in me, after me, creating a self that I could not quite recognize, with an intimacy that made them infinitely more confounding and scary.

During the time of occupation, I answered my phone with excessive cheerfulness, wrote reassuring notes to old girlfriends, and smiled knowingly whenever someone in a white coat revealed something sharp in his or her hands. I put my fingers in my ears and hummed tunelessly until someone told me the aliens were gone.

The flat, routine call from the surgeon confirming the bad news was an anticlimax. I asked him how bad the bad news was. "Well, it certainly is not a good thing," he said, getting in touch with his inner Martha Stewart. I hung up the phone and went in and looked at the girls, asleep already, and then went and looked in the mirror. I saw myself going away. Not dying, but not present.

I kept waiting for someone else to panic, but the doctors and nurses went about their business with remarkable calm. From the outset, I mimicked the detachment surrounding me. My general penchant for blind aggression in almost all matters receded, and the medical records from the time noted my plucky mien. I was described over and over in the medical record as a "gentleman," a term that did not land in my neighborhood a lot.

There is something embarrassing about having cancer, as if I had woken in the night and found someone I did not know touching me. Once the diagnosis was clear, I broke up with a girl I had been seeing— a smart, pretty girl I'd known in recovery—because I could not bear to have someone I knew casually watch me while I was under attack. Others were abashed by the diagnosis, preferring to refer euphemistically to the disease of cancer. There was enough avoidance in all that concern that I began to think I had a case of "It," instead of cancer. *How is It going? Did they get all of It? What's Its status?* Oh, do you mean this giant cancerous tumor on my neck that is tipping my head over? "It" seems to be doing fine. The host is a little freaked out, though.

I had many thoughts about what a juicy target I presented, the equivalent of the big-chested blond with suspect morals in the monster movie, the one who's got to be got. With a long, venal history of cigarettes, narcotics, and Pop-Tarts, having "It" should not have come as a surprise. But Hodgkin's is more random than that. It is a kind of malignant infection, an uncontrolled proliferation that lays siege to otherwise healthy people, regardless of their history. My suspicions came to rest on my old microwave. It had been a fixture in my parents' home for many years, an ancient appliance of doubtful structural integrity that throbbed and buzzed with radiant energy when I used it to make popcorn. Maybe, I thought, my microwave leaked cancer into my life.

Even though I had very little money and no insurance, I received excellent care—that Minnesota thing again—as I made my way from waiting room to waiting room. The guy who ran my case was an eminent hematologist named Greg, a man possessed of social skills rarely seen in his profession. We found ourselves cast in a 1960s-era television medical drama. He'd say things like, "We're going to beat this thing, David," and I suppressed a shameful urge to giggle, instead giving him the dude nod, full of resolve and confidence.

Some of the diagnostic work was misdemeanor—CAT scans, MRIs juiced with the injection of contrast dye—and some of it was appallingly aggressive, even though they called it the most "conservative" approach. In order to avoid chemotherapy, first they had to make sure the cancer had not spread.

I was a lucky guy in the context of some of those waiting rooms. Over the course of my treatment, I sat next to an eight-year-old girl who was being burned within an inch of her life by full-body radiation and a friendly dairy farmer from Luverne who had a steel hoop screwed into his skull so that they could pinpoint the tumor during radiation treatments. They may have smiled—humans generally respond to the absurd with some display of humor to make those around them feel better—but theirs were horrible battles, full of desperate measures and, often, disappointment.

I had enough medical history to be something of a connoisseur, and I preferred competence and directness. The guy who did my bone marrow biopsy had little of either. Bone doesn't anesthetize well, but has a surprising number of nerves. The doctor was nervously furtive and kept slipping off the pelvic bone he was attempting to perforate. He made grunting noises, and I even heard him quietly swear once, but he said nothing to me until he asked me to shift positions so he could get a more direct angle. "You might experience a bit of sharpness here," he said. He slipped again, driving the huge biopsy needle deep into soft tissue. Seeking to calm his nerves and steady his hand, I cracked wise: "Sharpness, huh? Where did you intern, Dachau?" He said nothing.

After the diagnosis, all the news was good, with nothing indicating that the alien was on the march. Dr. Greg recommended that we do a staging laparotomy, which involved making a midline incision in my abdomen, removing my spleen and squeezing it for evidence of cancer, and then taking out some lymph nodes and small chunks of my other major organs for further inquiry. I told Dr. Greg that it sounded a lot like something I had done to a frog in my high school biology class. The frog had been *dead* while I did all those things to it. "Yeah, well, it's a little like that," he said, but added that he thought it was the most prudent course of action.

People around me, some of whom I did not know very well, came alive with opinions. Wheatgrass, they'd say with surety. Vitamin C, others would say. Had I thought about yoga? No, I thought about cancer. I was all for sending in a fully armed medical landing party that would lay waste to anything it found. I was, after all, the one with cancer, and if they thought that burning sage and meditating would do the trick, they could give it a whirl when *their* turn came.

My parents were heartbroken and scared. They had watched me flop around for years, and finally, when I managed a bit of stability, it was DefCon 4 again. I can remember riding in the back of their car on the way to the staging laparotomy the day after Christmas. I don't remember who watched the twins that day and in the days that followed while I was hospitalized, but I thought of them constantly.

A half hour before the surgery to remove my spleen, a doctor whom I had not met came into the room and introduced himself as an oral surgeon. He and his "team" had determined that my mouth was going to be subjected to a great deal of radiation because the cancerous node was high in my neck. The team had decided to take out all of my molars as a preventive measure against radiation cavities and ensuing necrosis of the jaw. My parents merely nodded their assent to his brimming authority, but sitting in my surgical gown, I was loath to make a major life decision without my pants on.

I gathered my thoughts enough to tell the doctor, whose name I never knew, that his timing was poor and that on that particular day, I was willing only to donate my spleen. Without looking up from his chart, he indicated that I was going to dearly regret my decision and sent in a nurse to show me pictures of people whose faces had fallen off after necrosis of the jaw had set in. I remained steadfast, telling him I thought I had plenty on my plate. He smiled quietly and said, "I'm pretty familiar with the procedure you're going through today, and, believe me, you are not going to even notice that your teeth are gone."

My, thanks for that. I told him we were finished for the day. When my surgeon came in, I told him that if that doctor was in the operating room, I was going to get up off the table and leave.

Even three days after the operation, when I was short a spleen and immunocompromised, the oral surgeon was still after my teeth. I found out he was a visiting resident, and it gradually dawned on me that he had some kind of gap in his résumé he was trying to fill. I finally threw such a fit that the chief of residents came to talk to me. He flipped through my chart and said, "We don't want your teeth."

Good, I said, "howzzabout telling Dr. Joseph Mengele here?" I think of that asshole every time I order steak.

Treatment regimens for cancer are full of painful realities and powerful ironies: Radiation can cause cancer and wipe it out. Toxins in the body can create an opening for cancer as well as be used to shut the door against it. In order to fight cancer, you have to sit very still. A conservative approach required tactical aggression. It was, and still is, confusing. In that long clinical narrative, I am meat—diseased, if not condemned, meat. The meat is called "the patient." Patient is as patient does, sitting oh-so-still, waiting with hands folded and eyes gently closed, waiting for someone to blow a whistle and say that the patient is fine.

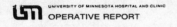

OPERATIVE REPORT

Name: CARR, DAVID
UH#   135-46-01-7
OR Date: 12/26/91   IP

/dm3603267

John Raines, M.D.
CUHCC
2000 Bloomington Avenue South
Minneapolis, MN 55404

OPERATIVE SITE: Main Operating Room Suite.

PREOPERATIVE STATUS & DIAGNOSIS: This thirty-five year old man recently
developed a mass in the left neck. I did a biopsy under local anesthesia and it
showed nodular sclerosing Hodgkins disease.

Dr. Vercellotti in the Hematology Section carried out an extensive workup
including abdominal CT, chest CT, and bone marrow biopsies, all of which proved
to be within normal limits, showed no evidence of Hodgkins disease.

After some deliberation, the Hematology Service recommended that the patient
be subjected to staging laparotomy. He clinically is Stage I-A and the use of
radiation versus chemotherapy was contingent upon establishing the status of the
abdomen.

NAME OF OPERATION:
1.   SPLENECTOMY
2.   MULTIPLE LIVER BIOPSIES
3.   MULTIPLE RETROPERITONEAL LYMPH NODE BIOPSIES.

ANESTHESIA: General.

OPERATIVE PROCEDURE: Under general anesthesia, the abdomen was prepared
with Betadine and draped. A midline incision was made from xiphoid to about two
inches below the umbilicus. Manual exploration of the abdomen revealed no
palpable abnormalities. The spleen was questionably generous in size. There were
a number of unusual adhesions of omentum to abdominal wall in the left upper
quadrant which had to be taken down before the spleen was exposed. We then
proceeded to clamp, divide and ligate the short gastric vessels. Then, we placed a
single tie around the main splenic artery and tied it. The spleen was then
mobilized up out of the retroperitoneum. Hilar vessels were then individually
clamped, divided and ligated. The spleen was not grossly abnormal. It was sent to
Pathology for permanent sectioning. After securing hemostasis over the bed of
the spleen, we then proceeded to carry out a wedge biopsy of the left lobe of the
liver, followed by the needle biopsy of the left lobe and another one of the right
lobe of the liver. The next step was to open the lesser omentum and expose the
retroperitoneal tissue lying just above the pancreas near the celiac axis. Here we
encountered a matt of normal looking nodes. We were unable to dissect out a
discrete node, but did obtain some fragments of nodal tissue from this celiac
lymphatic plexus. We then exposed the first portion of the jejunum and mobilized

the ligament of Treitz's so as to get into the retroperitoneum behind the
duodenum next to the aorta. There was a firm 1.5 centimeter node which was
probably within normal limits, but was certainly easily palpable. This was
dissected out and sent to Pathology for permanent sectioning. We then exposed
the right iliac by opening the retroperitoneum there and sent out some nodal and
peri-iliac soft tissue. The same procedure was carried out on the left side,
although we were less certain of a definite node. We carefully palpated up and
down the iliacs in the retroperitoneum and could identify no enlarged or suspicious
nodes. The external iliac was palpated through the intact peritoneum and again no
significant adenopathy could be palpated. The small bowel was then run and no
lesions identified. One mesenteric node from the jejunal mesentery was excised
and sent to Pathology. The abdomen was then closed using interrupted #1 Ticrons
on the fascia and a subcuticular stitch of 4-0 Dexon to approximate the skin
edges. The latter was supplemented with Steri-strips.

COMPLICATIONS: None.

JOHN P. DELANEY, M.D. (00/18)
LUIS SANTAMARINA, M.D.
ANDERS ULLAND, M.D.

JPD/70
D: 12/26/91
T: 12/26/91

cc: Gregory Vercellotti, M.D./UMHC

The ticktock of medical jargon in the record vibrates with subtext.

"The patient has no complaints."

Oh, but he does. They are legion and festering, and cannot be resolved by mumbled words of reassurance.

"The patient tolerated the procedure well and [was] taken to the recovery room in satisfactory condition."

As I remember, the patient felt as if he had been cleaved in half, and when he woke up in the recovery room, he took stock of his physical state and began vomiting, pulling hard at his newly installed stitches.

"The patient has had his spleen removed in the interval since the last examination."

Just like that? My spleen, what with all of the venting and expressing I have done throughout my life, would seem to have been a critically adaptive organ. You'd think the loss would be acknowledged with a little more than a lifetime of prophylactic antibiotics. How about a little sweet with the bitter, for mercy's sake?

"The patient continues to do well and is in complete remission of his Hodgkin's disease."

That's more like it. After having my life medicalized for months on end, I left on a dead run. Once the medical Borg has a fix on your coordinates, it can lock and load in a heartbeat. I have been back to many hospitals, many doctors, many waiting rooms, not because the cancer came back but because I once was cured of it.

Certainly the physical expression is still with me. I have no jowls—they were seared off during radiation—and I have a swanlike neck, although pocked by scars from all of the biopsies, both to see if the cancer was there in the first place and then to see if it came back. And when I go swimming, the people around me must wonder if I lost a really bad knife fight. I have what looks like the footprint of a machete in my abdomen: a thick, ropy scar that drops from my chest cavity down to, well, just below the belt buckle. There's a little jog around my belly button, lending it a bit of drama. Many hands have been inside there messing around, and I have no illusion that they won't be back.

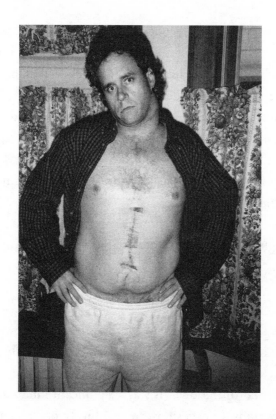

Cancer's ubiquity means that I, like everyone else, have lost many familiars, including my mother, to the alien. I could default to recovery speak—better them than me—but these many years later, I still feel very much at risk. Not clinically, but psychically. Even though I never talk about it much, having cancer scared the shit out of me. It kept seeming to come back, even when it didn't. I had forgotten about that part until I got the records and reviewed them from this distance. My neck kept getting big again, and at least one time, my doctor thought he felt an enlarged node under my arm. After stiff-upper-lipping it for six months of treatment—I didn't weep, except in the dead of night, when I wondered about bringing any more bad news to Meagan and Erin—the suggestion that the cancer was back caused a shutdown, a "vasovagal episode," as it was called. That means I fainted, not that I went all girly-man. It was, as they say, a false positive. I'm fine now.

But different. When life is good, which it often is, I always tell my children that "things will not always be thus." Peddling through files, buried beneath all of the clinicalspeak, it's clear that having cancer wounded me in a way that addiction never did. With addiction, I could look in the mirror and say, yes, the affliction nearly killed me and will finish the job if I am not vigilant. Cancer keeps its own appointment schedule. Your body belongs to you one day, and the next it becomes the host. That mystical power, its very ineffability, gives cancer traction on the soul that never goes away.

Sometimes when I sleep, I hear beeping, like the noise a medical apparatus might make, or the sound of a very tiny spaceship coming in for a landing.

———

I came home from the hospital with a one-foot gash down my abdomen. Doolie and I were seeing each other only occasionally at the time, but out of pity she came over and ever so gently made sure that all of the rest of me was operational. It was a significant kindness, especially because my wounds were, gosh, weeping a bit. (Not to get ahead of the story, but this "conservative" approach, meant to avoid the complications of chemo, began a surgical odyssey for me, with ventral hernia repair, surgery to repair surgical scars (which is sort of counterintuitive, when you think about it), acute necrotizing pancreatitis, gallbladder removal, and so on. If they were planning on using me as an ATM, I wish they had installed a hinge to start with rather than slicing their way in every time.)

I never came close to dying, but for the first month of my treatment, I looked like I might. In those thirty days I had a neck biopsy, a bone marrow biopsy, major abdominal surgery, and thousands of rads of radiation. I woke up in fistfuls of hair, and my ears, neck, and the inside of my throat got burned, but it seemed like a fair trade. I would lie there getting irradiated, and a mechanical voice would keep repeating instructions from a small speaker. "Hold your breath." "Relax." I spent a lot of time staring up at a tropical poster on the ceiling, taking in the Zen rhythm of the machine. (That poster may explain why I had an odd urge to go to Nicaragua when I finished my treatment, but I can't be sure. It was a good trip.)

I went from a fat, vaguely thuggish guy with a fresh, heinous scar to an almost beatific, skinny soul. Every time I caught my reflection, either in a mirror or in the face of a friend, I averted my eyes.

One night my friend Mary, a pal from the church we attended, was over at our house on Pillsbury making dinner for the twins. I was resting on the couch in the living room and listening to the music of Mary chattering to Erin and Meagan as she cooked. Without warning, a glass light fixture on the ceiling came loose, bonked Mary on the head, shattered, and sliced her forearm open. It turned out that the tenants upstairs had left the water running and the flood it had created weakened the ceiling. The fixture came down along with a rain that seemed almost biblical. As I helped her stanch the blood from the gaping wound, I thought, "This place is the fucking temple of doom. Nobody else in or out. Just us."

The girls and I developed a routine. Meagan, who was an almost pathological caretaker by disposition, began to take over all sorts of responsibilities as the girls edged toward four. From my couch in the living room, I would see her setting juice glasses on the counter above her head or mopping up a spill with the paper towels she knew were under the sink. (Meagan remembers precisely none of this, by the way.)

If I frightened my children, they didn't let on. In what became something of a pattern for us, I told them as much as I knew, even though they weren't yet four. Yes, I was sick, with something called cancer, but the doctors were pretty sure it would be OK. In the meantime, I might not look or feel that good. All of which was true. For their part, the girls hung tough, suggesting that something called "cancer" was no match for the likes of us.

When I was feeling good, I would spend time setting up the refrigerator so that all of the stuff that could be eaten raw was on the lower shelves—that way the girls could just grab some carrots or an apple if they were hungry. I sent Meagan to the door more than once to give the pizza man $10. "Keep the change," I'd hear her say per my instructions to some stunned guy who probably took the story back to the shop. On nights when I was too tired to tuck them in, I would lie there and hear her tell Erin it was time to say prayers before bed.

"Lovely lady, dressed in blue, teach me how to pray . . ."

I excused myself when friends called wanting to drop by, telling them that we were fine but couldn't accommodate company right now. Blood relations were a different matter. My mom came and went, bringing easy food to make and taking the laundry with her. My sister Coo, my longtime ally and familial jester, still had run of the place. She would burst through the door, arms full of junk food and her head full of capers, bringing the circus with her every time she came. I couldn't even stand the sound of a television set at the time, but her voice, her yelling, her goofiness, well, that somehow sounded celestial. When she asked me how I felt, I answered truthfully, telling her I felt like shit and "It" was scaring the hell out of me.

"Hey, what a coincidence! Me too! Well," she'd shout, turning to the girls, "what say that we go into your room and make a *huge* fort where no one is in a bad mood and everyone feels good!"

Whenever I go in for a CAT scan—which is scheduled when some new ailment occurs—the technician is always confused. "Where is your spleen?" "Hey, what happened to your kidney?" And, "You seem to be missing your gallbladder." He makes low, whistling sounds as he surveys the wreckage of my past on his screen.

For the record, I have had four concussions, I have no meniscus in my right knee, I was born with one kidney, I have half a pancreas, no spleen, no gallbladder, and what's left of my insides is all covered by a steel mesh to keep it in. I have scars on my neck and my abdomen where the surgeons hacked their way in. I have had two broken legs, a broken wrist, a broken arm, a broken foot, a broken nose (twice), a broken hand, and a broken finger. That oral surgeon was right in a way, it has been a battle to keep my teeth, but I still order steak, medium rare. My neck is chronically bent—dropped head syndrome—because the nerves and muscles that hold it aloft are compromised, shot out by all the radiation I absorbed so many years ago.

It all serves as a reminder of two points:

I may have gotten away with a few things, but I did not escape clean. I trailed parts behind me as I went.

You don't need much to get by. My donor card may be shot, but I am healthy enough to ride a bicycle hundreds of miles, I ski steep runs whenever I can, and I feel good enough every day to do honest labor. Best to keep moving, lest the alien get a fix on your coordinates.

47

THE VILLAGE PEOPLE

Tender, you're the princess who is looking for your mom, and I
am the mother, and we meet in the woods by the palace.

—MEAGAN TALKING TO ERIN IN THE BATHTUB WHEN
THEY WERE FIVE YEARS OLD, AS QUOTED IN A PARENTING
COLUMN IN *FAMILY TIMES*

The prerogatives of normal life—a middle-class version of it,
even—began to float back toward me and mine as I healed in
1991. On summer weekends we would go up to Blueberry Lake
in Wisconsin and a collection of dilapidated fishing shacks my
family had bought. It was sort of like the Kennedy compound in
Hyannisport, but without the football, ocean, or yachts—a white
trash nirvana. I would take the girls out for boat rides and fishing when the boat motors worked, or hold the wrenches while my
dad quietly swore when they didn't. Many times I would grab the
chance to sleep a bit while the rest of the family kept an eye on the
twins.

Blueberry was always more fun when my sister Coo was up there,
because it meant some kind of monkeyshines were under way. She'd
build some harebrained, patently unsafe contraption for land or water
and then plop the twins on it.

Coo taught my daughters that women make stuff—she adored power tools—and that there was no need to wait for a man to get things going. She had been married to a great guy, a farmer, who cracked the occasional fag joke. Having spent much of my college years hanging out with a coven of brilliant pot-smoking lesbians—and noticing how Coo's eyes got wide when she was around them—I knew that one day she would wake up and tell her husband she was one of those people.

It was a lesbian cartoon after that: She immediately met someone in a woman's group, one of them brought a U-Haul to the second date, and before you knew it, Coo was living with her partner in the Uptown neighborhood of Minneapolis and wearing those hideous silk pantsuits with the animal prints from the Lesbians "R" Us store. She was an incredibly powerful person, someone who could tilt a room with her presence, and she liked to come into my house and give the place a good tug. Sleepovers at her house with the twins began at an early age. There would be candles, movies, Skittles for everyone, and no set bedtime. I used to call those sleepovers Lesbian Indoctrination Camp.

The other early constant in my daughters' lives was Kathy, their day-care provider, also a lesbian, but less extravagantly so. A former nun, she lived on the south side. Through a network of referrals, she ended up as the go-to day-care provider to a group of mostly single parents who were struggling in one way or another.

I went back to see Kathy, now living far outside the city with her longtime partner Cynthia, and she began giving me all manner of pictures almost immediately. Diagnosed with stage 4 cancer, she was heading out the door and wanted to leave me some things. We talked for several hours and hugged big at the end, with talk of a visit to see the girls. We both knew better.

There was something pitch-perfect about her, a person of remarkable constancy. And she looked after the parents as well as the kids. I remembered those years, from the time the girls were three until they were six, as simple, wonderful times, but Kathy reminded me that they were hard days as well.

"When I look at how hard you were all working—all of you; one- and two-parent households, it doesn't matter—you were working your asses off, as was I," she said. "I worked hard and you parents worked hard and the kids, they just flourished, the kids blossomed. I did a good job with them. I found my niche."

She said I found mine in the time she came to know me. "It changed you, having those two girls. I bet if you had two boys, it would have been different. It's for a reason. I think they changed you."

She shifted an arm that was giving her obvious pain. Cancer was everywhere, and now it was here, with me, in my friend. She just kept talking. "It changed you from self-absorbed to absorbed in them. By doing that, that means you had to take care of yourself. I saw that, I just happened to be there at that turnaround. You cared deeply for them."

She reminded me that I was backed up by a tactical unit of pals and relatives who punched in as required. It happened a lot, either because of work or, in that time, my own cancer. "You were surrounded by people who were rooting for you all the way. I don't remember all your friends, but once in a while they came by to pick up the girls, and the girls would smile. The girls were used to having people in their lives."

It came in handy when I got sick.

"I remember you treating it as no big deal, like 'I have to do this,' meaning you have to keep going. I don't remember pitying you, I sort of remember going, 'Wow.' You had a lot of determination," she said. "I don't remember you looking like you should be pitied. I remember us being worried about you, all of us, when you were in the hospital. I remember your parents—your dad more than your mom—and I remember the girls going home with them or with Coo, and just all of us clucking."

I eventually got better, but Kathy did not. She died a few months after we got together. When I look at the pictures from day care, Kathy is mostly just out of the frame, but you can see her reflected in every single kid, including mine.

As a parent, I was the king of the ad hoc, scrambling not so much to keep up with the Joneses as to keep our heads above water and moving downstream. When the twins gazed lovingly at some expensive cowgirl outfits before Halloween, I bought only the hats and told them I would make them real ponies to ride. Some hobby horses, a bit of glitter, and two packing boxes later, those fillies were riding high. The Halloween cowgirls of 1993 was a moment of vivid personal triumph.

The twins were morphing into their own damn thing so quickly that sometimes when I would come to Kathy's at the end of the day to pick them up, they seemed discernibly different than when I dropped them off. They were a concept when I started taking care of them, little wiggling markers of responsibility, but then they started to talk, and talk back to me. Peddling back through the columns I wrote for *Family Times*, I realized that I had turned on a dime, morphing from a big, nasty thug into one of those horrible, gooey parents who thinks that everything his kids do is extraordinary. Small stuff was huge. Cooking an egg. Eating candy. Going for a ride.

FAMILY TIMES, OCTOBER 1992

Even old family recipes like "Egg in a Hole"—which has been handed down successfully for generations through the family tree—are being subjected to scrutiny. The other day, each girl was offered an opportunity to imprison their own egg in the hole of a piece of frying bread.

"More butter, Daddy. That's what makes them lots yummier," Meagan said, gesturing toward the margarine with a wave of the spatula.

"Hey, I have been turning out perfect Eggs in a Hole since dinosaurs roamed the earth," I said as I goosed a little more margarine into the pan. "My daddy taught me how."

"Well, he's your daddy, but he's our grandpa, and we know how to make 'em too," she said, deftly lifting off a corner of the bread to see how the egg was doing.

Erin followed and was so pleased with how her breakfast effort turned out that she offered me a rare kiss on the lips.

"Oh really," I said with mock amazement. "You don't usually go for that kissing stuff."

"Well, I switched my mind." Not so long ago, I made an impulse buy at the SuperAmerica of some Gummi Bears that boasted tropical fruit flavors. A sickly sweet odor poured through the car after I opened them for the girls, and then boxes of candy came flying back into the front seat with guffaws about how terrible they were.

"Those aren't Gummi Bears. Those are ishy bears," Meagan said, setting off a long, slippery peal of laughter from both of the big smart guys in the backseat. Thus emboldened, Erin found the words to describe just how awful my purchase on their behalf had turned out.

"They're so yucky they taste like broccoli trees."

My life, which I was worried would shrink when I took on responsibilities beyond my own needs, was exploding out in glorious, unforeseen ways.

48

A SAVAGE LOVE

As a family, we were ferocious toward one another. My brothers Jim and Joe developed whatever skills they have as pugilists by using me as a punching bag until I started hitting back. "We kept it up until you became a kind of monster, and then we kept our distance," Joe said. But we looked after each other. It was tribal stuff, something far older and more durable than the suburban idyll we grew up in. I can remember being a new freshman in high school when some upper classmen took me into the corner of the gym to pound me. I saw my brother Jimmy over their shoulders, running toward us. I assumed he wanted to join in the fun, since he had been doing the same thing for years. He was small, but not to be fucked with. We still call him Savage. He jumped on the guys' backs and did not stop until they ran. Tribal shit. Irish stuff. Nobody screws with anybody in our family. Still.

In a family of seven, there is a universe of skills. The youngest, Missy, got bossed around a lot and gave love in return. My sister Lisa was the only one in our family who got in the common-sense line when God was handing out that piece of treasure. Coo was an innovator, a what-if, blue-sky kind of gal. Joe was my mom's favorite—an unspeakable truth, but there it is—whose ability to charm did not end with her. And my brother John was the oldest, a man who helped negotiate peace in our family when he wasn't doing so in the Middle East or Northern Ireland, working on behalf of the Catholic bishops. Jim was the only Carr who could count. A former repo man with a good touch for collections, he knew and understood credit problems in a family that had a few of them. After I finally began to stabilize, I had about $30,000 in debt.

"Send me the file," he barked when I asked him for advice. It was a grocery bag of menacing letters, past-due notices, and threatened garnishments. Savage knew every corner of the game and negotiated on my behalf, using his unique touch with the phone, an instrument that turned him into a rapacious animal. He wrote letters, loaded the gun, and shot every bullet: I was a crackhead, cancer victim, single father of two, enclosing a clip to boot. He, um, fibbed a bit and said he was willing to pay the debts himself, but that was a limited-time offer. Most of my creditors eventually begged to settle for pennies on the dollar.

3/14/94
Betty Marks
Citicorp Legal Department
Re: David M. Carr

Betty, per our conversations last week, attached is an article outlining some of the problems David has had in the past.

As you will notice, he had quite the lifestyle, to say the least. He has kicked the cocaine problems and had a few other situations of note enter his life.

David is a single parent of twin 5-year-olds Meagan and Erin. Their mother, they were never married, had the same chemical problems as David and "took off" when they were young. David now has full custody of these great little girls.

Another situation that confronted David was cancer. David

was diagnosed with Hodgkin [sic] disease a year and a half ago. After months of therapy and radiation, it appears to be in remission.

I have told David that he should write a book about his little adventure over the last 10 years, but who would believe all of these things happening to the same guy.

Now for reality: David is in the process of getting his life back together, and the last major stumbling block has been his past credit history. To say the least, it is not very good. I helped David out on several occasions in the past including buying him a car which he "lost" (literally, he actually didn't remember where he left the car, and it never turned up). I paid off some other judgments he had so his ex-wife could get their home released which she sold, and he paid off a student loan which had turned to a judgment.

David has no money, but he does have a brother who knows that given the opportunity he can be successful and raise those two great kids. He can't get credit or buy a home as long as this judgment is still out there.

He is working, but the medical bills, child care and day-to-day living expenses do not provide enough to pay off an obligation as large as he has with your company.

Here is the deal: I will pay you $750.00 cash for full and final settlement for all monies owed by David—that includes the account at the agency.

This is my money, and it is all I have to take care of this obligation. If one of my debtors offered me 20¢ on the dollar on the principal after 7 years, I'd take it in a heartbeat.

Your kind consideration of this matter is greatly appreciated.

> *Jim Carr, brother of David Carr*

Even though we pounded each other with abandon when we were young, as we grew up, we became wise enough in the ways of the world to know that there is significant safety in numbers. We were remarkably different people but had shared characteristics, including an overly fond relationship with John Barleycorn—only Savage and my little sister Missy seemed to have dodged that bullet. One by one, four of us wheeled through the door of recovery, a path that had been laid down by my father. My oldest brother, John, was a former seminarian who ended his studies for the priesthood when he bumped into Linda, his soul mate and, eventually, his wife. A high-ranking official with the Catholic Church, he worked to very good effect on behalf of the poor, the dispossessed, the powerless. And then, in spite of continued success in professional and family life, his turn to admit he was powerless over at least one aspect of his life came some years ago. He saw his addiction as something of a weakness, a lack of personal rigor. When he went to treatment, I sent him a long letter detailing our family history in order to remind him that his father, his sister, and two of his brothers had been down this road. He sent me a copy of that letter after I interviewed him for the book.

> *There is a part of you that still sees drinking as a moral failing, but there is a lot of evidence to the contrary. You are both an alcoholic and a moral man. You don't cheat on your wife, or your taxes (not much, anyway). You have raised great kids with sound moral principles and demonstrated the power of faith in both personal and global ways. That makes you a good guy. But you are also a drunk.*
> *So what is a drunk?*
> *A drunk is a woman, born with birth defects of her own, who suffers terribly as a teenager, making significant mistakes. This woman finds a good man, makes a new life with him, but brings the bottle with her. Eventually a child is born to her who also has a birth defect. And that woman sobers up, loves that child and her others with all of her might, lifting them up, pulling them up, showing them a life that is good and true. She becomes a tower of quiet strength to everyone around her, a*

dynamo of unshowy love. That woman is a drunk, but one who has found recovery.

A drunk is a guy who lives a life of self-seeking. He is a good-time Charley who spreads joy where he goes. He is a lover of life and his family of origins, and he is loved in return. But a penchant for partying eventually overwhelms him, and he finds himself in the weeds time and time again. The good times recede and are replaced by a DWI, a solitary life of drinking in hotel rooms, and many mornings of ruthless suffering. Eventually he tires of the loneliness, the pain, the shittiness of it all and goes to treatment. He sobers up just in time to be there for his mom who is dying. And in the course of that, finds a woman from his past and true love with it. He marries that woman, and takes her into his arms, along with her children, and finds a way to make a new life among the chaos of little money and teenagers in full bloom. His new love is felled by illness, and he is there for every step back to stability. When the man's sister dies, he all but grabs the wheel and sets all her affairs in order. His love is huge, as are his abilities, and he spreads a lot more than good times where he goes. That man is a drunk, but he is living sober day to day.

A drunk is a guy who gets in trouble early and often, tumbling into a world of darkness and drugs. An early life of professional promise is snubbed out by a life of venality, of the endless search for the next high. Somewhere along the way, he gets his dope dealer pregnant, and the twins that pop out become his and his alone. He sobers up, sitting in a shithole for six months while he tries to remember who he is supposed to be. He finds a new way of living and begins to take responsibility for his own life and the lives of those who have been given to him. He struggles through cancer and many other threats to his health, but remains sober. He finds the love of his life, his professional career resumes and prospers, and he finds happiness

300

he has never known. That man is a drunk, but one who has chosen to embrace his powerlessness over alcohol and drugs, to win the fight by surrendering.

A drunk is a guy who is born to a good station in life, who has a leg up, but stumbles when he sets out on his own. He has many children with a woman he loves, starts and loses a business, and begins to drink too much. He hides bottles in the basement, slurping surreptitiously when he can get away with it. His business life is a mess, he is blown about by forces beyond his control until one day he decides that the grand experiment is over, that if he gets back in the ring with booze, he will surely be knocked on his ass. He sobers up, learns humility, and takes a job working for people half his age. He succeeds on his own terms and retires, having mentored many. In the fullness of time, the man prospers spiritually, becoming a leader of men and women. The woman he loves becomes very sick, and he nurses her with slavish love and attention. He comforts her within an inch of her life, and when that too is at end, he is completely present for her. He mourns, finds a new love, and settles into a life that is rich and full. He continues to love and parent his children for all they and he are worth. That man is a drunk, but one who has found God afoot in his life, a God that has left him awash in the promises of sobriety.

A drunk is a guy who comes out of the gate quick and stays there, a tremendously talented and charismatic leader. Instead of putting his talent to work building wealth for himself, he becomes a steward, a man who mines and encourages compassion. He finds and marries his true love, and his influence grows. He sits among world leaders and the least of us with equal ease. People come for miles to hear the man speak. But in the midst of it all, the man finds himself drinking far too much, using alcohol to blunt the pains that the world dishes out. His career continues to soar, but his soul is dark and tortured. Much of his work and effort is dented by the reckless *and godless behavior of others. He sinks further into depression, one that cannot be fully ameliorated by the wife and family he loves so much. And then one day he wakes up and says quietly: Enough. He enters treatment filled with apprehension, but goes nonetheless. That man is a drunk, but one who has taken his first step into the light of his future.*

49

MY PLOT TO TAKE OVER THE WORLD

I do not for a moment imagine that any part of what I have to relate can be interesting to the public as a narrative, or as being connected with myself.

—JOHN STUART MILL, *AUTOBIOGRAPHY*

After I went to Sam, my boss at *The New York Times,* to let him know about the book, we talked about what such a project might look like. "You know that part about where you dust yourself off and take over the world?" he asked. I said, yeah.

"That shit is *sooo booooooooring.* Nobody wants to read about that."

Still, the fundaments of the genre require me to run close and careful analysis on how exactly I reversed course from certain damnation and came to a professional life beyond all expectation. So here goes:

I worked a lot.

If memoir is an attempt to fashion the self through narrative, dreams simply reverse the polarity on the same imperative. The future is even more fungible than the past: We can make it up, assert it will be so, and no one can say it won't happen with any surety. Herman Melville, in talking about history, said that the past is the textbook of tyrants, while the future is the bible of the free.

Excelling in the rat race, whether it is hunting down the biggest boar or getting the biggest piece while others do the killing, is an act of self-deception. To begin with, the striver must believe that the world is a fundamentally meritocratic place, that hard work will out, that winning is a matter of effort. And if the goals are accomplished, that person will believe he lives in a just, beautiful world. And if things don't go well, he will be down at the bar muttering bitter oaths into cheap whiskey about what might have been.

In possession of my chemical health and professional life, finally or at least temporarily, I had a general goal. I wanted to have enough juice and accomplishment so that if somebody got up in my grille in an untoward way, I could simply say, "You are not the boss of me. *Fuck. Off.*" And then go on to something else. I had watched my father get pushed around by lesser men, men who lied as much as they spoke, and I decided that was not how it was going to end for me. Or at the very least, if I was going to be bossed around, it would be by women and men of accomplishment, people who knew things and were willing to teach me. Properly inspired, I am a worker among workers who requires a minimum of maintenance.

My professional life benefitted from the wisdom of others. The guys I ran with were still maniacs; they just didn't drink and drug. After I was sober for a while, we rented a houseboat and went down the Mississippi for some golf, onboard cooking, and a little fishing. It had rained a lot that summer, and the guy who rented the boat to us took one look at the motley bunch—even though we had not had a drink or a drug in years, we looked like the wall of the post office brought to life—and warned us to stay in the main channel. Many of the backwaters had flooded and looked inviting, but they were shallow and could take out the hugely expensive stern drive if we were not careful, he said gravely.

We were not careful. We made a try for the lee side of an island and got stuck, pinned hard against the current as we tried to back out. The motor became mired, and we more or less used it to dig through the mud bottom in an attempt to crawl back to where we were supposed to be. Just when we were about to make it, something snapped, and the high-pitched whine told us that there was no longer a connection between the motor and the screw driving the boat.

Magically, we floated back into the main channel and were able to beach on the side of the island where we should have been in the first place. Before one of us flagged down a passing boat, we huddled on the deck: eight guys who knew their way around a story trying to come up with a version of what happened. "Yeah, we were just idling along, and it let go." Or: "There was a huge submerged log, and we didn't see it until it was too late." The stories, all of them false, began to gather at our feet as we tried to come up with a version of what happened. My pal Steve, a big-deal musician and artist who once was showing off on the balcony of a New York loft and face-planted a few floors below, cleared his throat.

"The truth is always simpler," he said. When the guy came by, we simply told him that we broke it by going where we weren't supposed to. The truth, simple and unvarnished, is a kind of gift, as long as you accept it.

―――――

In my basement, there is a file called "Career Stuff". It's full of memos pitching for jobs, memos for setting course once I got them, and memos about course correcting thereafter. They reflect decent editorial thinking, a real urgency about excellence, and, oh, one other thing: The guy who wrote them seems to be a real jerk.

In 1993 the top editorial job at the *Twin Cities Reader* came open. The once-feisty weekly had moved to the suburbs and grown up, maybe a little too much. But without saying anything to anyone, I dropped a note to the publisher, Jeff, suggesting that his paper had lost its way and that if he hired me, I would arrive with a box of grenades.

Some of the people you will be considering for the position are
no doubt very bright, competent people, but I, frankly, wouldn't
follow them out of the room. You need someone with a
commitment to excellence who can communicate in a

*meaningful, direct way, offering a message and a demeanor
that will motivate people to consistently surpass themselves. By
definition, an editor should be a person with a strong sense of
purpose and conviction—people in and out of your shop will
tell you that I have my share of both. I'm frankly only interested
in the job if I can rock the boat out at the* Reader. *If you're
looking for someone who can respect precious staff sensibilities
and maintain the status quo, I'm not the person you'd want to
talk to. That said, I'd love the opportunity to chat with you
about interests we may have in common.*

I had no idea what Jeff thought of the paper, I only knew what I thought, and I said it: The paper needs work, anybody else you talk to will be too much of a pantywaist to change things, and I will menace or fire anybody who gets in the way of making it better. Jeff bought it. I called him after all these years and asked why he put his money on a maniac.

"I talked to several people, and several of them warned against you just because of the history," he remembered. "A few were indifferent, and a few were like, 'Yeah, David knows what he's doing, he's a good guy if you can keep him on the straight and narrow, everything is going to be fine.'"

That's a pretty big if.

As soon as I had thought there was a small chance that I would get the job, I had every lawyer, political hack, and business person I knew fax him, suggesting that I ranked right up there with sliced bread in terms of mankind's achievements.

"I thought we needed someone who was a little irreverent, someone who would project personality back into the paper. You knew what was going on. You had friends in high places—not to be gauche about it, but I was impressed by the number of calls I got in support of you; you did a great campaign."

For seven years at the *Reader* and later at the *Washington City Paper*, I was the boss. A penchant for personal franticness was now writ large over a roomful of people. Being the kind of person who is afraid of missing something is an adaptive skill for an editor, but you might not want to work with him. Paul, a writer at the Minneapolis *Star Tribune*, wrote a profile when I got the job that was triumphal in the extreme, a very kind and generous piece of work.

Under a massive headline, it read, "David Carr: Survivor, *Reader* Editor Beat Cancer, Cocaine, Custody Battle."

> When David Carr applied for his new job as editor of the *Twin Cities Reader*, he told the weekly's publisher, "If you're not ready to rock the boat, don't call me." As if to emphasize his point, a huge Super Soaker, a machine-gun-like water pistol, now hangs from the ceiling above Carr's desk.
>
> "Oh, that," mused Carr, 36. "It's there to remind anyone who walks into my office who's in control."
>
> Even coming from a man who can match wits with close friends like comedians Tom and Roseanne Arnold, Carr's remark smacks more of irony than humor. Sure, Carr's résumé includes the *Minnesota Monthly* piece in which the late Minneapolis councilman Brian Coyle revealed his fight for life against the AIDS virus; *Corporate Report Minnesota*'s chilling two-part series about John Chenoweth, former executive director of the Minneapolis Employees Retirement Fund who was found shot to death; and *Corporate Report Minnesota*'s confessional profile of the Northwest Airlines pilot who flew drunk.
>
> But David Carr in control? For more than a decade, Carr could hardly control himself, much less a group of others.

Nice, flattering words, but probably not the kind of thing that was ultimately good for a guy who already had some trouble sizing himself correctly. The quotes from me in the story are ridden with hubris and possessed very little in the way of humility or awareness.

Given that my primary management experience was collecting week-old drug debts, followed by a domestic stint running around after twin five-year-olds, there was a bit of a learning curve. Because the newspapers I ran were good, it has always been my quiet conceit that I was a wonderful boss, even though objectively, as seen through the memos and talking to the people who worked for me, I was loud, crude, and demanding.

"When I took this job, I said we were going to beat the shit out of the competition. That has not happened," read one memo from those early days. "I am proud of the strides we have made, and I think the papers of the last three weeks clearly indicate we are capable of putting out a book that is worth reading. But I can think of many, many other papers that I read with my eyes crossed because I didn't really wanna see how bad they, meaning we, were."

A newcomer to management, even the small-bore stuff I was involved in, I experienced the terrible beauty of power, and in the process, formed the kind of crucible that Nietzsche talked about, where people were annealed by my will. I was a parody of a boss, someone who knew how to motivate people to take a hill, but not that great at picking hills. And my tendency toward linguistic idiosyncrasy—what were known as "Carr-isms"—led to the development of a running database of translations that could be given to new arrivals, only half in jest. "I gotta be honest with you"—a trope I opened all manner of conversations with—suggested that I was less than honest the rest of the time. Stories needed to be "ramped up" (improved), because the reporting was too "open mouthed" (naive), resulting in a "C-minus" (crappy) story filled with clichés that were "on ban" (forbidden).

One of the people who made his way through the linguistic thicket was Brett, who was a runner for advertising when I first met him at the *Reader*. He wrote about rock music, and later, at the *Washington City*

Paper, he became a restaurant critic, a move I had offered him because he always seemed to be sweating people for their food at lunchtime. The son of a former governor of Minnesota, he blossomed into a remarkable writer who now works in New Orleans.

Brett liked working for me, but, then, we were friends. In his taxonomy of supervisors, I would be known as a yeller. "Some people just can't hang with getting yelled at. I'm not one of those people," he said, sitting on his patio in Faubourg Marigny, near the French Quarter. "Some people don't like the volatility.

"I always thought you were fair and honest. Honest not just about the work of your employees but also about yourself. When you blew up, and we had some sort of disagreement, I knew that you were open to the idea of being wrong and admitting it." I was, he said, a man in a hurry who expected others to hew to my schedule. "I thought you were trying to make up for lost time," he said. "I thought you were trying to make a better paper than the other guy and prove yourself and racing with the clock. I think you felt like you'd wasted maybe a decade of your life, and that while you were getting high and getting drunk, people who were less talented than you were climbing the ladder above you in your chosen profession. I don't think that set well with you."

Many good things happened while I was at the *Reader*. The next publisher, R.T., who would go on to become mayor of Minneapolis, engineered a deal to take us out of the horrid suburban office building we were in and bring us downtown, to the city we were trying to cover. I hired Rose, out of a T-shirt shop, who went on to become a very talented investigative reporter; Burl, a laconic but gorgeous and funny writer; and an assorted crew of misfits. We made a great paper and fought tooth and nail with *City Pages*, a very well-done weekly that had overtaken the *Reader* in the early nineties.

Some of my defects of character made it hard for me to run the place credibly. It was a fast and loose environment, full of smack talk. I stepped over the line more than once. People were complimenting the blouse that one of my coworkers was wearing, and I commented that it was hanging on a very "nice rack." Near the end of my tenure, I was pulled into the publisher's office and told that I made some of the women in the office uncomfortable. I failed to understand that my tendency to pop off about any old thing in any old way I wanted was less than adaptive now that I was in management. I made it a policy going forward not to offer any sexist annotation about people I was supervising and to keep my hands to myself. I grew up at the expense of the people around me, a persistent motif.

Claude became the managing editor at the *Reader*. When I was a freelancer and he'd put me through a tough rewrite, I vowed to hire him someday if I had the chance. Talking with him a dozen years later in Minneapolis, I got a clear feeling that he was describing a cartoon, one that more or less drew itself.

"The story meetings were always amusing. Oh my God, they were hysterical. They were fun, but you would read people's beads, and you'd jump up and down and get mad at people if they didn't have story ideas and if they were coming unprepared or didn't have anything to bring to the table.

"And then the interns," he said. "You would say something like, 'If you don't get this done by tomorrow, I'm going to have my foot so far up your ass you're going to be on the fifth floor.'"

He reminded me that we had a wonderful time, made a great paper, and I had a very loyal staff. Actually, by the time I left the *Reader* in 1995, I had *half* a ferociously loyal staff. The other half thought I was a coarse, abusive lout and could not wait for me to leave. A case could be made.

50

SHAKING HANDS WITH THE FUTURE

I never saw any reason to go looking for a wife.

By 1993 my physical and romantic interests no longer traced the edge of pathology and instead found expression in serial monogamy that may have lacked seriousness but was diverting enough. The waitress at my friend's restaurant whom I had a mad crush on; another smart, lovely waitress who had a crush on me; some women I met in recovery or parents' groups, or professionally. I was cancer free, working out at the Y, and was no longer fat, drunk, or addicted. Not a catch, exactly, but not nothing.

One night in the spring of 1993, Sarah, a Republican operative I had once waited tables with, said a bunch of people were getting together at the Monte Carlo, a downtown bar where lawyers, politicos, and journalists hung out. She said she had a friend she wanted me to meet. I told her that all of her friends smoked really long ciggies, drank too much brown liquor, and, besides, were probably Republicans who hated poor people, and I nearly qualified. Just come, she said.

I arrived with a date—we were going to a rock show later—but Sarah came up to me and said her friend was there; that we should meet.

"Well"—I indicated my attractive friend—"why would I want to meet anybody?"

"We're over by the bar," she said, walking away. (Jill had no idea that some sort of set-up was under way).

I liked Sarah. She was a friend and a source, and so after a bit, I excused myself and walked over. She introduced me to Jillie, a brown-eyed blond who was classically beautiful with a Lord & Taylor sort of refinement. We shook hands, and I heard Wagner, my face got hot, and I lost track of my surroundings. We just kept shaking hands and looking at each other until the people around us began blushing.

Everything right about her was wrong for me. I had generally gone out with women who had a lot of dark hair falling into their faces, bee-stung lips, and remarkable leather jackets, with more tattoos than jewelry. As my friend Eddie once observed, "The women you date don't just look bitchy. They are." This Danish-Icelandic-Norwegian-Irish girl had worked in the U.S. Senate for a Republican, had her own house in South Minneapolis, and was just coming off a sales job and getting ready to go to grad school to become a teacher. Not. My. Type.

My kind, though.

Sarah said that my memory of meeting Jill was not at all embellished. "I've never experienced that phenomenon in my life where I introduced you two, and it was like the rest of the world didn't exist. It was stunning. It was this chemical thing, an intellectual, chemical thing that is so rare that when you see it, it's spectacular."

I still stare at the girl, still wonder why she is with me.

Our first date, on Saint Patrick's Day of 1993, was a marathon, thirteen hours, but not in the way you're thinking. I picked her up for lunch, and she was leaning on a parking meter in downtown Minneapolis, smiling and looking all freaking adorable. Lunch dates usually mean no kissing. But when I got out of the car, I walked over and planted one right on the lips.

We went a few blocks away to a steak house called J. D. Hoyt's. When we sat down in a booth, she reached into her pocket and pulled out an antique green bow tie with shamrocks on it. I reached into my pocket and pulled out a green lightbulb for the lamp hanging over the booth. The mutuality of the gestures, unknown, unrehearsed, yet connected, was filled with portent. Until in the course of removing the bulb that was already there to replace it with the green one, I dropped it onto the table. Kismet, albeit now decorated with shards of broken glass.

We talked families. Her dad was bright, drunk, and itinerant. She grew up with her mom, a cancer nurse. "Is she retired now?" I asked helpfully. "My mom is eleven years older than you," she said. Hmmm, so lots of productive and wonderful time ahead of her. Her mom, she explained, was the kind that anybody would want—empathetic, intuitive, and careful with her opinions except on very significant matters.

She blew off work for the rest of the day, and I took her over to St. Paul, where my mom's side of the family, the O'Neills, were hosting a Saint Patrick's parade after-party at my cousin Giggle's joint. She met the whole messy tribe that first day: the drunk, the recovered, the loony, the successful. My folk. We proceeded on to Hopkins for my mom's kooky annual parade, and then I suggested dinner at my house. We picked up Jillie's dog at her house and my twins from day care, and then I made her dinner. Mac-and-cheese for the girls, Dover sole sautéed with plantains for us.

Things went quickly after that. We drove to Taos, New Mexico, in her new Saab for some skiing just weeks after we met. We skied together and we skied apart, with me getting tossed around the narrow, steep black diamonds on the high traverse. The butt-kicking I took on those huge moguls opened up my internal midline incision, and I started bulging like one of the crew members in *Alien* just before the monster came out. I palpated the spot until my insides went back in—I would get surgery when we got back. Rough and ready, she just rolled with it, no worries. On the whole trip, we had just one argument. When we crossed over into Iowa, I slipped in *Exile in Guyville* by Liz Phair. "If you think I'm going to live in her personal concentration camp for five more seconds, you're crazy." I decided right then and there I'd marry this sassy girl if I could talk her into it.

On its face, it seemed ludicrous. While Jillie began working as a scheduler in the U.S. Senate right out of college, I was working on my nascent career as a drug dealer. A sorority sister at the University of Minnesota, she had manners beyond reproach; I was, in general, reproachful. She liked guys with pressed trousers and nice loafers; I had two pairs of pants, both black, both jeans, and wore sneakers. She was a trained ballet dancer who grew up in the Minnesota Dance Theatre, while my dancing style could best be described as white soul on a rampage. While we both had deep, lasting roots in the Minneapolis music scene, she thought my taste in all other matters was appalling. She was irresistible in her audacious opinions, her decisiveness, who she was, and what that meant. Her status as a committed, converted Catholic who actually went to church sent my mother into spasms of joy. I never really expected to get married, and if I did, I didn't think it would be to someone like her: a churchgoing Republican who had done her share of fooling around as a kid but was now a grown-up in all regards.

Before I decided to ask Jill to become my wife, there were certain matters to attend to. I did not remember precisely how I shared the news with the twins, but then I remembered I had written about the conversation for *Family Times*. Annie the editor sent along a clip I did not have.

The day before Christmas Eve, I loaded the girls into the car and explained we were going shopping for Jill, who is my sweetie and their very special friend. Before the car had even warmed up, they started peppering me with questions.

"Whaddaya gonna get her?" Erin said directly. "Maybe some jewels," suggested Meagan.

"You're getting very warm," I replied.

I knew we were about to have one of those important little family chats that generally begins with some difficulty and usually ends in a fair amount of accord.

I asked the girls if they knew what getting a ring was about. They both nodded after a bit and Erin added she thought it meant that "You love somebody." I explained that it also indicated you wanted to spend the rest of your life with that person.

"I want to marry Jill and make her part of our family."

There, I said it. I watched in the mirror as they traded glances from under their winter hats. Meagan spoke first.

"We already have a mother," she said quietly.

Erin and Meagan had just come back from spending ten days in Tucson with their mother, including a side trip to Mexico. By all accounts, it had been a time of re-connection and renewal. Our primary family value is loyalty and it made me proud that they were making their own little loyalties clear.

I explained the proposed arrangement in terms that went something like: "Your mother will still be your mother. That isn't going to change regardless of who I marry or who we live with. Jill is going to get married to me and be part of our family, but your mom will be your mom for the rest of your life." Erin saw the trend and interrupted. "But we don't want a stepmother." Meagan nodded vigorously in agreement. All of the literature and pop culture symbolism which had been piled up around the notion of step-parenting apparently had an impact on both of them. If they had their druthers, there would be no evil, wicked stepmother tucking them in at night. I suggested that Jill could be what she always had been: a friend.

315

In addition to getting the twins' approval, I needed them to keep a secret. I was hoping surprise would work in my favor in getting Jillie to say yes. In the days before Christmas of 1993, I said to her, "I'm going to get you something that you don't know you want but are really going to like." Jillie is a complete busybody—we call her "Krav," as in Gladys Kravitz on *Bewitched*—who has to know everything, and it drove her crazy. She surveyed my history, my penchants, and my former girlfriends, and then finally said, "If you get me a leather jacket for Christmas, I'm going to hate it. I'm going to be really pissed, and I will never wear it. Never." I played along, getting a huge box that might hold such a jacket, wrapping it elaborately and placing it under the tree.

On Christmas Eve I made her wait for hours while Santa Claus put toys and clothes all over the living room for the girls. She sat down, and I finally handed her the big, heavy box. Inside was a large antique teddy bear. He had a small box between his paws. She opened it and beheld a custom engagement ring with a moderate-size diamond. Jillie put it on and admired it, speechless. Meanwhile, I was on a knee chanting something about her marrying me and making me the happiest man alive. She continued to admire the ring. I finally told her that if she liked the ring, she'd have to also accept the two hundred pounds of goofy that it was coming from. She said yes.

It was a massive wedding: cops and robbers, judges and crooks, politicos and fixers. Erin and Meagan were heartbreakingly beautiful flower girls standing beside Jill, whose appearance in the doorway of the church made me catch my breath. The gospel was the parable of the prodigal, but I felt that I was coming into riches that far surpassed any fatted calf.

Our partnership was romantic and practical, with the pants going back and forth between us as the situation required and a shared appetite for adventure driving us around every bend, together. If marriage is about deciding to love on a daily basis, I have woken up to a no-brainer every day since.

Jill was raised by a single parent, so she had a regard for what me and mine had accomplished, but she had trouble finding a place to stand in a family that was already rolling. If there has been a disappointment, and it is a significant one, it is that she never knit together with Erin and Meagan in the way that I had hoped. When they were little, it was easy for everyone. But as they grew, I frequently found myself in the middle of a quiet but very real struggle for my loyalties. The girls felt her watchful eye every time they moved about the house, and sometimes the disapproval that went with it. It is the common strife of blended families of all kinds, but I felt like I needed goggles to protect my eyes from all the estrogen. When I was granted custody of Erin and Meagan, I made a commitment in my heart that I would protect them from anyone and anything that got in their way, but I had no idea that part of the trouble would come from such an intimate distance; in this instance, the person I chose to marry. Jill was a good parent, making the kind of home that anyone would be proud of, while working hard at good, interesting jobs. But even though she clearly loved the twins, there were times when she didn't seem to like them very much. Part of it was predestined: She did much of the heavy lifting of parenting, but the twins took her for granted and then treated me like I hung the moon when I walked in from a day's work.

Like all functioning families, we have made accomodations and found a place to put our disappointments. In the main, it has been a long and glorious run, anchored by two people who shook hands on the future the day they met.

Jillie had watched me come and go for a year on the book, digging up a past that she had some awareness of but little experience with. When I sat down with her in our cabin in the Adirondacks at the end of the summer of 2007, she said she never doubted for a minute that we would have a grand life together. Still, when we first met, she had every reason in the world to keep her distance. My reputation was still trashed in some corners. We knew people in common, some of whom did not hold me in high esteem.

"There were people that were leery of you, and maybe not so much in your present state when you and I met, but certainly of your past. I

317

don't remember what they said, but they implied, you know, 'Stand clear, be clear, be leery of him.' You had quite a reputation as being a maniac and a troublemaker."

So why not take the advice?

"Because I sensed something very different. I knew, when I started to learn of those things, it was mainly through you because of your very honest disclosure, and so I was never uncomfortable with your image and the reputation that preceded you and who I felt I was getting to know. I was never afraid of you. I never said, 'He gives me the creeps; I don't want to be around him,' never once.

"I just think we were of like minds. Not that I was like you or you were like me, but we just connected in a way that we wanted to be around each other, and we felt that our time with each other was cooler than our time without each other."

And the fact that I had kids?

"You were in a tough, tough situation, and part of your appeal to me was how you could be this amazing person, work your ass off, and be raising these two small children. That was entirely attractive to me," she said. "You were doing that alone, and you didn't have very much money, and all the while having a really good attitude. Just seeming like, well, yeah, this is what I do, this is who I am."

Sometime before we were engaged, we were lying in the bedroom of her little house on Pleasant Avenue. The room was painted Chinese red, with an arrangement of decorative tree branches and white lights on the ceiling. It was singular and compelling, like the girl who slept there. As couples will when they may have a future in common, we were discussing our dreams going forward.

"You said that your intention was to become a major figure on the national media scene," she recalled.

Just like that?

"It didn't strike me as weird at all. That's the kind of thing you can say, and maybe it will be and maybe it won't. People can have dreams."

Given that I was fresh off welfare, cancer, and had my first real job in years as editor of the *Twin Cities Reader*, it seems obnoxious and far-fetched to have made that kind of assertion even in the intimacy of a lover's bedroom.

"You work hard, you're smart, you are, um, without fail. I can't think of anything in our time together where you failed and screwed up and just blew it off and didn't care. Never once, can't think of a time."

Sort of cunning as well?

"That implies negative, and I would say none of it was negative," she said. "Not cunning; probably a planner, but in a kind of methodical way and a big-picture way without maybe connecting all the dots of how that comes to be."

I watched her as she talked, thinking back to our honeymoon, when I spent a fair amount of time staring at her and thinking about my great, good fortune.

We talked for a bit about the blending of our little family, the fact that although as partners we were deeply in love, we had some significant bumps as I sought to look after both the girls and her. She said I was just being who I was.

"You were very empathetic, very lovey, affectionate, a lot of natural inclination toward responding to needs, way more so than me," she said. "I tried to do what I was good at. I wasn't very empathetic. The fact that there were two was never that easy for me, either. If one was zigging, the other one was zagging."

Regardless, she said, I almost always took their side. (They say precisely the opposite was true, by the way.)

"That comes from your family. You are tribal in every respect. Obviously there was a great deal of indebtedness that you felt you owed them. You needed to make up for the fact that their mom was who their mom was, and that when they came into this world, it was a less than perfect situation in a lot of ways. So you were not only just being the best dad you could, you were making up for a lot of crap too."

Apart from my decision to start drinking again later in our marriage, we rarely fought, even about the twins. But when I brought up the idea of moving to Washington, DC, a place she had just left after four years, to become editor of the *City Paper,* she went off on me. She was glad to be back in Minneapolis, glad to be back near her mother, and planning on having a baby near her.

"If you think I am moving thousands of miles away to a place I have already left and having a baby so far from my mother, you're crazy."

We moved to Washington a month later.

51

WELCOME TO OUR NATION'S CAPITAL, YOU APRIL FOOL

When I got to Washington, I was excited to exercise new muscles over the *Washington City Paper,* a much bigger enterprise with a history of excellence. But I quickly found out that I was landing in a complicated place. My reputation had preceded me.

NEW EDITOR FOR *CITY PAPER*

Washington City Paper, the District's feisty free weekly, has a new editor who is a recovering cocaine addict. David Carr, whose appointment was announced yesterday by the alternative paper's Chicago-based owner, comes here from Minneapolis, where for the past two years he's been at the helm of the weekly *Twin Cities Reader.*

"As a person in recovery, I have a fundamental belief in the redemptive power of people, of human beings and mayors and all that, and so, yes, I do feel some kinship [here]," said Carr, 38, from his hotel yesterday, where he was taking a break from house hunting. "I am pro-District. I think the city has lots of potential."

At *City Paper's* offices, the announcement got a lukewarm reception. "There's been guarded dismay, guarded optimism," said one staffer who asked not to be identified. "His colorful background has been the source of chuckles, but no one's passed judgment."

Carr, who says he's been clean for six years, takes pains to point out that he also was for five years the single parent of twin girls, now 6 (he married four months ago), and is an experienced journalist. "I was clearly the best person for the job," he says. "I'm a person who's been places and done things . . . I'm not interested in coming to this town as 'the man who stuck things up his nose.'"

"He put it on his résumé," said Mike Lenehan, an owner of Washington Free Weekly in Chicago, of Carr's drug use. "It was never an issue for us." Carr replaces longtime *City Paper* editor Jack Shafer, who resigned in November.

—*THE WASHINGTON POST,* APRIL 1, 1995

52

THE SKUNK AT THE GARDEN PARTY

A long shot for the job of running one of the best weeklies in the business, I was running a small newspaper in Minneapolis and the interviews did not seem to go well. But Jane, the head of operations for the outfit, surprised me with a call and an offer. In the summer of 2007, I called her to ask why they'd handed me a job that seemed a bit beyond my ken. By then, she had retired from most of her duties.

"My memory is, we decided to hire the person, not the paper," she said. "We wanted a leader. They were a dysfunctional bunch. They were not very mature as employees. It was clear that we needed someone who would be a leader in whatever peculiar kind of leadership style you have or had at that point. It looked to us that you would be able to, maybe not happily, but you would be able to wrangle them."

With its history of narrative glories, *City Paper* was a kind of literary fantasy to the likes of me. I could recruit from the top of a class of nascent journalists, young people in a hurry who had come to Washington, DC, looking for a fast track. The staff ran the gamut from Eddie, a former ice-cream truck driver who generated legendary portraits of entropy; to John, who wrote tart political features with frightening ease; to Stephanie, with her big investigative heaves; to Amanda, a student of the District life, who did amazing profiles. We had Jason on cops, Erik doing the "Loose Lips" column, and Brad, an arts editor who was actually a newsman. Darrow, a quiet, hugely talented photographer, gave the paper its trademark black-and-white elegance. And when I was finally able to recruit and publish great black writers who reflected the majority culture—Neil, Ta-nehesi, Jonetta, Jelani, Holly, Paul—it gave the paper a new measure of credibility and salience.

When I first arrived, in 1995, I was full of plans and full of shit. At our first meeting, the staff got a load of me and my brutal Midwestern accent and decided I wouldn't last long. They had run the interim editor out on a rail with such ferocity that he had felt compelled to leave behind a dead fish in the ventilation system.

It was not that they weren't talented—many of them went on to do great work at the *City Paper* and elsewhere—they were just privileged young people who had never experienced much of life beyond the hothouse of the fancy colleges in which they had come of age. There was a lot of smirking, eye rolling, and note passing—it reminded me a lot of high school. I took their manifest disrespect as a kind of provocation. They were, collectively, smarter than me. But tougher? Not so much. Having been in rooms with people I owed money to—people who had guns and unknown intent—working in an office where people gossiped about what an idiot I was did not make a strong impression.

There were some issues of adjustment. Coming from Minnesota, a land of white people who eat white food in a frequently white landscape, Chocolate City, with its black middle class, political leadership, and cultural legacy was a complete mystery to me. My first week, Jonetta, a black writer with deep connections in the political community, wrote a scathing indictment of the talent and intentions of the city's leadership. Always in search of a snappy headline, I slapped this one on the cover: "Black Hole: Why Isn't the Black Community Producing Leaders Worth Following?" I got mau-maued from every corner, but it both reminded me to watch my cracker mouth and steeled me to push back when it was required. Some marginal dude self-selected as a spokesperson would call and say, "We in the community have discussed your most recent issue . . ." and I'd say, "You mean the community I work in, live in, my kids go to school in, and I pay taxes in, or some other community I don't know about?" Or they'd begin with, "You can't say that," and I would respond, "Well, we just did, so let's work from there."

Headlines got me into trouble more than once. A few years in, having noticed that there was an entire class of self-seeking party kids from far-flung lands—embassy brats, the progeny of international power brokers, minor royalty from places you never heard of—I came up with a headline in search of a story that read, "I'm OK, Eurotrash." Roberto, the son of an ambassador, wrote a scabrous social portrait of the denizens of Georgetown nightlife who screwed around, did dope, and drank like goats. For reasons I am at a loss to explain, I ordered up party pictures of real people to decorate the piece. Ooops. The ownership, which had left me pretty much to my own devices and supported me in good times and bad, was tested by that fiasco.

Erik, who worked as a freelancer, a columnist, a deputy editor, and eventually ran the place, talked about that when I went to see him on a trip to Washington in 2006.

"I do believe that I heard whispers among really smart people around Washington or people who had known you that held the view that your ambition was greater than your skill. There was a disparity there that was eventually going to have to play itself out."

As I had done in the past, I wrote a column that used media as a prism on the broader aspects of culture and began to demonstrate an understanding of the place.

Jill, in spite of her adamant misgivings, loved our little house in American University Park and found work as the director of administration for the Republican National Convention, where they anointed Robert Dole to go down in flames.

My daughters thought the place was amazing. "I remember pulling up in Washington, DC," said Meagan, "Erin and I bickering about something, and pulling up to the actual house and seeing it and how big it was and being utterly convinced that it was a mansion. There were more doors then we were used to. More windows, there was a yard, there were other houses on the street like it. It was different."

It actually was a tiny three-bedroom house, but given what they had come from, it probably looked gigantic.

In 1996 Jill got pregnant. It was joyful news, a new step for all of us, and she was thrilled. I could not wait to see the little round ball of love as she grew. But Jill was, without a doubt, one of the meanest pregnant ladies who ever lived, like Sigourney Weaver in *Alien*, guns blazing in all directions. The twins and I cowered behind furniture for the duration. When Madeline popped out on November 13 with a full head of dark, curly hair with inexplicable white tips, I took her from the nurses and plopped her into Jillie's arms. My wife took one look at her and said, "Had I known it was you, I wouldn't have been so crabby."

Maddie was the real wiseguy in the family. At eighteen months, she would respond to a long, loving look by saying, "Don't see me." But it was kind of hard to look away.

While we lived in the District, I went to recovery meetings but was far less connected to recovery than I had been in Minneapolis. There, every Thursday night, I went to a meeting at the House of Charity food center with a group of men who knew my story. Millionaires, cab-drivers, junkies, common drunks, and lots of new guys rolling in off the street. I liked a men's meeting—still do—because I can't help but be strategic in my communication around women. It's a kind of gender-based Heisenberg principle, where the presence of women changed what was said. In the District, I sort of hopped around, sat in the back row, and didn't get connected. Every time I went back to Minneapolis, I remembered how much I missed that meeting.

And I partied. Not drinking or using, but lots of going out, lots of dinners, lots of people over. The work was objectively good. My job was not to screw up a good paper, and I managed that. We beat the *Washington Post* on a couple of important stories, and published a paper that people talked about—perhaps not always with a great deal of fondness.

I still had some growing to do as a manager. I often treated people's carefully wrought stories as little more than dots on the screen and then more or less dared them to take issue with what I had done. Not that I could not pull good work out of people—I just had a tendency to grind them down at the same time. The office of Brad, the empathetic and talented arts editor, was known as the Cape of Good Hope, while my end of the office was known as Cape Fear.

One of the people who taught me how to be a boss was Amanda. She would come in to talk about a story, and I'd wave her off and tell her to just bring me copy. "Carr, you have to talk to us. You have to take the time to work through these stories," she'd say.

I had never been good at the nomenclature of editing. I have good skills at the keyboard—I can imitate almost any voice—but was weak on structure and organization. I shoot off my mouth and think with my hands, but Amanda and others gradually introduced me to the concept of reasoned discourse about editorial strategies, writing, and execution. She busted my balls plenty along the way, and even though she is a diminutive person, I always thought her comic impression of me was brutally close. She reminded me of my sister Coo, a small person who made a large impression, mostly by taking the big people around her down a notch.

I e-mailed Amanda—she was in the middle of writing a real book about something besides herself, so I didn't want to interrupt—about my reputation as a despot.

"You were the best boss I ever had," she said. "Although that was also the only job I ever had that gave me chest pains. I was twenty-two and I used to get chest pains walking up Champlain Street. I went to the doctor, and he told me it might be my job. Sometimes you were an asshole, but I think it was a strategy to motivate us.

"But mostly we worked really hard at *CP* because you had that ineffable effect on a room. That energy that good and dangerous leaders give off. That kind of aura that makes you want to please them, even when you're not sure why. I don't know what that comes from. Partly passion for the job, partly credibility. But some part of it you're born with. And you have it. I'd say ninety-nine percent of managers don't have it."

The newspaper turned over, as young reporters with lots of future advanced to other jobs, and the staff was gradually replaced with other talented skeptics, but ones that I had hired. My management skills had grown, but not that much. My tendency toward linguistic invention often left the people I worked with more confused than inspired. Neil, who moved on to a great career in New York, came out of my office after one of my special closed-door talks and told people, "I either just got fired or got a raise, but I'm not sure which."

At one point, in the middle of my tenure at the *City Paper*, I got a long voice mail from my pal David, who was one of the people writing and producing *The Corner*, an HBO series about drug dealing in the projects. I got very excited because I thought he might be looking for some script work. Instead he said, "I have a one-line speaking part for a white-boy drug buyer, and I think you'd be perfect." There I was in one of the episodes, pulling a car up to "Fat Curt" and handing him some money. "You're coming back, right?" Even though I had very little acting experience, it was not much of a reach.

On January 1, 1999, I appointed Michael, a twenty-five-year-old former Fulbright scholar, as deputy editor of the *City Paper*. On January 3 I tipped over into the hospital with something called acute necrotizing pancreatitis. I was in the ICU for four days, the hospital for sixteen days, and off the job for a month. I was so sick and full of pain that they filled me with narcotics and put me on complete bed rest, which meant no eating or drinking. Jill, who had never seen me high, came to the hospital one night when I was really flying. I ripped out all of the tubes and went storming down the hall, telling her and anyone else who would listen that I was actually a member of the Kennedy family and had important things to do. "You were incredibly nasty," she now recalls. "I got a glimpse of what you must have been like back in the old days."

I didn't die, but it sort of looked like I might. Again. The pancreatitis failed to fully resolve, and I was left with a cyst and chronic abdominal pain. I received a lot of lectures about the mysteriousness of the pancreas at medical institutions all over the region, including Baltimore's Johns Hopkins. I ended up at a pain clinic where a doctor gave me a relatively new drug called OxyContin. It made the pain manageable but put me at risk because of my other chronic health issue: the tendency to use mood-altering chemicals to excessive ends. I ended up obsessing over and counting the pills, and finally called the doctor to tell him that I needed to find another way. He offered me a different narcotic. I flushed the massive supply down the toilet, but I was on and off pain meds because of the pancreatic issues and surgical adhesion for years to come. At the time, it seemed like a necessary evil, but it left a huge gap in the perimeter of my defenses, a place where the pirate could slip through. The illness had other legacy effects, including leaving my pancreas impaired enough so that down the road I developed insulin-dependent diabetes.

On June 16, 1999, my brother John called me and told me to meet him at Washington National Airport. My mom, diagnosed a few months before with lung cancer, was dying. The hospice nurse had not been sure she would still be alive when we arrived in Minneapolis, so we phoned my mother. "I'll wait for you," she said as we both leaned in on John's cell.

When my brother and I walked in, dozens of people were streaming in and out of her room. My father was leading them in an impromptu song/prayer. The whole thing gave me the willies. They all gathered around, singing songs, telling jokes, talking about "their" Joanie. I didn't even know some of them and found it completely weird. But my brother Joe reminded me, "Hey, kid, that girl always loved a party. Why should today be any different?"

The twins—my twins, her twins—were one of her crowning achievements. She insisted they call her Jo-Jo, which I thought was off-the-hook dorky, but they joyfully complied. When the room finally emptied out for a bit I read the last few entries of her journal: " . . . my cup runneth over, Lord. I will be with you in days," said one. I leaned in and reminded her of the times she taped bows on the girls' heads because they had no hair. Of all the matching outfits. Of how their clothes arrived at our house magically folded and matched. She didn't talk, but she smiled.

And then a new group of people came wheeling through. My mother collected people along the way: the homeless, the learning disabled, the knucklehead son. She taught me how to button a shirt and iron it as well, how to serve, how to pray, how to be a mom, and now she taught me how to say good-bye. Watching her die was like watching a giant parade float roll slowly and gracefully into the water.

In 2000, five years after I first started working at *City Paper,* I started to get itchy. I worked for nice people, the town and its story were highly engaging, but just about the time the people I'd trained were doing great stories, they'd leave for bigger jobs. Although my bedside manner as a boss had improved somewhat, I was frustrated by always typing into the work of others, nipping and tucking their work to make it presentable. It was a lot like parenting but without the added benefit of helping build people that you brought into the world.

Brett, my buddy from Minneapolis who was now writing about food for the *City Paper,* said he had seen news reports about Inside.com, a digital media news site being put together by Kurt, one of the guys who had launched *Spy* magazine, and Michael, an editor from *New York* magazine and *Spin.* Why didn't I apply? he wondered. "Brett, those guys could swing a dead cat the next time they are out for lunch and find five people more qualified to write for them than me," I lectured. He shrugged and walked off.

An hour after that, some dweeb at a party, in between showering me with a fine mist of beer and pretzels, began hammering me about how the *City Paper* needed to start covering the Hill, where the stories were "falling from the sky." Staring at his congressional ID badge, I repeated a conversation I'd had dozens of times and explained to him that when he came up at the Dupont Circle Metro station, there were thirty newspaper boxes. Only one of those boxes contained a paper about the District itself: *City Paper.* He said I just didn't get it.

I walked the few blocks to the office, even though it was past two in the morning, tapped out a note to an address I had seen for Kurt, attached links to some of my clips, sent it, and forgot about it.

A few days later, Kurt appeared on my e-mail and invited me to take the shuttle up to New York to talk. I rode in from LaGuardia Airport looking at the density of the city with new eyes, as a guy who had a family of five, and began shaking my head. The whole dot-com thing was beginning to look a bit shaky, I had a good job, and who knew if I could even cover media in a city where I had never lived?

Inside.com's offices were at the end of a freight elevator ride in the Starrett-Lehigh Building on the West Side. There were rows of jelly-bean Macs and people sitting at them who had worked at the *Wall Street Journal, Fortune,* and *McSweeney's.* All of the dot-com trademarks were there: the cappuccino machine, the gee-whiz whiz kids, and an ambient insouciance that all of the rules had changed. If there had been a big vat of Kool-Aid, I would have jumped in and started backstroking.

That explains me, but why did Kurt walk by all of the people he could have acquired with a flick of the wrist?

I called Kurt. He said he didn't exactly remember, but took a guess.

"I figure it must have been your e-mail; you know, your quirky and ineffable charm was evident in your e-mail. And then I read your stuff and thought it was good," he said. "I liked the idea of working with someone else over forty, somebody who had some interesting miles on the tires. And you told me right off about your druggy past—and I was probably impressed by the fact of it, both the grisliness and the recovery, and by your candor about it. And I think I thought the down-and-dirty alternative-paper experience was a good thing to have on our make-it-up-as-we-went startup team." He paused. "And I thought you'd be fun."

53

DAVID BOWIE DID NOT SING TO ME, BUT HE COULD HAVE

Memory can change the shape of a room; it can change the color of a car.

—LEONARD, A MAN WHO CANNOT MAKE NEW MEMORIES AND IS SEARCHING FOR HIS WIFE'S KILLER, *MEMENTO.*

People often use personal fables as a way of answering the question of who they are. My current fable is that I fell off a turnip truck in Lower Manhattan—at night, of course—in 2000, and the city, as is its habit, clutched another émigré to its ample bosom. I may or may not have been a rube, but I didn't know anyone or anything. In the first three months before my family arrived, I sat in a bug-infested rental in Independence Plaza and read the daily papers, trying to diagram this new, strange place. A lot of my tutorial came from Page Six in the *New York Post,* where I kept reading about this large, powerful movie guy named Harvey, who could block out the sun. Sometimes when I was taking my ease at the window with the papers, I would look out and see a big black car pull up; a large man got out, and everyone around him on Greenwich Street would begin scurrying. He would be flipping pages in his hands, barking orders I couldn't hear, and then disappear into the TriBeCa Film Center. Some weeks passed, my worlds merged, and I realized that the man on Page Six was the man on Greenwich Street. And sometime after that, I ended up in that car interviewing Harvey for a story.

That's how I think of my introduction to New York, but thinking, with its symbolic and representational constructs, is actually the opposite of remembering. Memories may be based on what happened to begin with, but they are reconstituted each time they are recalled—with the most-remembered events frequently the least accurate. What one is remembering is the memory, not the event. And memory uses the building blocks of fiction—physical detail, arc, character, and consequence—to help us explain ourselves to ourselves and to others. As such, remembering is an act of assertion as much as recollection. The neuroscientific term is *reconsolidation*. We accessorize the memory with the present tense.

Sitting in the space between dendrites, memories wait to be brushed by a smell or a taste, and then they roar back to life, but it is always in service of the current narrative. Who is really to say that our mind, which is to say our brain, is not engaged in some biological poetics when we are not looking? A dialogue is often under way in the subcortex that has nothing to do with the conscious participation of the host. Throughout my life, I have turned out the light on some knotty, insoluble linguistic or logical issue, only to wake up in the morning with a fully formed fix in mind. I was asleep, but someone, or some part of me, was awake and processing. So why wouldn't memories frolic in a REM state, rearranging themselves into a more coherent narrative, conjuring a history that comports with the present moment?

If, by virtue of neuroscience and human nature, every soul is a fiction of his own creation, what happens when those fictions come into conflict with someone else's memory of hard-and-fast events? Who wins? The one who tells the story the loudest? The one who remembers the most detail, however false? Or is it the one who finds the lie in the other's tale first?

———

More than once I have told a story about my first night out living in New York. The shopping magazine *Lucky* was getting its opening bow at Housing Works Bookstore on Crosby Street. As the publishing reporter for Inside.com, I was aware of the fashion subtext of the event—

a magazine about shopping, for chrissakes—so I decided to wear a houndstooth shirt under a houndstooth suit coat, my own dweeby attempt at sartorial fashion transgressiveness. You know, so wrong it's right? (It was just wrong.)

So in this memory/story/myth, I am pinned against a wall. I don't drink, you couldn't smoke, and the room was incredibly packed, mostly by the same two hundred girls who are at every New York party. After a time, I decided I either had to speak to someone or leave. I picked out a guy with a Pet Shop Boys haircut who looked harmless enough. I gave him a rat-a-tat hello, saying I was from Inside.com, that I was a reporter, and that I covered the magazine industry. "So that's me," I said, all gee-whiz-nice-to-meet-ya. "What are you doing here?"

"Well, I'm James Truman, I'm the host," he said.

Shit. I knew that. Certainly, I knew he was the editorial director of Conde Nast, intellectual swami of the death star. Actually, I had no idea. I slunk back to the wall.

A woman, impossibly tiny, noticed me standing bereft and wobbled over on shoes that were tall enough to qualify as superstructure and outré enough to make a statement.

"You don't belong here," she said, but in a friendly, nice way. No shit. We had a flirty, fun few minutes, with her reassuring me that this gossamer world would all too soon take on prosaic, predictable dimensions. We later had lunch, and, as I recall, she invited me to a David Bowie show. It was—again, as I recall—an incandescent night, with seats in the VIP area next to Iman and a serenade from Bowie from about four feet away, who was probably singing to his wife. In my version of the story, Mim, my guide to this splendid new place, leaned over and said, "You're in."

I called Mim. We have remained friends, even though by the time I met her, she was completely bored by a scene I was just feeling my way around. My daughters thought she was the coolest person they had ever met. I found her intimidating and remarkable. A New York writer and editor with a massive, throbbing brain, she was and is neurotically brilliant, as capable of winning a throwdown over rock trivia as debating government black ops during the cold war. I have never won an argument with her, and this one would be no different.

She said she did not come up to me at the party, we were introduced. She did not say I did not belong there. She said that although we did see Bowie, we did not sit anywhere near Iman. Iman was sitting stage right, Mim said, and we were stage left. And she did not say, "You're in." Mim speaks forcefully in the recollection. I believe her, not my own story.

"We had excellent, incredible, privileged house seats," she said. "They have always been very, very kind to me, David Bowie's people, and we had a little table that was in the best spot. That was thrilling to me also because I usually don't have enough clout to merit the little table, the best little table."

So it was groovy, but not Iman-sitting-next-to-you, David-Bowie-singing-to-you groovy?

"He did not sing to us particularly, but it was a really, really good show. He sang to us and everybody else in the Roseland because he is Mr. Bowie. They did every song on *Station to Station* except for 'Word on a Wing' and 'TVC15,' about which we later talked."

There is, she said, "nothing that you told me about our meeting that I know to be wrong, because I was a firsthand witness to it," but then added, "From what you're saying now, your memory is emotionally honest. It's just factually wildly inaccurate."

───────

When I moved to work in New York, I asked my pal Amanda how she thought I'd like it. "It's a fight. And if you want the fight, it's great. And if you don't want the fight, it sucks."

I liked the fight. Unlike Washington and Los Angeles, where people rise and fall based on some secret chart, New York is a place where the wiring diagram is very visible and fundamentally, oddly, just. If you are good at what you do, work hard, and don't back down, you can make a place to stand on the island.

The trick of enjoying New York is to not be so busy grinding your way to the center of the earth that you fail to notice the sparkle of the place, a scale and a kind of wonder that put all human endeavors in their proper place. One night soon after I started working, I was on the thirteenth floor of the Starrett-Lehigh, staring out at the lights of New York as dusk fell, a Midwestern rube literally gaping up at the tall buildings. I was in full reverie, and my mouth was probably open at the majesty of it. "It keeps on happening," said Kurt, another former Midwesterner. "You never get tired of looking."

I don't. After a year at Inside, the money ran out, and I found gigs as a contract writer for *New York* magazine and the *Atlantic Monthly.* And then, suddenly, that view, which I had already come to cherish, changed for me and everyone else.

54

A COMMON STORY

Writing is an act of faith, not a trick of grammar.

—E. B. WHITE

On the morning of September 11, 2001, I was in the wrong state for a newsman. Jillie was in the city and called me at nine o'clock at home in Montclair, New Jersey, and said that a plane had crashed into the north tower of the World Trade Center. I turned on the television while we talked and remarked that they were replaying the crash, that someone had got it on tape, and she said, no, you are seeing a second event.

I went to the top of the hill over Montclair and watched the towers burn for a few minutes, and by the time I got back to my house, my editors from *New York* and *Atlantic Monthly* had both left messages saying my presence was required in the city. I grabbed maps, water, a kerchief, food, a flashlight, notebooks, and put on every press ID I had ever owned. Traveling in from twelve miles west of the city was like rowing upstream. Everything was cordoned off every which way. I drove over medians, highway cones, and the wrong way down a ramp up above the helix. And I finally got to the tunnel and told the cop standing there that I had talked to the Port Authority, and they said if I got there, I could park at the Port. He said, "I *am* the Port Authority, and you are full of shit."

I eventually talked my way onto one of the evacuation boats at Hoboken—I had to turn on the water works, weeping and saying I would lose my job, but I made it. I crossed the Hudson and started walking downtown. By the time I got there, it was past noon, and both towers were down, and, of course, the dust was everywhere. I had no specific instructions, so I began interviewing everybody walking around. One man in particular was full of information. He told me that after the south tower fell, dust obscured the entire bottom of the north tower until it fell. And he said that minutes later, he had seen someone jump from very high up and land on a fireman or a policeman walking near the base of the north tower. Both things, of course, could not be true. His memory, confronted by the most horrible human events imaginable, was beginning to rewire what he had seen into a narrative he could understand.

Like everyone else down there, I was just improvising, trying to be of some small use. I would get close and then get barked back out to the perimeter. I was standing at Church and Chambers streets, and a guy who ran a bodega there saw my notebook and started talking to me. "You see this spot right here?" he said, pointing to a large depression in the dust. "A jet engine landed right here. The FBI came with a truck and took it away." We were six blocks up the street from the site, and I just wrote down what he said, shaking my head in disbelief. On a day when so many terrifying things had happened, why would people manufacture more?

At 5:20 p.m., I was standing near that corner, and Building 7 fell, sending a wall of debris up the street. I dove under a car and found a lone pigeon and a book, torn and full of dust, that had blown out of the towers. *The Elements of Style*, E. B. White's ur-text about writing.

Jillie stayed in the city that night and was able to get the key to a friend's parents' place, a massive apartment in the seventies on the Upper East Side. She had gotten through to our nanny and spoken with Erin, Meagan, and Maddie. After a long walk to the apartment, I plopped down on the couch and began watching the images of that day. No one knew less than the people who were down there about what happened, including me. And I watched the video of the second plane, hitting the southeast corner of the south tower. The engine broke loose and was clearly visible, flying up Church Street and landing where the guy at the bodega said it did.

I worked for great editors. Caroline and John at *New York* magazine found me amusing and gave me a desk and some nice assignments. I was the staff rustic in a room full of cool, gorgeous people. Immediately after September 11, they guided a room full of reporters more used to covering the gossamer exterior of the city and went tactical, producing a weekly magazine that rose, and then rose some more, to the occasion. My own stories were terrible—all dust and mood and no substance. But Caroline got me involved writing text and headlines for a photo book about that day's events, and I finally felt like I added a small bit to a very large story.

Michael, the editor of the *Atlantic*, was the king of mission creep, having hired me to do media stories, but then changing his mind after the attacks. I had gotten to know Michael back in Washington. Jason, our cops reporter at the *City Paper*, had zeroed in on a square block of Capitol Hill that had a murderous history—it seemed to present the perfect urban ecosystem for violence. While he was working on the story, it became apparent that the *Atlantic* was doing the very same piece. I called Michael, and we engaged in a round of strategic blarney.

"We've been working on this story for months," I said. "And people who live on the block tell us they are 'waiting for the *Atlantic* story.' Well, aren't we all? We will be out months before you." Michael, who had retained an eminent urban writer who lived in the very place we were talking about, ignored my challenge.

"Did you hear about what's going on at the Washington zoo?" he said. "I hear the zookeepers are fucking the pandas there! Huge scandal! You guys need to turn some attention that way. It's a great big story."

Funny guy. We came out first. The *Atlantic*'s story smashed ours flat.

Michael was a reporter in his bones, and I would hang up the phone after talking with him wanting to go through walls. He talked me into the homeland security story measuring various vulnerabilities, something I was manifestly unqualified to do, but through a kind of hypnosis, he convinced me I could do a credible job. (And he was right. For years, I have gotten a residual check from a military college because the story is part of its curriculum.)

But working at home on and off for two different magazines, I missed the metabolism and urgency of a newsroom, the feeling of being a part of something. I got a call from Dave, the media editor at *The New York Times,* who had read some of my work at Inside, and he asked if I was interested in talking about a job. I thought it was the most preposterous thing I had ever heard. My dad, on hearing about the discussion, said, "Well, you've always wanted to work at *The New York Times.*" Which is a damn lie. I had never said that in my life.

Like every other working journalist, I had read and admired the paper all of my life, but I never saw myself as a *Times* guy. Besides, I felt I had unfinished business, especially at the *Atlantic.* I called Michael to say that I had been tentatively offered a job at the *Times.* He said, and I am paraphrasing from memory here, that since I had received what seemed to be a nice offer, he would buy out my *New York* contract, give me a raise, and quit changing my job around every other month.

"There," he said, "that is my offer to you as your editor." And then he said this, and I remember every word: "As your friend, I need to tell you that if you go to that place, and they like you and you like them, it will change your life. I can't offer you that. Why not take the job, see how you like it, and if you don't, just come back?"

I took the job. Michael, a reporter who could not resist a good story, set down the editor's pencil and went to cover the opening of the Iraq war. After the first Gulf War, he had written the book *Martyrs' Day* and went back to write a second book. During the initial dash to Baghdad, he was killed when his Humvee came under fire and overturned into a flooded ditch. I wrote his obit at the *Times.*

55

THE NEEDS OF THE MANY

When I interviewed at the *Times* at the end of 2001, I was doing fine until I bumped into Al, a large, indomitable masthead presence. He glanced skeptically over my background of magazines, alt weeklies, and dot-coms—not a whit of daily newspaper work—and probably saw a hot dog. The only way I got out of his office alive was by stating in plain terms that I clearly understood that the needs of the many frequently supersede the needs of the one. I could see him brighten when I said I was more interested in fitting in than sticking out.

I meant it. I felt like an eight-year-old boy who wakes up inside his father's body and is handed his briefcase. Shouldn't someone more competent, more skilled, more grown-up be doing this job? Still, I went to work in the business section, writing stories that were put through edit and published for all to see.

Dave, the media editor, broke me in, and he was old school all the way. I picked up a few corrections early on—a dread that snapped me awake in the long sewery parts of the night—and he talked me off the ledge, patiently explaining that my tendency to lard a lot of detail into my stories was a great way to pick up minor corrections. "If you aren't absolutely sure, just rip it out. Who's going to know? You can't get in trouble for something that didn't run."

That basic newspapering stuff was not lost on me. The baked-in folkways at *The New York Times* have made most people who ever worked there, including me, better than they were. Imagine working in a place where everybody—the dour middle manager, the fresh-faced gunner down the hall, the big cheese who walks by every once in a while—is trying to make it better. Even when they are stapling you to the wall, or pointing out an error in your work, or changing it fundamentally after you thought you were finished, they are trying to make it better.

The New York Times is weird—freaky, even—that way. I am the first to admit that the majesty of the endeavor is much more apparent to the people who read the paper than to those who make it, but the institutional muscles of the place are hard to deny. The people who run the paper have generally kept me away from breaking news, but I have caught a few red balls—working against an impossible deadline with little information, no time to write and bombs going off everywhere. And just when all is lost, when you are quietly but noticeably freaking the hell out, the place picks you up and carries you across the goal line.

If some of the darkness that lives in the walls there got to me— big-city journalism is a very serious undertaking that, done incorrectly, can ruin lives—the broader impulse of making it better had a profound effect on me as well.

———

The *Times* sort of shifted under my feet and everyone else's in 2003. Howell, the executive editor, seemed like he would be lord god of everything for eternity, and then he was gone. Jayson was the necessary figure, a guy who spent a great deal of time on the margins of the newspaper and then moved to its white-hot center before setting himself on fire. He created a massive scandal. Howell and his deputy, Gerald, left the paper after it became clear that Jayson had invented stories and sources out of whole cloth.

I knew Jayson as a friend in recovery who I smoked cigarettes with. He was plugged into the paper in a way I never was and never will be, so I always learned something juicy when we talked. Jayson was socially adept, the kind of high/low cat who could hit almost anyone's happy buttons, unless that person was trying to supervise him. I knew that he was viewed as a handful—he had been in and out of jams working in the metro section—but I was no longer in the business of supervising or judging young reporters.

Near Christmas of 2002, I was sitting in the smoking room back when there was such a thing, bemoaning that when I walked out after a play in New York, I took custody of a wish list from some kids whose families couldn't afford presents. It was full of all manner of urban wear that was not only beyond my budget but beyond my ken. Jayson grabbed the list, gave it a once-over, and said he would split it with me. We went shopping. He negotiated with clerks, enrolling them in what we were doing, and soon enough we had a big bag of presents. He had forgotten his credit card that day, natch, but he promised to deliver the presents to the house in outer Brooklyn. He came back and described how the mother's eyes were shiny with tears and the kids totally freaking because we had pretty much nailed their Christmas list.

Things seemed to get better for Jayson, who got a hot hand in the fall of 2002 as a reporter during the story about the Washington, DC, snipers. But the stories he filed proved to be his undoing, and by extension, Howell's, who had pushed his thinly sourced, partly fabricated reports onto the front page. Early in 2003, I was sent down to Washington to do a story about Ari Fleischer, the White House press secretary. I called Jayson while I was on my way down and asked him where he was staying, and he mentioned the Jefferson. I asked if they had broadband. He said yes. We made plans to have dinner at Georgia Brown's, an upscale restaurant with down-home cooking. Almost immediately Jayson called me back and said he had been called out of town to Virginia Beach. When I got to the Jefferson, there was no broadband, and they had never heard of Jayson. All of that should have sent my bullshit meter to 11, but I just kept rolling. He called me when I was on the train home, saying he was coming back to DC.

We didn't work in the same department or cover the same stuff, and I didn't buy into his theory that the masthead was out to get him. I believed him to be a good-hearted guy who had recovered from a go-round with crack cocaine and a real, if somewhat conflicted, journalist. As it turned out, he deceived his editors and his readers, and brought tremendous shame to the paper. His caper was an ornate one and involved all sorts of machinations. I remain convinced that simply going and doing the stories would have been easier, but then again, I'm not him.

When it became clear that a massive con was under way, I was dumbfounded. On the day he left, Gerald, the managing editor, was less worried about Jayson the journalist and more concerned about what might happen to Jayson the human being. He sent me out to look for him. I found him just down Forty-third Street with his friend Zuza. I was worried he might do himself harm and/or tip back over into crack. It was an emotional moment. Part of me wanted to strangle him for lying, lying to me about lying, but there was plenty of that to go around, so I thought I should show compassion. I gave him a panicky little speech, but I don't remember any specifics. Later, when his book, *Burning Down My Masters' House*, came out, that moment was in there. He describes standing there with Zuza and spotting me.

> We could see him across the street, standing alone, his black bag over his shoulder, black sunglasses on. He was nervously rocking back and forth.
>
> "Carr!" I yelled.
>
> David made his way across the street, and I introduced him to Zuza.
>
> "Oh God, I am so glad you are here," he said, giving her a big hug. "I am so glad you are here." David embraced me. He was crying, tears pouring down his face under his sunglasses. "You're not going to go west, are you?" he plaintively and emo-

tionally wailed. West was toward where the drugs were, my spots. "I don't want to man, I don't want to." I too was crying.

"Don't go, don't go. I don't want you to die, man. I don't want you to die. Listen, I don't know what happened, but I know that you were not honest with me, and a time will come when we will sort that all out, but I just don't want you to do something stupid. I just don't want you to go west, I don't want you to pick up, I don't want you to kill yourself, and you know that picking up is just killing yourself slowly. Whatever shit you have going on that you think it will make better, it's just going to make it ten times worse. Ten times worse, and you are just going to kill yourself. This time it might not be all that slow. Don't do it. Just don't do it."

Here's the weird thing: Give or take hyperbolic description, it was probably word-for-word what I said, better than anything I could have done from memory. This guy was in the middle of the worst day of his life, and months later he writes a book and remembers almost exactly what I said. It was almost like a parlor trick. When it came time to write my book, I called Jayson and asked him how he did it.

"I think I recounted it and replayed it in my head when I was in the hospital, and I was worried about going out and, like, not having a job and being in the middle of New York City—having some money in my pocket, at least forty dollars, and being able to use, and I recounted that story to myself even when I got out of the hospital." (After he left the *Times,* he entered the hospital to deal with some mental health issues.)

I read his book and ingested all the coverage about the scandal after he was fired, and I still have no idea why he did what he did. He more or less grabbed a rope, tied it around his neck, tied the other end around all of our feet at the newspaper, and then jumped. But I did have some basic questions. What about the time when you were at the Jefferson in DC but maybe in Brooklyn?

"I don't know about that specific date, but in the beginning of the sniper shootings, I *was* at the Jefferson," he said, adding that he stayed in another reporter's room.

And what about the big bag of presents and the touching family story?

"You should note for your story that you and I talked a couple times after it all happened, and then there was a period of silence," he recalled. "I called you, and you said, 'The one thing I want to know is, Is it true?' And I'm like, 'Is *what* true?' And you say, 'Did you take the presents to them?' And that just blew me away. I don't know how to describe how I wasn't offended by it, because it fit within the whole genre of everything that was going on, but I was, like, it made me think people are even questioning that shit."

So I asked again, is it true?

"One hundred percent," he said.

I believe him, but maybe that's just me.

56

THE VILLAGE TAKES A HIT

I haven't seen you in ages, but it's not as bleak as it seems.
We still dance in my outrageously beautiful Busby Berkeley
dreams.

—MAGNETIC FIELDS, "BUSBY BERKELEY DREAMS"

I took a flight on February 27, 2004. I wanted to remain there, in the brutally clear blue sky, where the sun was shining on everyone, including my sister Coo. While I was up there, Coo, a bad singer, a good dancer, and a person with a fetish for both power tools and her nieces, was still alive. "Coo was the fun one," Erin says now. While Coo was cooking dinner for her partner, Laurie, an unseen hand in the form of an aneurysm reached up and snatched her. She was still breathing, but gone. I wrote my way to her bedside and then said good-bye. I later published what I wrote in the *Family Times*.

> *Our family loves drama. Take any misdemeanor—the stumble of an alcoholic brother or a new boyfriend for the baby in the family—and we can crank up a hailstorm of phone calls full of theoretics, palliatives, and advice. We recount these dramas to each other, and they usually end sweetly, with the teller and the family held harmless, a life beyond real consequence. The last sentence of those stories has become a family trademark: "And nobody died."*

My sister Coo is/was the master of the nobody-died stem-winder. A gifted communicator who could talk more smack than a corner boy, she was able to take and hold the floor in a family full of loudmouths. She was a smart one, with perfect comic pitch arrayed over stories that were the audible manifestations of her expansive range of interests.

This story began the night before. My brother in Washington called to say that Coo had fallen down and begun babbling incoherently. Her partner, Laurie, called an ambulance, and they went to a nearby hospital. It was determined that she had suffered an aneurysm and had to be stabilized and transported to another hospital for surgery.

The ticktock of calls through the night each carried more weight, more portent. I dozed with the phone in my hand. In the morning there was one bump of hope as the drugs lowered her blood pressure and stanched the flow, but then new leaks, new horrors. There would be no transport, at least not to another hospital. Shaking off the shock, but not the implication, I booked the earliest flight. As I frantically packed, Jillie nixed the black suit as too morbid.

Fifteen minutes before my plane left Newark for Minneapolis, the call from my brother Joe came to me saying that Coo's big throbbing brain was dead. There would be a reassessment later, but all indications suggested we would have to make some decisions when we arrived.

I will need that suit. But before we bury Coo, we have to go to the hospital and admit that she is dead. Admit that the otherwise lifeless slab whose chest is animated by a ventilator has nothing to do with my sister. I know without checking that she is a donor—generous of spirit with a massive heart.

I know how it will go. My older brother John, a man who spends many of his days defending the sanctity of human life in all its iterations, will nonetheless lay out the endgame after meeting with the doctor. There will be no side doors, only a long, dark hall we walk down with my sister and then come out, one by one, without her. We will pull the plug—the scrim of our Irish ancestry has taught us that you don't mess around with death. You shake its hand grimly, and then look for a bottle of brown liquor, or if that might kill you too, a meeting with other like minds.

But for now, I want to stay up here where my sister is not dead, where the blue is endless and the clouds are just decorations, not wisps of dread.

Two years younger, she loved me with inconsistent ferocity, a hurricane of sibling love when she was not otherwise occupied by a complicated, busy life. Her fealty to me—in a big family, we were a powerful alliance for a time—was payback for times in her young years when I beat the hell out of anyone who dared tease her about her nasal voice and stubby nose, legacies of a cleft palate. When she turned twenty, she saved her money and had bones in her face surgically broken and the original intent of the creator restored. After that, she was unstoppable.

Moderation is something she and I were always moderate about. I lovingly corrupted her for years, taking her to throbbing punk bars and parties full of skeevy people. We shared a manic dancing style, and most of my great rock moments include her joyous, upturned face. She was down for a taste of coke, but she mostly did line after line of everything around her. She inhaled whatever was on hand—people, far-flung lands, weirdos of all manner.

I eventually began moving around, while she switched jobs, towns, and affectional preferences. We shared secrets, but only when things were really bad or really good. Last week, when I called her for some family gossip, she self-described as "Fabulous." She remains fabulous, because I am in the air, and I will keep heading straight for a horizon where my sister is still alive. Still fabulous.

57

ADDITIONAL RESEARCH

There is no passion in nature so demoniacally impatient as that of him who, shuddering upon the edge of a precipice, thus meditates a plunge. To indulge for a moment, in any attempt at *thought*, is to be inevitably lost; for reflection but urges us to forbear, and *therefore* it is, I say, that we *cannot*. If there be no friendly arm to check us, or if we fail in a sudden effort to prostrate ourselves backward from the abyss, we plunge, and are destroyed.

—EDGAR ALLAN POE, "THE IMP OF PERVERSE"

There is a Delphic component to addiction. Anyone who denies that has no idea what he is talking about. On November 23, 2002, almost fourteen years to the day after I entered Eden House, I found myself in my kitchen with a drink in my hand. And not just any old drink. I had been cleaning up during a party, pouring one glass of leftovers into another, and without much thought, I put that disgusting concoction to my lips. And then a few more. One would think that if a person were going to do something as momentous as take a drink after umpty-ump years, he'd make a plan—you know, put on a nice suit, go to the Pen-Top bar, and order up a proper martini. For fourteen years I had walked by precious single-malt Scotch, exotic tequilas, and in one particularly difficult moment, an ice-cold beer after they ran out of Coca-Cola at an open-air disco overlooking an active volcano in Nicaragua. But no, I was drinking the equivalent of college wapatuli.

Somewhere in the move from Washington, DC, to New York, I had stopped going to recovery meetings. But still, why get back in the ring? The heedlessness of that act is beyond comprehension, in part because I was sitting atop all the promises that sobriety brings: a wife and family I adored, a job I was proud of, and enough income to live comfortably.

With that drink, consciously or unconsciously, I set out to become a nice suburban alcoholic and succeeded. Having profiled as a nondrinker in all my endeavors, at first I told no one. A few weeks later, Jill was sitting on the back deck of our house and noticed the odor of alcohol. Five years later, she has very little trouble recalling that morning.

"We're on the back porch, it's Saturday morning, I had been running errands and doing things, you were going to put Christmas lights on the outside of the house, which required a ladder. We were sitting at the table, and I could swear I could smell alcohol—and it's like ten-thirty in the morning," she said. "I'm like, This can't be, I'm imagining this. I convinced myself that I was imagining it. So then you were either outside or went somewhere, and I went and opened your bag that was on the side table in the dining room—your briefcase bag—and there was a bottle of half-drunk vodka in a paper bag, and it was sloppy and messy and spilled and stinky."

Sort of like the guy the bag belonged to. She called my father and her mother, there was a lot of drama, and then I started going back to meetings and didn't drink for months. I was at a loss to explain myself. For years I had been the life of the party without doing any drinking, and now I was back in the ditch. It seemed to come out of nowhere, except it didn't.

Some of my old buddies in recovery back in Minneapolis saw it coming, or something like it. Sitting over a burger in the summer of 2006, Dave C., my pal the businessman who brought Christmas presents when the twins were little, said that even over a distant phone line, he wondered whether I was having my way with New York or, more likely, the other way around.

"I was worried about you," he said. "When you started talking about some of these people you're interviewing and the access that you have, these powerful people who know what you could do for them, they're gonna bait you and gonna give you stuff or offer you stuff, you're going to be in situations that are unlike, you know, something we see here in Minneapolis, which makes you very vulnerable. I was just worried about that. It's a big lure, especially when you're traveling and stuff like that."

A chaotic pattern emerged. I would be sober for weeks or months, take a trip somewhere, go buck wild, then return and stumble back into meetings. I got drunk in Los Angeles, London, Montreal, and Chicago, but was very careful to do my work and turn in my assignments. I never really came out as a drinker, never joined the huge social swirl as a party person. Because nothing was going horribly wrong, I eventually wore Jill down and began drinking at home, at the end of the day, when the kids were in bed.

I tried snorting coke a few times, but I was older, more scared. I knew that if I jumped down that hobbit hole, I would lose my job and my family in short order. I'm sure there are plenty of fifty-year-old white males who still do coke, but even drunk, even stupid, I had no real interest in another go-round with illicit drugs. Still, the progression of the disease had its way with me even without narcotics. Booze is a cunning, baffling opponent. I never turned into a mean, fulminating drunk, just a quiet, morose one. I knew in my bones that what I was doing would not work. I never took a drink under the illusion that I was a normal person, but something in me wanted to screw things up. I was in and out of meetings, in and out of sobriety, in and out of trouble.

There were some fun moments in there. Jill and I partied our way through Paris and points beyond in 2003, but there were significant signs that the center would not hold. In February of 2004, Jill and I got dressed up and went to the opening of the Time Warner Center in

Manhattan. I drank early in the evening, but, mindful of the fact that it was a very public event and that I would likely be the one driving home, I backed off and started eating. When we drove to the entrance of the Lincoln Tunnel, there was a sobriety checkpoint, a frequent phenomenon that I had breezed through many times as a sober person. I still wasn't worried, but when the cop checked my BAC level, he said it was on the borderline and that I would have to wait to make sure it went down. It did not.

I was booked, in a tuxedo, for driving while impaired. Not legally drunk, but not legal to drive. I was locked up in a West Side precinct during the night—Jill was looked after in the lobby until she was judged OK to drive—and then I was brought to Midtown for a hearing in the morning. It was jail: a grisly cell, and the food was rancid. The day passed, and no one came to get the guy in the tuxedo, and I began to go into diabetic shock because I had not eaten. As the end of the day neared, I told the jailer that I was in some medical distress. He said that was fine, that they would just transfer me downtown to the Tombs, the legendary holding pen for Manhattan. Yeow. I talked my way in front of the judge and got kicked loose, finally, onto the streets of New York in a day-old tuxedo. I pled guilty, paid fines, and went to alcohol education classes and got back into meetings, but not for long.

Each time I went back out into the drinking world, worse things would happen. In June of 2004, I went to San Antonio, Texas, and gave a speech, which went very well. I celebrated by going up into the hill country, drinking and driving and carousing. The next day I missed my flight and then finally left San Antonio without my good shoes or my car keys. I came home and went straight to a meeting. I sat in an L-shaped room and poured out my heart, talking about the ass-kicking I had just put myself through. When I got up to leave, I recognized a guy I knew who had been sitting around the corner where I could not see. He had a position of some leadership at the *Times*. I was horrified that he had heard my story, but when I got back to work, there was an e-mail from him reminding me that he was at the meeting for the same reason I was, and that if I ever needed to talk, he was available.

Being in those meetings made me feel like a bit of a fraud. I was surrounded by people with years of recovery, years that I had drop-kicked away. I came late, left early, sat in the back row, not talking to much of anyone. I went months—sometimes as many as eight—without a drink, but every time I picked up again, I would end up passing out or driving drunk or wandering around in parts of cities I knew nothing about. I didn't hit anyone, I didn't sleep around, and I did not fall back into a life of drugs. My career continued to prosper, in part because I drew a bold white line around it—if I felt a bit overmatched at the *Times* sober, I was toast as an active drunk. Still, I was failing to notice the trend, failing to realize that one of these times, I wouldn't make it back.

Once again, I began handing out different versions of the truth. I told many people, including my boss Sam, that I was back to having a few drinks very occasionally and, boy, it was going swell. One night, maybe after he got a promotion, we had a spontaneous dinner. We walked into Bar Americain, a popular spot that had to be booked weeks in advance, and using nothing more than his charm and directness, Sam got us a table right in the middle of the room. He never mentioned *The New York Times*, an invocation that I always took as a sign of weakness when a story wasn't involved. It was a stupendous night, one of those magical New York evenings when possibility seems everywhere. Two martinis, half the menu, and many toasts to the fact that a couple schmucks like us would end up with the jobs, families, and lives we had. Of course, Sam hopped the subway home to that lovely family with a nice little glow on. I took off for the West Side and drank alone.

The only person I told the unalloyed truth to was Seth, a writer I knew. We had been introduced by mutual friends in the belief that we might hit it off, and we did. I was older and had more years in recovery under my belt, and he'd been involved in heroin, but we both took journalism and sobriety very seriously. When I was going good, I talked to him about that. When I was in the ditch, I talked to him about that as well. He ran a straight, simple program of recovery and had, as they say, something I wanted.

Seth was really the only one apart from Jill who knew my whole story during that time. I called him in the summer of 2007 and was very surprised to find out he had worried about me long before 2003.

In 2001 we'd been walking toward a party in the Village for some dot-com, a party where we would both not drink.

"You had been going through some of the health stuff, and you were taking Oxy," he said. "We're talking about how that was fine, and you said you had to take it sometimes slightly different than it was being prescribed, but it wasn't a problem. I was about ninety-eight percent sure that you had taken some that day that kind of blurred the line between need and recreation.

"There were three things going on. Like, you're telling me what was going on with yourself, and you're trying to convince yourself what was going on was OK, and you're asking me if I felt what was going on was OK," he said. He did not think what was going on was OK.

Stripped of pretension, you could say I was born a drunk and merely acted like one after many years of being in remission. Regardless of health issues, sobriety will do nice things for your life if you follow some kind of program, and almost any will do. Mine sort of begins and ends with an admission of powerlessness, attendance at meetings, and, when I get in a jam, a power greater than myself. Stick to those basics and you can live congruently, stay married, and keep out of jail. But what you can't do is change channels. If you are filled with quiet ennui, you can't go to the cupboard and suck down several ounces of booze so you no longer care or smoke a doobie on the porch so you no longer notice. Sobriety means that wherever you go, there you are, for good or ill.

My decision to do further empirical research on my relationship with alcohol when the data were already clear still leaves me baffled. For me it was less about having scrambled to the top of some greasy career pole and finding not much, and probably more about some venal, long-brewing urge to take a sledgehammer to things I adore. We,

I, you tend to feel unworthy of some of the blessings that come our way, perhaps because, in our darker moments, it is so much more than we think we deserve. If that seems a bit ardent, a flourish of therapy-speak in what is a fairly black-and-white matter—there are some people, millions, in fact, who should not use mood-altering chemicals—how else to explain the very common story of relapse among people who have a decade or more of sobriety? Perhaps it has less to do with Freudian imperatives and is more as simple as the fact that human beings have a tendency to forget. You might say I had a lapse of memory.

I stopped in Chicago to see my pal Ike, a rock singer and songwriter, a former doorman at the Park Hyatt, and an astute student of the human condition. Sitting in the studio he had built in his house, he considered the riddle of why people, people like me, choose chaos. He knows the syndrome, and me, pretty well.

"We're talking about middle-class white Americans that have an inside track to any success they want, and yet a great portion of the people have fucked it up," he said. "You have, I have, guys we pass through town have. Why? I don't know. Greed and insecurity are obvious; the guy is greedy. What's the cliché? Pigs get fat, hogs get slaughtered. Greedy people should be punished. I'm all for that."

While Ike tends toward the biblical in the wiseguy epics he writes and performs, he suggested that my decision might have been as basic as a longing for the dark aspects of life, in spite of its downsides.

"Is it an escape from the monotony of the white middle-class lifestyle in this era?" he asked. "Were you tempting fate?"

Yes.

"Maybe you found that—and I found this—it's too straight, and because of something in you that relates—to the tenets of the rock lifestyle or the journalistic lifestyle or the addict—to what's happening, where the action is."

Sometimes, he suggested, it was less about engaging in bar talk with some nitwit twenty-three-year-old at four in the morning—a little of that will go a long way, especially after awhile—than having trouble knowing where to stand at the kids' soccer game.

"I can't even go to the school where my kids go because it creeps me out so much. I don't want to go to the church. I don't hate those people, but it reminds me of everything I wanted to escape as a kid. And so it's midnight, everyone else is going to sleep to get up for work, I'm still living in the same town, I'm going to get fucked up tonight, and I'm going to walk through the streets, I'm going to stay up all night, I'm going to run through my yard in my underwear in a thunderstorm. Is that the same thing as giving the suburban drunk a try?"

Almost precisely, come to think of it.

"I drink too much," Ike went on. "I clearly don't have a history of addiction and programs like you, maybe because I haven't gone to any meetings, but I haven't bottomed out like you. I haven't jeopardized the loves of my life. You gotta work, you gotta be a man. There's nothing wrong with being a man and taking care of people, and with that comes compromise. We go back to the discussion of great artists, great writers, who forego all that shit—family, homes—and are they men? Are they *loyal?*" he asked, pausing on a word he probably knows comes freighted with meaning in my neighborhood.

"What are you going to do?" he asked. "Are you going to be loyal to a fucking concept like being an artist, or are you going to be loyal to human beings that you're responsible for?"

———

Barring a necessary and opposing force, the obsession that lives in an addict is always in the basement, doing push-ups, waiting for an opening. And all the treasure, human and otherwise, will not change that math. That's why reading all the junkie memoirs that ridicule various programs of recovery makes me laugh. As opposed to what? Free will? Moderation? A flash of self-realization followed by a lifetime of self-control? Gee, that sounds like a plan, except an addict alone—me, for instance—is in a very bad neighborhood. Millions of lives have been saved by gathering like minds in a church basement. You don't like the slogans? Make up some new ones.

In various programs of recovery, adherents will talk about "slips"; but the collapse into drinking and drugging can take a very long time. In that process, the prospect of getting high or drunk, unimpeded by obeisance to a higher power or a program of daily living, is rolled around in the mouth absently, surreptitiously, long before it is actually swallowed, to see how it might taste. That's how I finally found myself in my kitchen with that disgusting drink.

When I really think about it, somewhere in the late nineties and into 2000, I stopped identifying myself as an alcoholic and an addict and began thinking of myself as someone who just didn't drink or do drugs. It took about four years to make that nasty drink in my kitchen, four years of not going to meetings, four years of not speaking honestly with people in recovery, four years of a long conversation in my head, before the thought became deed.

Each time I would come back, I would bounce a little lower. I filled Seth in here and there during that slide. "You would say, you know, I'm having, like, a drink, and it's fine. Whenever that happened, I sort of said, 'Well, isn't that always what you hear?' And you said, 'Well, no, it's not like I'm smoking crack.' Well, there's a lot that's not fine before you hit that.

"I was less worried about work than just worried about whether I was gonna wake up one day and get a phone call that you were either in the hospital or you had died," he said, recalling the times when we would walk and talk after a meeting. "Maybe, again, this was stupid of me, but I sort of had confidence that no matter what happened at work, you were talented enough and skilled enough to kind of be able to bullshit your way out of it."

For a guy like me, the work is always the last thing to go. It is, in some twisted way, more sacred, more worthy of protection, than friends, loved ones, and family.

It wasn't that I wasn't trying. At the end of 2004 and into 2005, I put together eight months sober. But on the Fourth of July weekend,

I found myself at loose ends. I was in Mississippi and Louisiana, writing about an author who was using a raft to do a book tour, a juicy, wonderful assignment. As I was driving toward St. Joseph's, Louisiana, I called the guy who was advising me on sobriety matters, and we talked until the cell coverage ran out. I was feeling itchy, but determined. I was tired and hungry and a long way from home, but the motel I was staying at was supposed to be on a lake. I envisioned a nice dinner followed by a cup of coffee with a good book on the porch.

I pulled up to the place, and it was a cinder-block building on a swamp. I checked into my room, and it was beyond bleak. The restaurant was closed, and I went to the store at the front of the motel, which sold mostly two product lines: whiskey and guns. In my rattled state, I thought, God either wants me to drink or blow my brains out. I bought some Jack Daniel's.

I made it through the weekend, but another spiral commenced. In August while Jill was traveling in France, I drove the girls to the cabin in the Adirondacks. It was late, I was bombed, and got lost because of a detour. When we stopped to get gas, I nearly pulled into an oncoming car. Only Meagan's shout from the passenger seat stopped me. The gas station attendant, a man who spoke very few words of English, saw me, saw the girls, saw what happened.

"Go home, mister. It is time for you to go home."

I remember the silent vow that I made to those children when I took custody of their lives, that I would lay low anyone or anything who put them at risk. What to do when that malevolence comes from the self?

Sitting at that same cabin near the end of the summer of 2007, Erin remembers it vividly. Of all these interviews, the ones with the twins are the most uncomfortable. I still have an enormously tender relationship with each of them, one that was built early and strong, but it took a huge hit when I started drinking. It wasn't that I drank around them a lot. I would often wait until they went to bed, but that only meant that when things went wrong, they were all the more surprised.

They had never seen me drunk or high in their entire lives, and they certainly weren't expecting it.

Erin looks at me for a second when it comes up, and then looks away into the camera. She says I told them to stick around on that Friday night, that we were going to drive to our place in the Adirondacks, which was three and a half hours north under the best conditions.

"We took off from work for it, and you said we couldn't be with our friends, so we just kept waiting and waiting, and we kept asking when we were going to go, and you're sitting outside smoking on the porch and kind of bumbling around. And I was like, What's dad doing? What the hell? I was just frustrated. You came in the room, and you're all packed up, and your face was sort of red, but I didn't grow up with you drinking. I have no idea what that is. I had never seen that before.

"We got in the car, and you seemed out of it, but I thought you were tired. Maddie whispered to me, 'I think Dad's been drinking.'" Maddie was eight years old at the time. "I was like, 'No! What are you talking about? Shut up, don't say those things! That's not true.' Meagan was like, 'I don't know, Erin, I'm a little nervous about it.' We were still in New Jersey, I think only, like, twenty minutes from the house. We had to pull into a gas station, and you didn't see an oncoming car, and we were, like, *this close* to hitting it. That's when everyone knew for sure that you were just completely ass-faced drunk. It was the most irresponsible thing you could ever do."

She is still pissed. And I am still sorry. It did not rub out the fourteen years of sobriety that came before it, but it placed more import on the years of sobriety since. She could have happily gone through life without ever seeing me head into the ditch.

What looked like a quick spiral into alcoholism—to my kids, and, really, to me—looked a lot more like a long, slow slide, with plenty of rumination along the way, once I started reporting it out.

I stopped in South Minneapolis to see my friend Cathy, whose ex-husband Patrick is now in prison. She knows plenty about how things can appear to be wonderful but still go very wrong.

She mentioned something odd that I said back in 2000, when she and her husband, along with their daughter Grace and son Jack, who is my godson, were staying in my house and visiting the sights in the city. "You were bringing us to the airport, and you said, 'Hey, I got something to float by you guys. You think I could pick a city and go there and drink there and then walk away from it?'"

I was joking, or thought so, but she said I had a city all picked out: New Orleans.

When Hurricane Katrina happened, I was adamant about going, but Jill was dead set against it, worried that I would slip again and suffer the consequences. I went down a few days after the flood, and the work went fine, but when I wasn't working, I was lurching around a chaotic, dark New Orleans with a bottle of brown liquor in my backpack.

With most of the city under water, hotel rooms were at a premium, and I invited Brett, my pal from both the *City Paper* and the *Reader,* who was now the restaurant guy at the New Orleans *Times-Picayune,* to stay in a room I had cadged off a colleague. We did our stories and went out at night, but I stayed up long after he went to bed. I went to New Orleans to talk to Brett about those chaotic days. We sat at the back of his house in the Faubourg Marigny, which had made it through Katrina.

"It was a difficult professional situation. I'm a restaurant critic, and I was all of a sudden doing a very different duty and also wondering what this was going to mean for my life because I live here. That was a very difficult time for me.

"I didn't see you as a wreck. Part of it was because I don't feel like your personality changes dramatically when you drink. You're not a person who is, you don't have a lot of inhibitions, so it's not like loosening up for you. That's the way I've experienced your personality; you're very uninhibited."

And the context provided cover. "At that time, a journalist going off on some kind of bender is going to blend in quite nicely." And it did. I had plenty of company.

"I remember admiring the stuff you did from here," he said. "I thought it was really well written and had the right level of empathy and irreverence, even, and I remember thinking that you were able to twist that off."

My brother John called me when my second column from New Orleans ran, amazed that someone who was living a sober life could walk the edge and not go flying off. I merely thanked him for the read and got off the phone as quickly as I could. And when it came time to look back, I checked the clip. You could smell the whiskey. Good work, but not the kind of approach to a story that I could sustain:

> The French Quarter, which has served as the television backdrop for so many stories, is empty, save the drunks and lunatics at Johnny White's, a bar that never closes. The rest of the Quarter is block after block of pitch black. Is this Bourbon Street or Royal Street? Which way is the hotel? Is my flashlight running out of batteries?
>
> On Wednesday night in the midst of the gloom, at St. Louis and Royal streets, the shadow of a figure over a big kettle appeared. Finis Shelnutt, the owner of Kelsto Club, had cooked up a huge batch of jambalaya and had a cooler of cold beer to go with it. It was a hopeful gesture, not a commercial one.
>
> "I don't want your money," he said. "I just want to know what you think of the food. Right now, I need to give back, not take." A group of newspaper people—print journalists filing string that may or may not be used—nodded their assent. For the record, the jambalaya was incredibly spicy, with a burn that provided a shock, in a good way, to the ghosts and sleepwalkers who came by to eat.

Perhaps the Katrina story resonated so keenly because somewhere inside me, muddy waters were rising and beginning to overtake me. I filed my stories and wanted to stay, but Jill heard something in my voice she did not like. When a second hurricane threatened, she barked me onto an airplane. I made it, but this time I could not bring it in for a landing.

When I returned to New York, I started in right away on a story about Caris, an actress who was incapable of forming memories because of a brain injury. A former Broadway ingenue, she was putting on a one-woman show with the aid of note cards. Jill and I went to see her play on Sunday, September 25, 2005. This is what I wrote:

> The first time I met Caris Corfman after her one-woman show at the Flea Theater, she looked—almost stared—into the very backs of my eyes as I told her how I enjoyed her performance. She was flattered and incredibly gracious.
>
> The second time I met Ms. Corfman, she again stared and responded graciously. But she had no idea who I was. It was exactly five minutes later.
>
> She can't remember. Ten years ago doctors detected a benign tumor in her brain. A series of four operations removed the tumor but damaged the part of the brain that regulates short-term memory. As a result, she not only forgets who she met five minutes ago, but she also can't remember if she took her medicine, if she ate, if she should go right or left or just stay put.

That I found her riveting may have had something to do with the fact that I was in the middle of forgetting something very important: that for a guy like me, forgetting could be a fatal error. Or as she put it in her play, "No memory, no life; no memory, no career; no memory."

Because I had spent three years on and off booze, but mostly off, I had been able to stop in the past. Not drink like a normal person—my idea of a social cocktail was sitting alone on the porch of my house drinking four ounces of vodka on ice, followed by four more ounces on ice, followed by vodka from the bottle mixed with spit until a fifth was gone—but stop drinking long enough to do the normal things like go to work and attend functions. But somewhere in there, a progressive pathology took over, and I could not stop. The Sunday after Caris's performance, I drank on the patio of the TriBeCa Grand with Jill, lulled by the martinis and the gorgeous surroundings into thinking all was well.

I struggled through work on Monday, all itchy and clock watching, which is not my way, and then drank Monday night. On Tuesday, September 27, I got halfway through the day and left work, my skin crawling and my cells—my very synapses—now devoid of relevant memory, calling out for beverage alcohol. Up until that time, I had never left work to drink. I wandered up Eighth Avenue, drinking at anonymous bars with others like me, people who stared at the bartender and wondered when he was going to get around to pouring them another goddamn drink.

I called Jill, and she knew I was off my rocker. She said it was college night at the girls' high school, and I should not come. I said I was coming. She said I should take the train home. I said I would drive. She said they were leaving without me, and she hoped I did not make an appearance. I drove home to an empty house. For reasons that I'm sure were clear to me at the time, I showered and put on a suit. There is some logic there. If you can't be sharp, look sharp. And then I drank about a half bottle of vodka.

I was late, drunk, but nicely coiffed. At the crest of the hill heading into Verona on the way to the girls' school, the guy in the left lane slowed, and I gunned the engine and sped by in the right lane.

58

STUMBLEBUM

Through the windows, bright red strobe lights flashed across the walls accompanied by a high-pitched wailing. The sound was nagging and accusatory. It was nothing, nothing like song.

—ANN PATCHETT, *BEL CANTO*

DEPARTMENT OF POLICE
VERONA, NEW JERSEY
DRINKING – DRIVING REPORT
(page 2 of 3)

DATE: 09/27/05   CC# 5009736

OPERATION OF THE MOTOR VEHICLE:

On Tuesday September 27, 2005 I was assigned to the 1500-2300 tour of duty in marked patrol vehicle #4. At approximately 1929 hours I was northbound on Grove Ave in the area of number 24 when I observed NJ-KRT57R traveling southbound at a speed of 44 MPH. I then turned my patrol vehicle around in an attempted to stop the above vehicle. As I attempted to position my vehicle behind the above vehicle the driver began to accelerate to speeds over 50 MPH. At this time I activated my overhead lights and affected a motor vehicle stop on Bloomfield Ave near Elm Rd in North Caldwell. The driver of the vehicle abruptly stopped the vehicle and pulled to the side of the road approximately three feet into the driveway of the "Exxon" gas station.

WHEN STOPPED:

Upon approaching the vehicle I observed the driver with his hand out of the driver side window holding what appeared to be his New Jersey Drivers License. The driver of the vehicle was found to be David M. Carr from his New Jersey (picture type) Drivers License. At this time I detected a strong odor of an alcoholic beverage emanating from the interior of the vehicle. Mr. Carr was then asked for his registration and insurance card. Mr. Carr fumbled through paperwork in an attempted to find the documents but was unsuccessful in his attempts. At this time I observed that his eyes were blood shot and watery and that he had white saliva buildup on his lips and in the corners of his mouth. I then asked Mr. Carr if was feeling okay to which he replied, "Yes." At this time I asked if he had been drinking, to which he also replied, "Yes." Mr. Carr was then asked where he was coming from and he stated, "Mount Saint Dominic." It was later discovered that Mr. Carr was in route to Mount Saint Dominic. I asked Mr. Carr where he had been drinking and he answered, "90 Cooper Ave." I then asked Mr. Carr to exit his vehicle and walk to the sidewalk, which was well lit, free of debris and level. Mr. Carr walked around the rear of his vehicle swaying and used his left hand for support on the rear of his vehicle as he approached the sidewalk. At this time I advised Mr. Carr that I was going to conduct field sobriety tests. Mr. Carr was asked his level of education to which he responded, "I graduated college." Mr. Carr was asked if he had any injuries or illnesses which would cause him to have a problem completing any of the tests to which he responded, "No." Before beginning I advised Mr. Carr to listen to all of the instructions carefully and not to begin each test until he was told to. At this time I demonstrated the walk and turn test. I advised Mr. Carr, with his arms at his sides, take nine heel-to-toe steps, turn, and take nine heel-to-toe steps back, while counting each step out loud, while watching his feet. Mr. Carr was asked if he understood these instructions to which he

366

replied, "Yes." Mr. Carr started to perform the test before instructions were complete. He also didn't touch heel-to-toe, lost his balance while walking, used his arms for balance, turned incorrectly, and took the incorrect number of steps (7). I then demonstrated the one-leg-stand test, I advised the Mr. Carr to stand with his feet together with his arms at his sides and listen to his instructions. I demonstrated by lifting my left foot approximately 6 inches off the ground keeping both legs straight and my toe pointed out. Mr. Carr was asked if he understood the instructions to which he replied, "Yes." Mr. Carr started to perform the test before instructions were complete. He also used his arms for balance and put his foot down 4 times. At this time I advised Mr. Carr that I believed he operated his vehicle under the influence of intoxicating liquor or drugs.

DRINKING – DRIVING REPORT
(Continuation page 3 of 3)

DATE: 09/27/2005   CC# 5009736

Mr. Carr was advised that he was being placed under arrest, he was then handcuffed, read his Miranda rights and placed in the rear of marked patrol vehicle #4.

ENROUTE TO STATION:

While being transported to Headquarters, Mr. Carr apologized several times for his actions and stated that he would be more than cooperative if he could contact his wife.

AT THE STATION:

While at headquarters, Mr. Carr was again was advised of his rights under Miranda. Mr. Carr stated that he understood his rights verbally and also shook his head that he understood his rights, however he would not sign the waiver. Mr. Carr was cooperative in answering any pedigree information questions. During conversation with Mr. Carr he stated that he had earlier spoken to his wife and that she told him not to drive. Mr. Carr further stated that he was going to Mount Saint Dominic from work in New York City, which contradicted his previous statements. Mr. Carr repeatedly stated that he was wrong and that I, Officer Shafer was right to pull him over and that it was a, "good stop." Mr. Carr was read The Standard Statement and when asked if he would submit to breathe testing he replied, "I am consenting to the testing of my breath for alcohol content." Mr. Carr was cooperative while giving breath samples. Refer to Alcohol Influence Report for results. This Officer contacted Mr. Carr's wife, Jill Rooney Carr, to arrange to pick up her husband from Headquarters. Mr. Carr was issued five traffic summonses and released to his wife, who signed the Potential Liability Warning at 2142 hrs.

TRAFFFIC OFFENSES:

Summons # A-083296 39:4-98
            A-083297 39:4-50
            A-083298 39:3-76.2f
            A-083299 39:3-29
            A-083300 39:3-29

OFFICERS SIGNATURE: _Ptlm. Robert Shafer_ # 0487
                     Ptlm. Robert Shafer

59

RE-LOADED

So now what?

The drinking life provides a few signs that things are not going your way. Arrests tend to be a good indicator, and I had a few new ones under my belt. An inability to confine drinking to appropriate times of day would be another. But as Jill and I sat on the back porch staring at each other on the morning after my arrest, the options seemed limited. I had been in treatment four times—five, actually, but I didn't know that at the time—and I had been a speaker and consultant on recovery issues. I could give a pretty good presentation off the top of my head on the disease concept of alcoholism, so more information did not seem warranted. Nor did further research, given that I was fresh out of handcuffs and in the midst of physical withdrawal from alcohol. Being a drunk does not require the lunacy and lawlessness that coke addiction provokes, but it will still take down your life one brick at a time and leave you a shuddering, needy mess.

When I was in the Parkview treatment facility in 1984 for the first time, a nice place in St. Louis Park with good food and serious counselors, I did not know much about booze and had no physical addiction. My roommate, Mike, a retired dentist from International

Falls, was near the end of his treatment, which had gone very well. Mike was the old head in group, a reasonable guy with a sort of Norwegian Zen about him. All is well, he'd say, all is well. He returned from a weekend pass and confided to me that he had drunk a fifth or two during his time away and was going to act as if nothing happened. But something did. The next morning while we were getting dressed, he went into withdrawal, and his upper dentures—go figure, a dentist with no teeth—came clattering out. I called the nurse, there was all this stuff on the PA about code blue and Mr. Red, but it was all to no avail. He left our room dead on a gurney. I was dumbfounded.

By both heritage and preference, I was a substantial drinker, mostly brown liquor and lots of gin, which I always thought made me win, until it did not. But that same genetic loading meant that I could drink for years without suffering grievous medical consequences. And the pace of my lifestyle and the heedlessness that went with it masked the fact that somewhere in there I crossed a line to clinical alcoholism. By the time I got to my third treatment, at St. Mary's hospital in early 1988, I was drinking a fifth a day in one form or another. Some hours after I was admitted to St. Mary's with a garbage bag of stuff, I came up to the nurses' station, telling them that I felt unwell, my vision was blurry, my skin felt tingly, and my heart was pounding.

"You are in withdrawal from alcohol," the nurse said flatly. "We will give you something to ease the transition."

The sheer horror of that almost dropped me. I was fine with being a coke addict—there was some measure of transgression and hipness in that—but a common drunk? And now, twenty years later, those shakes that rattle the soul and everything else were back. Alcohol withdrawal is profoundly uncomfortable to host and no picnic to stare at. I was a pitiful wreck. In desultory fashion, Jill and I went through all of the people we could call or institutions we could check out. And then Jill said, "What about that guy at work? The one you told me you saw at a meeting. Didn't he say to call if you needed help?"

What about that guy? I didn't really know him other than the fact that I had seen him at a meeting, he had seen me, and that he had a significant job. After some false starts, I got ahold of him.

I said that I did not want to put him in any sort of position because he was a boss at the *Times* but that I was pretty much flat on my ass with the drinking stuff. Should I go to the booby hatch, call my supervisor, what?

The guy told me that work was a nonissue, that he was interested in helping me in any way he could. He was full of concern and empathy in spite of the fact that he did not really know me from a load of hay. He listened as I ran my story. He said it sounded like I needed to go to detox. I said I might have to go somewhere after that. What would I tell work? He said I was an employee in good standing, with no work issues, none, and a lot of time off coming. "Tell them nothing." The guy said to call him when I got out of detox, and we would take it from there.

Sam, I decided, was another matter. He was both a friend and a direct supervisor. I would fill him in.

It is a rule of thumb that when it comes time to detox, it's best to head for the sticks, but for reasons having to do with insurance and a lack of clear thinking, Jill and I decided that I would go to a detox in the city the following morning. I got very drunk that night and made a fool of myself saying good-bye to my children. The suddenness, the uncertainty of it, along with my intoxicated apology, scared all of the kids.

"I don't remember you ever being unreliable," Meagan said. "I don't remember ever feeling like you're making choices that could put us in danger, and when it did happen—even though it was for a limited time—it was very scary. You're a stable parent, you're the good parent, you're all those things. When it's not there, it's pretty scary."

In the morning, we went to the detox in Midtown, and I knew I was in for a complicated few days. It was a medically advanced, serious place, but a quick look around the waiting room indicated that most of the patients were heroin folks off the street; there were no special accommodations for the sloppy drunk from the suburbs. But the place had a bed, and Jill pretty much did not know what else to do with me. I wondered what lay upstairs on the unit, but I was sure there would be no duck pond.

I got up there and it was epic, like a B horror flick that was scheduled to run continuously for days. Plastic mattresses, twitches scratching themselves, and me, sweaty and shaking apart. I paced in my room for a half hour, looking out at the city through a dirty window and thinking about all the overt acts that had brought me to this place. Rube that I was—I really had become a nice suburban alcoholic—I took a fresh pack of cigarettes into the smoking room. A dude with greasy dreads and very live eyes started sweating me right away.

"In here, we share and share alike," he said.

Oh, really, like what?

"Like you give me half that pack to share with the people in here, and you keep the other half," he said, not smiling. Everybody else in the smoking room turned away from the television and looked at me.

"How about we keep this civilized. You ask me if I have an extra cigarette, and I give you one," I said.

Otherwise what? he wanted to know.

"Otherwise I poke your fucking eyes out."

Now he smiled and looked me over in all my sweaty, shaky glory. "You don't look like you're going to be poking anybody's eyes out."

"Maybe not today," I said. "But I will be better tomorrow." He snatched the cig out of my hand and walked off.

When I saw the doctor, he asked what my objectives were at the detox. I said I wanted to get detoxed from alcohol as quickly as possible and get back home. He wrote me up an order for Librium and said that if I woke up on the fourth day and could function without it, he would discharge me.

I battened down the hatches and went fetal in my room. My friend John from the *Times* walked over and left cigs, a phone card, and small money for me downstairs. I used the phone card to call Jill and whine about how mean and shitty the place was. I was pathetic, a drunk and a big fat baby.

Walking aimlessly around a locked ward, sleeping in a place where others came in my room and rooted around, I was back to where I had been so many years before, standing with a bunch of my peers who were hugging their marks and asking when the next pill roll was. It had been seventeen years, but I remembered all of it.

The message conveyed by waking up with your face suctioned to a plastic institutional mattress by your own sweat is elegant and direct. You are not a nice suburban drunk. Play with whiskey, it will play with you. No, I didn't shoot dope in my neck or hit anyone or supply hookers with drugs. The bottom still arrived.

I skipped the dance of the low-sloping foreheads—oh, I mean quality time with my fellow addicts in the meds line—on my fourth day, Sunday morning, October 2. True to his word, the doc kicked me loose. "Good luck out there," he said with a wave.

I waited for Jill on the street. She walked up, took a hard look at me, and asked if I was sure I was ready to come home. "Why, you want me to head back up to Happy Acres? No thanks. Let's go."

I got home and had a long talk on the phone with my new friend at work about treatment, about inpatient versus out, about the next step. Money was an issue, and treatment was going to be expensive. I was a little beside myself, not knowing how to act now that I was back to being the problem. "Who is to say that you don't just need to get back into meetings? Intensely, like ninety in ninety days?" my friend suggested.

"Remember," he said, before he hung up, "you don't ever have to feel like this again." I mentioned that I had been in and out of meetings, that I had drop-kicked away fourteen hard-earned years of sobriety. "Those fourteen years and everything you accomplished are still yours," he said, adding that this was about the next fourteen.

I went to a beginner's meeting near my office, raising my hand and offering my paltry count of days sober. Five days, eleven, twenty-three, and so on. I went to meetings in Montclair, downtown, uptown, but mostly in Midtown. I rejoined the cult, showed up early, said hello to people, drank my share of the Kool-Aid, and was suddenly counting weeks, months, now years, and if things go my way, many more.

Sam had told me in very simple words when I got back to work that his support and that of the institution were unconditional. He'd wink when he would see me tearing out for my twelve-thirty recovery meeting. Some of my close friends at work noticed that I had put a cork in it, but it was not a major topic of discussion. Drinking was not something I was anxious to speak about.

Slowly, I remembered who I was. Hope floats. The small pleasures of being a man, of being a drunk who doesn't drink, an addict who doesn't use, buoyed me. One thing led to another, as they say. After a couple of years of in and out, drunk and not, I had two-going-on-three years, and not once has the monster snuck up on me, made me feel like I might go back. Beyond experiencing a nice, firm bottom and sticking with the meetings, I started to remember how straightforward and manageable my life had been before I picked up that first drink in the kitchen.

When I went up to the Adirondacks to start on the book in the summer of 2007, I got a call from my friend in recovery at work, who had by now retired. He had a friend who was running a meeting and needed a speaker at a certain Midtown detox, mentioning the place I had flopped into two years before. Had I ever heard of it?

I went down to the city and took the meeting. The place was rugged, like I remembered it. There was a major beef in the middle of the proceedings, and a few of the guys had fresh scars from the street, but this time, remarkably, I felt like I fit right in. Then again, at the end of the meeting, they let me out.

As I sat in our cabin and wrote the book, every day I stared at the wreckage of my past. I went to more meetings. The nice, friendly one in Saratoga, New York, where people talked about parking tickets, sick parents, and their cats having Leukemia. The scary, dark one down the mountain in the washed-up mill town where the meeting is called to order by a gavel that consists of a screwdriver jammed into a piece of wood. I could be picky, but they all look and feel sort of the same to me. No more Goldilocks—this one is too soft, this one is too hard— they all feel just right.

60

HALF-ZEIMERS

The final interviews of the summer confronted me. The twins.

Neither of them knew me as an addict or drunk, but they were now nineteen, and after growing up thinking that I hung the moon, they had watched me face-plant. When the twins did their respective essays for college, what I had thought was a fairly straightforward story—boy meets girl, girl and boy have twins, boy and girl combust, boy and twins live happily ever after—in their eyes had deepened and become more complicated. They were the ones, after all, who grew up without their mother. They were the ones who had to teach me how to be a parent. They were the ones who had to find a place to stand after I got married. And after hearing me say all their lives that all good things came from sobriety, they watched me throw that down a rat hole.

I have enormous regard for who Erin and Meagan have become and how they run their shows. They came from nothing and became their own damn things. I don't own their successes. Their status as independent, brilliant young women is something that fills me with the kind of wonder I suppose all parents have, but their trip has been all the more remarkable. After spending months staring at the medical records, the pictures, the journals, I think about how much they have gone through traveling in the vapor trail of adults who had a lot of growing up to do themselves.

But to ask them, to talk to them, was a different matter. If they were the nicest things that ever happened to me, was something even close to the reverse true?

Erin and I spent the summer in the Adirondacks together. She tended bar and waited tables, and I was locked in a room typing. We were uneasy roommates—a first-time book writer and a nineteen-year-old soon-to-be college sophomore, two of the most self-involved humans on earth. And now it was time to talk. Erin is a reflexive bright-sider and a bit of a sensualist. When we went for a ride in the car when she was little, she would say, "I love this world because there are so many things I love in it." She is a kid, by now a person, who has always seen the glass as half full, and when it's empty, simply finds a way to fill it herself. A pop-culture savant and a very gifted writer and talker, her sunny affect hides abundant resolve.

She is just about to head back to the University of Wisconsin, and you get a clear feeling that she can't wait—not just to get away from me and the skeevy book I am working on, but because she is building a life there. When we talk, it is clear that she wishes her mom had been different, wishes Jill had been different, wishes I had been different, but she believes that everybody did the best that they could, including her.

"Just looking at my origins and what I was brought up like, the two-pound baby, and all that," she said. "I read the health records, had so many problems back then, and look at me now. I'm going into my sophomore year of college, I did pretty good, have friends, am smart, I can do certain things well. Yeah, I would say life was kind to me.

"Meagan and I, we're smarter because you are our dad," she said, looking into the camera and not to me. "We learned a lot from you." She turned toward me. "You're an intelligent guy. Courtesy, respect, all those things that I see some of my peers lacking, I know it's because of my upbringing, not just solely because of you but because of Kathy, our day-care person, because of Jo-Jo, because of Grandma Diane. It was a group effort, and it turned out. You were our tribal leader."

Erin is a changeling, ambling through hair colors, piercings, and fashions like other people flick channels. She judges no one and expects no judgment in return. She has little relationship with her mother to speak of—too much drama for her—and an indifferent one with Jill that is morphing into something more substantial now that they are out of each other's hair.

She and I are connected, not just by our common history but by a love of all forms of pop culture. We trade movies and MP3s, spending hours chatting about the aesthetic value of various artifacts. The week before she heads back to college, we get in the car and drive to a run-down but wonderful supper club/bar thirty miles away. Like always, she has an iPod along, rifling through all the songs she wants me to hear. With a bit of a drumroll, she cues up "At the Bottom of Everything" by Bright Eyes, a band we both adore that sings about meeting the future with "our flashlights and our love." It is ostensibly about a plane crash, but its raucous chorus reminds that there is happiness in taking any trip, even one that ends in a fiery death, together. It's a gorgeous song, full of hope, terror, and portent, all leavened by the power of human love. We are having a moment. The sun is beginning to hide in the valleys we tear past, and as dusk becomes dark, a very full moon makes a spectacular appearance. Her hand slips into mine. We will be fine.

———

Much of the collateral damage that went with the life I chose landed on Meagan. She spent her time as a toddler entwined in my legs and became a young girl who wondered if anyone she came across might be her mother, and that search did not yield the warmth and affection she sought. She began to achieve amazing things in school and in sports to bring her a measure of value, but when that didn't work, she began to comfort herself in negative ways. Food became a measure of worthiness and punishment, while depression joined her for many long nights and days. She ended up in the hospital several times, and we became joined anew in a series of medical appointments, crisscrossing New Jersey in search of some respite for her. Throughout high school, she needed me to be present and attentive. We had many talks in the dark parts of the night. It stressed our relationship and knit it together at the same time. College, despite her achievements, began to seem like a receding hope. And then she took custody of her life, her body, her destiny. There was a lot of discussion about her going to college someplace nearby, but when it came down to it, she chose to go to the University of Michigan, a massive school that was not exactly right down the road.

She is excelling in her course work and seems to be absorbing the bumps that go with living independently. From the time she was an itty bitty, Meagan has been freakishly verbal and extremely direct when speaking about herself or others. As a sophomore, she is already focused on getting a master's in social work and healing others. And she worries endlessly, as she always has.

"I think I was acutely aware of stress. I don't really remember being stressed, but I remember being an anxious child at a very, very early age," she said. But she remembers nothing of being poor, of taking care of me at a very tender age when I had cancer, and has no early memories of her time either with me or her mother. She said we got by because I had a very "practical intelligence. You're very resourceful."

Much more so than Erin, Meagan has always had empathy for her mother and her battles. She never wanted to come home after visiting her mother when she was young, and I always thought that part of the reason she wanted to stay on was to take care of her. By now, some of that empathy has worn away.

"People live like they know how, even if it's not productive, and I think my mom learned very early on how to live life in a pretty destructive way and still get by," she said. "I don't think she ever learned any other way. If it's not drugs, it's men; if it's not men, it's money; if it's not that, it's loneliness; if it's not that, it's mental illness. There is always just some form of destruction she facilitates for herself."

It left a gap that no one, not me, not the village, not Jill, could fill. She learned how to be the woman she is mostly by herself.

"I felt like I was watching through, like, a glass, like trying to see," she said of growing up in our house. "And I don't think it ever worked very well."

We are sitting in our kitchen in Montclair. She will be leaving for Michigan soon, and it suddenly seems very important for me to tell her that everything good started with her.

"You tell me that on a regular basis. I have no reason not to believe you," she said. "It was always made clear that you guys had your own life, and your children weren't your whole life, but you also made it clear at the same time that us becoming part of your life was integral, like saving it. I always believed you when you said that."

Even when I ended up drunk after all those years?

"I knew you were going to screw up, and I knew it was gonna be tough, but I never pictured you throwing your life away."

Something else she never planned on? A book coming out of all that.

"I just never pictured you to be someone who would find this type of thing cathartic."

Bingo. That's my girl.

61

NOT NEARLY NORMAL

Every normal person, in fact, is only normal on the average. His ego approximates to that of the psychotic in some part or other and to a greater or lesser extent.

—SIGMUND FREUD

In the spring of 2007, I returned to New Orleans. The trip included a bit of reporting on the resurgence of the *Times-Picayune* there, but anybody who checked the calendar would have noticed that it was the first weekend of Jazz Fest, the annual hoedown to celebrate indigenous music. Jill and I have dear friends in New Orleans and make a point of going as often as we can. It was a last hurrah: Joan and Jeff, longtime New Orleanians, were pulling out because they could not abide raising their little girls in a city that had quit working in many respects and showed no signs of coming back soon.

When Jill and I were discussing the trip, Maddie, ten at the time, spoke up and said it sounded like fun. You're in, I told her. The three of us pulled into Louis Armstrong Airport. The last time I was there, the luggage carousels were serving as a triage point for evacuees who were ill or weak. I had made my way out to the airport along with the throng—there was talk of another hurricane on the way—and then proceeded to sit on the floor and get morosely hammered before getting on my flight. I can remember staring at the scene and thinking dark thoughts about the world, about this place, about my future.

On my return, the casualties had been replaced by plain old luggage, and the place had the generic look and feel of all airports. The metaphorical allusion was not lost on me, having brushed aside recently acquired rubble and now standing on safe ground. We grabbed a rental car and tore off to our pals' house on Esplanade, just a few blocks from the fairgrounds.

For the next three days, we grabbed all the food and music we could with both hands. At night when a big group of us went out to eat, I'd flip my wineglass over when the time came. And in the morning, before the house stirred, I walked over to a meeting of like minds at a nearby coffee shop and talked about the joys of the Jazz Fest and how to navigate its boozy shoals. There is a saying that wherever there is heavy drinking, there is heavy recovery, and the meetings were a revelation, full of frank talk and dead serious commitment. Those small efforts to mind my sobriety seemed like a tiny price to pay for all the fun I had.

Which raised the question of why I flopped around for three years before admitting that I was right the first time when I said I was powerless over alcohol. But there are benefits to a long, hot soak in booze, especially for the drunk. You say you're a bit bored by the banal splendors of everyday life? Try taking them away. When I was in the midst of an off-and-on jag with booze, I would have given anything to go to bed like a normal person and get up and go to work, with no consideration of dosage the night before or the shakes that inevitably arrived the following morning. As a drunk, every question asked of me seemed freighted with threat. A simple inquiry like, "What have you been up to?" becomes an indictment in the drunk's ears. *Oh, not much, sneaking drinks at every opportunity, having occasional blackouts, and doing my level best to generate a patina of normalcy over all the mayhem.*

Being normal has some significant practical upsides. In the years that I have been back sober, I have navigated three full seasons of Oscar reporting that were marked with alcohol-fueled parties at every turn and occasional bathrooms where every other stall seemed to have a bad case of the sniffles. I mingled, made the rounds, and then went happily back to the hotel to work.

As a sober person, I drove cross-country to drop Erin and Meagan off at college, and when we had dinner in South Bend, Indiana, the girls had their first legit drink with their parents. I was able to talk credibly about the benefits and drawbacks of the drinking life, and the role their heritage might play in their choices and the ensuing consequences.

Clear eyed and in the moment, I have put my hands in the air at a Hold Steady show, pushed my family down double-black-diamond ski runs at Lake Tahoe, gone ocean kayaking in Maine, and laid on the dock on a small lake in the Adirondacks, waiting to show Maddie her first "real" shooting star. It arrived on schedule.

None of that would have happened for the drinking version of me. I might still have a job, I might have stayed away from the coke, I might still be married, and I might still have a relationship with my kids, but all those bets were on the table.

To people who do not have the allergy, there is no clear way to explain the unmanageability that goes with addiction. A drunk or an addict picks up a shot or a dose because, same as everyone, he just wants to feel a little different. But it never stops there. I could be drunk tomorrow or shooting dope even as you read this, but the chances of that are low as long as I make a daily decision to embrace who I really am and then be satisfied with that at the end of the day.

I have my regrets at having had to spin out again to remember those very basic lessons, but I wasn't done. It took that trip, all of it, to realize that I'm not normal. Part of the reason that I tried drinking after fourteen years was that I had become so comfortable in a life that was wrapped in the raiment of the normal that I thought I *was* normal. Not cured, not remade, just normal. Two years of reporting and a lot of awkward conversations later, I realized that even though I live in a normal midcentury Colonial on a normal street in a normal town, that doesn't mean I am too. I'm nice—friendly, even—but I am a maniac who simply enjoys the fruits of acting normal.

In reductive psychoanalytic terms, I have achieved a measure of integration, not just between That Guy and This Guy, but between my past and my present. Carl Jung suggested that until we express both our masculine and feminine sides, we can't be made whole. For all the testosterone I have deployed in my affairs, I experienced salvation in expressing common maternal behavior. You are always told to recover for yourself, but the only way I got my head out of my own ass was to remember that there were other asses to consider.

I now inhabit a life I don't deserve, but we all walk this earth feeling we are frauds. The trick is to be grateful and hope the caper doesn't end any time soon.

62

TRUE STORY

When I started trying to remember who I was, I bought an external hard drive, a piece of technology that is designed to preserve the past. But the clerk at Best Buy asked how big it needed to be. How big?

19.3 gigabytes.

That's how much my life came out to be, measured in bits on that drive. Over the course of two years of reporting and writing, the data accumulated and began to tell a story that I thought I knew, but didn't.

The video of Donald, a combination of angel and ghost, swigging out of a bottle of Old Grand-Dad telling me, yes, there may have been a gun that night, but no, he did not have it? **166,631 kilobytes.**

The video of the interview with Chris suggesting that he was probably right? **205,375 kilobytes.**

The PDF of the police report involving the assault of one William C. Mikhil, aka the cabdriver I never knew? **1,025 kilobytes.**

The DDS audio file—there is no video—of Doolie talking about how I sat on her chest and hit her? **7,098 kilobytes.**

The JPEG file of Meagan as a newborn, surrounded by all manner of machines, fighting for a life that would turn out to be splendid? **773 kilobytes.**

The video of my wife in our cabin, looking into the camera and saying matter-of-factly that she knew every single day of her life would be an adventure and a fine one at that? **230,032 kilobytes.**

The music I listened to all summer to write the book, to hear something besides the voice of regret from me and others in those long nights of writing? (Songs most frequently played: "Chillout Tent" by the Hold Steady, "Bastards of Young" by the Replacements, "You Love to Fail" by the Magnetic Fields, Symphony No. 9 in D Minor, by Beethoven, "Whatever Happened to the Girl in Me?" by Ike Reilly—2,836 songs, all listened to at least once.) **6.94 gigabytes.**

The typed interview with Bob, the guy who ran Hennepin County treatment programs and who told me that I had one thing in my favor: a "soft piece of the statistical end of this business"; what he called the "ability to be hopeful"? **27 kilobytes.**

The book that folded all of it—the audio/video interviews, the lies, the true stories, the scans, the pictures, the arrest reports, the medical documents, the amends, the accusations, the promises of love, forgiveness, and vengeance—into one not-so-tidy package? **37,586 kilobytes.**

At the end of the night, when I would finish writing, I would plug the hard drive into the computer, always caught by the symbolism of my own need for an external memory. I would transfer the data from the computer to the little box and then hold it by the cord, staring at the shiny metal exterior and gaping in wonder at a box that knew more about me than I did.

The box knew that I had the gun, that I did not steal my children, but that I was not an obvious choice for a custodial parent. It noticed that my first counselor lost his license, my criminal attorney was disbarred, and my mentor went to prison, while all the while I was held more or less harmless. The memory card knows that I stiffed every attorney who helped me but paid every drug dealer I owed. It knows that David Bowie did not sing to me and that cancer hurt me, even though I pretended it didn't. The box knows the real name of the cabdriver I beat up, and somewhere amid all the 1s and 0s, that others corrupted me as I corrupted them. The box did the math and found I went to treatment five times, not four, and narrowly avoided a sixth. The box is aware that I was a rotten coke dealer and a serious journalist. The data in the box surmised that God did not forsake me, perhaps because nuns prayed for me.

————

The hard drive was sitting on the car seat next to me on Monday, June 4, 2007, filled with everything I had learned about a story I thought I already knew. I was heading up to our cabin, and I was in a hurry. I got caught speeding outside Saratoga Springs. It was the day I was to begin writing the book, and I took it as an omen that the halo of flies I used to wear could be summoned as needed.

I sat there holding my license out the window with my seat belt securely fastened. The cop asked me if I had my belt on when I flew by him.

"I can't help you with that, officer."

It wasn't that I didn't remember, I just didn't want to say it.

"Oh really," he said, leaning in. "Is there anything I should know about your history?"

Ummmmm, no. I squirmed a bit, swallowing the urge to crack wise. *Maybe you could check the database, sir, and tell me, did Donald have the gun or did I?* I already knew that if he dialed me up on the computer, he wouldn't find much. Twenty years is a long time, and even my face-plant a few years earlier was in a different state. So really, what did he need to know, apart from the fact that I wasn't wearing a belt when I went by him, a fact that he could ascertain without my assistance?

The cop, who was young and friendly, was still standing there as I was running all that history in my head. I heard myself open my mouth, speaking about the recent past instead.

"I did not have my seat belt on when I went by you."

He went back to the car, wrote me up a ticket for no seat belt and said he was going to let me slide on the speeding. I thanked him and went on my way.

ACKNOWLEDGMENTS

BOOK: Flip, David, Ruth, Cynthia, DonJack, Michelle, Peter, Jonathan, Phil, Jaime, Carolyn, Alexis, Sharon

WEB: Nick, Jigar

REPORTING: Anna, Donald, Chris, Doolie, Tommy, Brett, Marion, Barbara, Phil, Mickey, Peter, Todd, Pat, Terry, Deborah, Brian, Frank, Cathy, Barb, Emily, Rose, Daniel, Scott, Scotty, Seth, Mim, Bob, Dave, David, Annie, Steve, Lizzy, Nancy, John, Tony, Paul, Cute Michael, Peter, Emily, Julie, Zelda, Patrick, Steve, Dan, Tak

WORK: Sam, Bruce, Lorne, Bill, Jill, John, Dave, Danielle, Scott, Larry, Campbell, Randy, Tim, Anne, Julie, Chip, Rick

LIFE: Bill, Eddie, Erik, Kurt, Dave, Claude, Brett, Seth, Tommy, John, Burl, Oats, Bill W.

FAMILY: Joanie, John Sr., John Jr., Joe, Jim, Coo, Lisa, Missy, Diane, Linda, Mary, Mary, John, Don

BUT FOR: Jill, Meagan, Erin, Madeline

The story belongs to me, but the book does not. Sincere thanks for guidance, indulgence, and truth-telling.

THE NIGHT OF THE GUN ONLINE

A companion site for this book can be found at www.nightofthegun.com. It contains video and audio interviews, documents, transcripts, and pictures, along with a blog, an excerpt, and additional narrative elements not contained in this book. The site is a digital expression of this book and a reminder that the past continues to evolve.